BLAKE'S CONTRARY STATES

BLAKE'S
CONTRARY STATES

THE 'SONGS OF INNOCENCE AND OF EXPERIENCE' AS DRAMATIC POEMS

BY

D. G. GILLHAM

Senior Lecturer in English
University of Stellenbosch

CAMBRIDGE
AT THE UNIVERSITY PRESS
1966

Published by the Syndics of the Cambridge University Press
Bentley House, 200 Euston Road, London, N.W.1
American Branch: 32 East 57th Street, New York, N.Y. 10022

Library of Congress Catalogue Card Number: 66-15939

Printed in Great Britain
at the University Printing House, Cambridge
(Brooke Crutchley, University Printer)

CONTENTS

v

PREFATORY NOTE

CONSIDERABLE use has been made, in this work, of Sir Geoffrey Keynes's *Complete Writings of William Blake* (1957), and his text of the *Songs* is used throughout, together with his punctuation. Various copies and facsimile copies of the *Songs* have been examined, but the reproduction that has been most frequently consulted is the facsimile edition issued in two volumes by Benn, Ltd., in 1926 and 1927.

The author is deeply indebted for advice to Professor L. C. Knights and also to Sheila Gillham.

INTRODUCTION

M ost Blake studies are based on the assumption that the poet requires allowances to be made for his unusual manner of writing. The *Songs of Innocence and of Experience* most decidedly do not require a special critical technique, and this study is made according to the most conservative and orthodox principles. No attempt has been made to go far afield for material to assist the study of the *Songs*—quite the contrary. It has been assumed that Blake's intention may best be discovered by a patient reading of the poems themselves without forcing on to them assistance that only a specialized knowledge can give. The purpose of the following pages is to present the outcome of a reading of the *Songs* which assumes that they explain themselves if they are read together. Each poem must be read for its own sake, but it may most adequately be read by a mind that is informed by the remainder of the poems.

No period of history is very remote when seen through the eyes of a poet, and Blake is very much our contemporary because we are still attempting to come to terms with the rationalism that, by stimulating his antagonism, provoked his complex insight. Though we do not need the help of a special knowledge in order to understand the problems of our poet, reference is made, throughout this study, to thinkers of Blake's own time. This is not done on the supposition that the poetry can be explained in terms of influences that were brought to bear upon Blake, but in order to remind us of our own problems, and to throw into relief the qualities of Blake's peculiar genius in meeting those problems.

During the twentieth century a great deal has been written about Blake; most commentators have had something to say about the *Songs*, but for a number of reasons the commentaries on these short poems have been disappointing.

Perhaps Blake is, himself, partly to blame for this. His 'Prophetic Books', by their obscure and involved construction, invite a ponderous and mysterious explanation, and the *Songs*, regarded as an adjunct of the 'Prophecies', are crushed beneath the weight of an exegesis they cannot bear. This is true even of Joseph Wicksteed's work[1] on the *Songs*, which sets out to make a restrained and unpretentious examination of the poems, which succeeds in making many valuable observations, but cannot sustain its moderation. Wicksteed falls often into sentimentality[2] and sometimes overloads the poems with 'symbolic' significances culled from his knowledge of the 'Prophetic Works'.

Since the publication of Wicksteed's book three others have appeared which concentrate their attention on Blake's earlier and shorter writings. Stanley Gardner insists, in his work, that 'We cannot find the key to the meaning of the early books by reading the final books'; we must 'interpret the symbolism in its interrelationship, each symbol in its context'.[3] This is a sensible approach, and Gardner's discussion of the *Songs of Experience* is particularly valuable. In R. F. Gleckner's work[4] the *Songs* are forced into a rigid framework of 'symbolic' meanings derived from the 'Prophecies', and the analysis distorts the poetry. In the most recent work, E. D. Hirsch discusses the two sets of songs on the assumption that they 'express two distinct outlooks that Blake in each case held with an unqualified vigor and fervor of belief'.[5] This assumption seems wrong, but the critical insights of the writer are good, especially in discussion of *The Songs of Innocence*.

The reader's attention is beckoned away from the *Songs* by Blake's eccentric manner of composing his poetry as well as by

[1] *Blake's Innocence and Experience* (1928).
[2] See D. W. Harding's remarks on Wicksteed in his fine essay: 'William Blake', *The Pelican Guide to English Literature*, v (1957).
[3] *Infinity on the Anvil* (1954), p. 13.
[4] *The Piper and the Bard* (Detroit, 1959).
[5] *Innocence and Experience* (New Haven, 1964), p. 7.

2

the 'mythology' of the 'Prophetic Books'. In putting together his verse he was in the habit of using fragments ('odds and ends', as Eliot calls them) from his wide and unusual reading. Much careful research has gone into tracing the influence on Blake's verse of various philosophers,[1] of writers in the Hermetic tradition,[2] and of the tensions and events of his day.[3] For the reader of the *Songs*, however, the fruits of this research are not very helpful, and may even obscure the poetry by demanding a kind of attention that is not warranted. Blake so radically transformed the material he used, it became so very much subordinated to his own way of looking at things, that a knowledge of its origins usually seems irrelevant.

The complicated 'mythology' of Blake's later works and the idiosyncratic manner in which he chose to write them have both militated against the *Songs* receiving what they most need: a careful appreciation of their tone. Overwhelmed by the apparent need for a special exegetical apparatus, the reader is distracted from applying to the poems the sort of sensitivity that would be given poetry found in a less unusual setting. The *Songs* themselves are not idiosyncratic, but it is supposed that they should be, and the accepted tools of the reader are abandoned. Normally, we realize very soon whether a poet is speaking on his own behalf (through the mouth of an imagined character, perhaps) or is presenting us with a persona (with some character whom we cannot take as being the poet's direct representative). In lyrical poetry, it is true, we may very often take the sentiments offered as being the poet's very own, but this is not always so. In the *Songs* this decidedly cannot be the case, certainly not always—there is too marked a diversity in the attitudes presented.

[1] For example: Northrop Frye, *Fearful Symmetry* (Boston, 1947).
[2] For example: S. Foster Damon, *Blake: His Philosophy and Symbols* (Boston, 1924).
[3] For example: J. Bronowski, *William Blake, A Man Without a Mask* (1944); Mark Schorer, *William Blake* (New York, 1946); D. V. Erdman, *Blake: Prophet against Empire* (Princeton, 1954).

One would expect the reader of the *Songs*, on making this discovery, to take all the poems with some caution; to wonder, when reading every one of them, if Blake is speaking in his own voice, or if he is presenting a possible attitude for our inspection. The outcome of such an examination should be the realization that none of the *Songs* can be taken simply as a direct personal utterance. Innocence is not self-aware in a way that allows it to describe itself, and the poet must stand outside the state. From the mocking tone of many of the *Songs of Experience* it is clear that the poet does not suffer from the delusions he associates with that condition. Again, the poet stands beyond the state depicted. Blake, in short, is detached from the conditions of awareness imposed on the speakers of his poems.

Blake's critics do not follow the clue given by his tone, however, and, although the best commentaries all have glimpses of the detachment, the insight is sporadic and soon set aside. The poet is identified with one selection from the *Songs* or another, or, in an attempt to make them all emanate from the poet, it is stated that we may take the *Songs of Innocence* to belong to an earlier and hopeful period while the *Songs of Experience* belong to a later condition of disillusionment. The critics have been determined that Blake should commit himself in some part of the *Songs*, and this determination is understandable. The poems are obviously the work of a thinker, and this thinker identifies himself, sometimes, with the prophet, which suggests that he might wish to lay down some definite guide to conduct. The philosopher and the prophet are usually men with a message, are men with formed and finalized ideas, and the poet appears to resemble them, particularly a poet with the decided manner of speaking shown by Blake. Wicksteed, for example, will sometimes find Blake's commitment in such songs as 'London' or 'The Garden of Love', which show natural human propensities being smothered by institution. But Blake is too good a thinker to be putting forward the Godwinian idea as an explanation of man, though he does put it forward as being indicative of one of the shoals on which the human vessel may run itself aground. The idea may chart a point in Blake's psychology but it does not define his 'philosophy'. In 'London' Blake does not express his despair of the human condition, but depicts a condition of despair, not necessarily his own. All the songs depict 'states of the soul', as the title-page tells us, and Blake's own voice is detected in the purpose that governs the assembly of the *Songs* rather than in any particular utterance.

Blake has no message, or 'philosophy', and would not be more worth reading as a poet if he had. He offers something better: a serious and responsible consideration of the ways in which human energy may manifest itself. In the course of his study he touches on various ideas of the nature of man, but not because he regards any of them as absolutely true, as saying the last word on what we are. His concern is a moral one and he makes (or implies) a judgement of the positions he describes, though he does not dispute their truth. Any -ism is true for the person who believes it to be so, though it does not follow that all such truths may be said to reflect a decent condition of the mind. They are to be judged according to the fullness of the life that (it may be inferred) supports them. Although he refers us to various dogmas in his description of the states, Blake subscribes to no one of them, he presents no ultimate truths but leaves us to forge our own. He does attempt to awaken us to the responsibility of becoming alive to the best truths of which we are capable, but the poet detaches himself from the task of saying what those truths should be.

There was a strong tendency during the eighteenth century to view man simply as the outcome of education and conditioning. He was seen as an intelligent animal, but the intelligence itself was conceived as a calculating faculty, enabling him to make use of his experience to civilize himself. There were no fundamental impulses in the individual that could properly be called moral, but men could estimate that it would serve them well to behave according to an accepted morality. In the course of the *Songs of Experience* Blake often presents us with this conception of human nature, and implies that it may appear true to those who have lost their benign impulses. They need control from without and the restraint of self-interested conformity if they are to behave well. In the *Songs of Innocence*, however, Blake presents us with beings who cannot be accounted for on this explanation. These songs do not present us with persons equipped with premeditated or formulated moral notions, it is true, but we are shown individuals with affectionate and sympathetic impulses that dispose them to benign forms of conduct.

In *The Songs of Experience* Blake allows some of his characters to affirm the values and theories of rationalism, but he emphasizes that these are valid for the mind working in a superficial way only, and he describes the alternative mentality of Innocence. This alternative is not put forward as an original character or as a stage in the development of man, but as a condition of perfection, a completeness and harmony of being. Because we usually recognize this in children, we associate it with ignorance—the child shows its simple faith and wholehearted vitality because it knows so little, has not entered into the cares of a more responsible time of life. Blake is not setting up an ideal of childishness, however, and his Innocents are not all children. All men have their innocent moments, though what constitutes an innocent poise at one time of life will not be proper at another, and what will indicate perfection of balance for one person will not do so for some other. What is important is that we have known the perfection of Innocence, and though we can no more induce a state of perfection in ourselves than we can return to childhood, we are provided, by this knowledge, with a measure of the success of our more deliberate activities.[1]

[1] Blake explores the distinction between different qualities of experience. A similar distinction is examined, philosophically, in our own time by such writers as Martin Buber (*I and Thou*, 1937) and Martin Foss (*Symbol and Metaphor in Human Experience*, 1949).

Introduction

The measure is an inarticulate one, is an intuition of the sort of thing we can hope for and not a programme we can follow, but it does provide us with a more fundamental and constant guide than convention or rational argument can offer. One convention can drive out another and arguments are subject to endless amendment, but as they pass into the mind they come under the control of a being who has known affection, sympathy, fascination and delight, and who, therefore, has a touchstone (a sort of conscience) which, without our being able to give a detailed and explicit account of what it is, directs our more articulate and deliberate impulses. By introducing us, in the *Songs*, to the concept of Innocence Blake shows a dimension of the mind which the eighteenth century chose to ignore because there was no formula for it.

CHAPTER 1

THE POET AS SOCIAL CRITIC

BLAKE'S 'London', one of the *Songs of Experience*, was written in the early 1790s, but expresses a state of mind that may easily be recognized in our own time. The poem presents us with a series of allusions to regulation, law and institution, set against the distressed cries of individuals. The speaker is kept at a curious distance from those who surround him in the streets, encountering them as marks, faces, cries and voices. All takes place at a level of signs, signs that others carry the same feeling of forlorn incapacity as himself, though he has no intimate knowledge of their weakness or woe. It is a poem of façades, solid ones in the third stanza, and no less impenetrable human façades in the rest of the poem.

LONDON

I wander thro' each charter'd street,
Near where the charter'd Thames does flow,
And mark in every face I meet
Marks of weakness, marks of woe.

In every cry of every Man,
In every Infant's cry of fear,
In every voice, in every ban,
The mind-forg'd manacles I hear.

How the Chimney-sweeper's cry
Every black'ning Church appalls;
And the hapless Soldier's sigh
Runs in blood down Palace walls.

But most thro' midnight streets I hear
How the youthful Harlot's curse
Blasts the new born Infant's tear,
And blights with plagues the Marriage hearse.

The Poet as Social Critic

The highly personal and interpretative cast of the meditation of the man who wanders through the streets of the city is emphasized by the superficial nature of the encounters he makes. There is a vague bustle in the poem interrupted by the calls of tradesmen, of the sweeper, by the bawl of a child. The speaker idly picks up these sounds but they have a subjective meaning upon which he ruminates until a new sight or a new sound breaks in to add itself to his impressions. He hardly notices the persons about him. They are not seen, but 'marked'. What the faces reveal are: 'Marks of weakness, marks of woe'—the speaker finds what he expected, but the emotions are not shared or felt, though they might be a replica of the speaker's own. The evidence of emotion is noted but nothing further can be glimpsed, and no closer knowledge is desired or attempted. The repetitions and alliterations of the first two stanzas stress the indwelling melancholy of the speaker. But though he is used to this condition and regards it as inevitable, he is not so accustomed that he is indifferent. There is no resignation, particularly in the last two stanzas where the words used are bitter: 'black'ning', 'blood', 'curse', 'blasts', 'blights' and 'hearse'.

The thoughts of this lonely monad centre chiefly about the 'pre-established harmony' that keeps in order the strangers who inhabit the city. The first line of the poem contrasts the aimlessness of the individual with the organization that surrounds him: 'I wander thro' each charter'd street'. He has no direction of his own but is led along ways that are obligatory. In the city, order is imposed by institutions. The Law, the Church, the State, the family are all mentioned in the poem, and even the streets are presented, in the first stanza, in their institutional aspect. Against the background of this organization the individual wanders, his life so regimented that it has lost its own purpose and he is helpless and insignificant. Man appears to be in control of the city he has made. The streets have been 'charter'd', permitted to be just so, but, in fact, the orderly arrangement of streets which seems the result of planning and directing is the outcome of accretion. The streets of London are like all the institutions of man. There appears to be a deliberate control over their development, but they display an independent life of their own, growing up next to the men, or despite the men who must 'direct' them. The word 'charter'd', implying freedom, is ironical, and the irony is pointed by its application to the Thames. The river is given a mandate to flow within such and such bounds, but the act of will apparently exerted over the river is, in reality, an acceptance of its inevitable presence.

The cries of men and infants that break into the silence of the reverie are the abrupt utterances of beings suffering under the controls that man has imposed upon himself:

> In every voice, in every ban,
> The mind-forg'd manacles I hear.

Man is isolated, has no sensitive knowledge of the feelings of others, and must control his relationships by means of the 'thou shalt nots' of formally and informally imposed prohibitions. Law, regulation and code direct the commerce of the men who impinge upon each other and the inhabitants of the city are in the position of a man who has never learned to walk because he has always used a crutch. They cannot love because they have never had an opportunity to exercise love in a world of perfected institutions. For love to grow it must have an opportunity to exercise resource; it must make its own decisions.

Man has built himself an amazingly elaborate prison by the use of his mind. Too faithless or too clever to rely on the impulse of the moment, he has evolved a system of controls that manage every part of life. But these controls *are* the mind. The wanderer refers directly to no spontaneous impulse that might be an alternative to restraint. He regards the manacles as inescapable, an iron law of our condition. They are 'mind-forg'd', the result of intelligence and industry and not of stupidity and laziness. The cruelty of our position as it is envisaged is that we are required to use our talents against ourselves. Men labour to set up their controls, more obviously in the way of chartered institutions: schools, academies, councils, benches, companies, etc., and, less obviously, as the underlying policy, theory, loyalty, convention, tradition, method, etc., that penetrate to every part of the social body like a nervous system. In performing their labour men are guided by what they find—circumstances determine the shaping of policy, the intellectual climate determines what direction thought must follow. Not only are the larger movements of society determined (according to the wanderer), but every individual, conformist and non-conformist alike, must labour with his mind to form his mind out of the ideas current in his time. The wanderer insists on this aspect of our lives, that men are the outcome of a culture and cannot disengage themselves from it, nor escape the labour of acquiring it.

Stanza three is directed against the institutions of Church and State in particular:

> How the Chimney-sweeper's cry
> Every black'ning Church appalls;
> And the hapless Soldier's sigh
> Runs in blood down Palace walls.

Here, the very personal utterances of the sweeper and the soldier are, figuratively, up against the solidly built façades of impersonal organization. The tradesman's cry of the sweeper ('weep! 'weep!) is interpreted as a cry of distress from what we would now call the victim of a social evil, just as the cries of men in the second stanza are cries of pain, and the cries of infants are uttered in terror at the life they sense as theirs to come. In the world pictured in 'London', everyone is, in some degree, the victim of social evil, because society, through its institutions, is an evil of impersonality. The Church, however divine its origin, is placed as an instrument in man's hand, and so subject to the same deterioration as his other instruments. It is 'black'ning', becoming unsightly

11

with the accumulations of age as a legal and political and doctrinal crust covers its original impulse. Presumably, the message of the New Testament, if taken seriously, would render poverty and ill-usage quite impossible. Each man is responsible for the relief of misery. A wrong would no sooner appear than be recognized, no sooner recognized than every man's hand stretched out to right it. As things are, however, the Church is horrified at the evil of the sweeper's condition, but it is helpless to do much about it—no vigorous remedy may be undertaken because institutions are, by nature, conservative.

The sister institution of the Church, the State, shows no emotion at all. Here all is as stony and official as the exterior of an administrative building, represented by the palace. However terrible the soldier may be as the licensed bully of the administrator, he is a peculiarly unfortunate being as a person. Professionally he does what he is told, and so cannot be held responsible for his actions. The 'blood' he sheds is not on his head and so he is, morally, the epitome of weakness. Also, we cannot expect those who gave the soldier his orders to take responsibility. They are placed behind a wall of facts, statistics, precedents and regulations. The last thing that a bad administrator would think of doing, and the last thing that a good administrator could afford to do, would be to consider too minutely the effects of his work on any particular individual. He is impervious to what goes on beyond the palace walls because his is the world of affairs not of men, and he is as much in fetters as those who obey him.

The image used in the last two lines of the stanza to describe the weakness of the apparently strong may have been privately suggested to Blake by Burke's contemporaneous description of the King of France. Burke gives an account of the King as acting under the National Assembly to execute those orders which carry odium. Even as no more than a 'political executive magistrate' the King ought to have dignity, authority and consideration, but has none:

His functions of internal coercion are as odious as those which he exercises in the department of justice. If relief is to be given any municipality, the assembly gives it. If troops are to be sent to reduce them to obedience to the assembly, the King is to execute the order; and upon every occasion he is to be spattered over with the blood of his people. He has no negative; yet his name and authority is used to enforce every harsh decree.[1]

The wanderer completes Burke's picture by extending the helplessness of the King to all types of governor. Elsewhere in the *Reflections* Burke makes it clear that this is the case in France, that the Assembly which uses the King is subject to the compulsions of expediency, circumstances and the pressure of interests, and cannot be supposed to govern by 'reason'. Burke's insight is given a different twist by the wanderer. He sees that administration, good or bad, does not involve the administrator as human individual, but as officer. Institutions engage men impersonally, and this is true, even of an institution like the Church, which provides spiritual guidance. Under the control of proper institutions man is prevented from doing much harm and from coming to much hurt, but he is also prevented from being much more than a machine, prevented from doing 'good' in any sense of the word that implies personal choice or a sensitive consideration of others.

The impulses of fellow-feeling and communication, the desire to love, are referred to in the last stanza of the poem, though the wanderer does not 'believe in' such urges. In the society of 'London' the exercise even of sexual love has been replaced by a joyless and mercenary self-gratification, by recourse to the prostitute:

> But most thro' midnight streets I hear
> How the youthful Harlot's curse
> Blasts the new born Infant's tear,
> And blights with plagues the Marriage hearse.

The harlot is the source of disease. The third line of the stanza refers to the effects of gonorrhoea on the baby, and the fourth

---

[1] *Reflections on the Revolution in France* (World's Classics edn.), p. 222.

line to it entering into the home. But as well as source of this disease, she is symptom of a more serious disease, as is implied by the word 'hearse'. The city has rendered those who marry unfit to love. Marriage is a ceremony of mourning because the products of London are incapable of meeting, only of self-gratification. Love itself is withered, for if it were vigorous the harlot could have no attractions. She blasts the new-born infant with disease, but the infant cries because it knows that it is born into isolation. He will be incapable of love because he will never know what it is to be loved, and he will, in his turn, render others incapable. The harlot, who is youthful, and the infant, who is tearful, are creatures to be pitied, if the wanderer can feel pity, for their young life is made unnatural, their promise cankered before it can be shown. The wanderer sees man as too rigidly thrust into a social and institutional role ever to achieve proper humanity. He must become an isolated creature, living mechanically and unhappily. The unhappiness is felt, and the intuition that the condition of life is unfulfilment calls up the curse of the harlot and the cry of the child, though they do not have the satisfaction, even, of knowing what is missing, for they have never experienced it.

It is generally assumed that in 'London' Blake speaks in his own voice, that the wanderer is Blake himself, the lament his own, and that the condemnation of human muddle contained in the poem is that of the poet. Thus Wicksteed says:

Men become the hedged-in victims of system . . . It is startling to reflect how far Blake was in advance of his age in attributing these tragedies (poverty, prostitution) not to the individual's own fault but to the Society which tolerated them.[1]

Wicksteed is wrong, however, in saying that the sociological content of 'London' is in advance of its age. As a criticism of the effect of society on the individual (and we shall see that the intention is not merely that), the poem is original only in

---

[1] *Blake's Innocence and Experience*, p. 190.

the force and particular emphasis it gives to a topic that was being much discussed at the time.

Godwin, in *Political Justice* (1793), sees man as entirely the product of circumstances:

In the life of every human being there is a chain of causes, generated in the lap of ages which preceded his birth, and going on in regular procession through the whole period of his existence, in consequence of which it was impossible for him to act in any instance otherwise than he has acted.[1]

Social necessities conspire against the wanderer, who is miserable. The universe conspires against Godwin, but he finds, in this, a reason for elation:

Nothing is more unreasonable than that the idea of necessity should produce a spirit of neutrality and indifference. The more certain is the connection between effects and causes, the more chearfulness should I feel in yielding to painful and laborious employments.[2]

So complete is Godwin's determinism, however, that very little choice seems possible, even in the feelings one is to have about the matter. At other times Godwin is less contented in his necessitarianism and he takes up an attitude related to the wanderer's in respect to institutions. He regards them as a tyranny and sees their modification and eventual abolition being brought about as a result of (necessary) alteration of men's opinions.[3]

Burke, also writing at about the time that 'London' was composed, is more penetrating than Godwin. He does not go to the same extremes in denying free will to man, though he does see him as a limited and imperfect creature. Man stands very much in need of his institutions to give him a stiffening of purpose, method and tradition. But he is not so helpless that he is unable to look at those institutions critically, or to attempt their gradual improvement. Burke avoids Godwin's error of making man utterly determined. On the other hand,

---

[1] 1796 edn. IV, viii.   [2] *Loc. cit.*   [3] *Political Justice*, I, v.

he avoids Paine's mistake of supposing that man can scrap his *'organized* character' in order to return to an *'original* character'. Even Paine has his doubts about the return:

Man cannot, properly speaking, make circumstances for his purpose, but he always has it in his power to improve them when they occur, and this was the case in France.[1]

Paine's reservations, however, occur to him infrequently, and his usual attitude is one of full confidence in man's power to control his destiny:

The progress of time and circumstances, which men assign to the accomplishment of great changes, is too mechanical to measure the force of the mind, and the rapidity of reflection by which Revolutions are generated.[2]

In opposition to Paine, Burke shows that if man supposes himself so much the master of his fate that he undertakes to destroy institutions which regulate his affairs, and which are the foundation of his rights, he will find himself without regulation and without rights. Man has no 'original character'—none that is recognizably human or that can be returned to. Burke accepts the idea of human weakness and consequent need for support as a fact seriously to be taken into account:

We are afraid to put men to live and trade each on his own private stock of reason; because we suspect that the stock in each man is small, and that the individuals would do better to avail themselves of the general bank and capital of nations and of ages.[3]

Paine cannot understand Burke because he works from an opposed idea of the nature of man. Burke supposes that man is man because his history and development culminate at any particular time in an organization that determines the nature of the individual. Each individual's humanity is the outcome of the history of humanity and our thoughts and our principles are related to, are an outcome of, what has been thought

[1] *The Rights of Man* (Everyman edn.), p. 78.
[2] *Ibid.* p. 133.　　　　　　　　[3] *Reflections*, p. 95.

before. Burke does not see this as a supine process—we must labour for our humanity—but he does see each man's task as a given one. Paine, on the other hand, assumes the independence of reason and mind from any circumstances which might go to form them. His notion of thought is Platonic. Principles are absolute and independent, and man, by nature in possession of those principles, may, at any time, judge his circumstances, his government, his institutions in the light of an innate knowledge. He assumes that man is free to start his history afresh, that any generation may wipe out its institutions and find enough guidance in natural humanity to start with new institutions, in no way indebted to the old.

Godwin sees man as passive in his necessitarian state and finds this a cause for rejoicing. As we have no option but to be swept along by the current, we may find it exhilarating to swim with it. Paine assumes that the force of the current is negligible. Burke suggests swimming across the current, and so achieving a limited headway of one's own. The humanity of Blake's wanderer is drowned in the current that he drifts with and there is nothing to rejoice about, nothing to achieve.

If we are to identify the wanderer with Blake, then it is with Blake only in a certain mood. Blake achieves several purposes in his poem, and the least important is to convey the beliefs and vision of that mood. The poem summarizes the beliefs held by a large number of human beings about the situation of mankind. What gives the poem, together with the other *Songs*, innocent and experienced, a compelling and dramatic force is the fact that its beliefs are true. The wanderer has not formulated or selected his social philosophy as an academic exercise but to account for the facts of his existence. A different man would give a different account as his life would be different, and that account would also be a true one. What is sad is that the wanderer speaks the truth for so many men. Blake, the writer of 'London', stands away from the truth of the poem and away from the mood in which the poem might be true for himself. The reader is aware of a second voice speaking behind that of the wanderer: Blake's voice speaking in such close harmony as to be difficult to separate into its independent part. Nearly all of the *Songs of Experience* are counterpointed in this way—an ironical commentary is contained in them.

We arrive at the truth that the wanderer tells us, not only by listening to the sense of his words but by looking at the way in which his attention works. His thoughts turn on a central theme, and his reverie is jarred by the evidence of his fellow-men. Yet that evidence is so subjectively experienced and fits so well with his thoughts. We are aware of Blake pointing this out. The reader is asked to look at a mental and emotional state, to assess, to work by sign and evidence as well as by giving credit, and this places us, with Blake, at a slight distance.

The wanderer's forlorn mood in the first two stanzas and his disillusion in the third turn, in the last stanza, to acrid disgust. Despite this, the poem carries the weight of a much more forceful attack than these tactics would suggest. It is as though a steadier mind—realistic but not disillusioned, critical but not disgusted, more sensitive and more vigorous—were in control of the strategy of the poem. This is noticed, for instance, in the ironical overtones of the 'charter'd' of lines 1 and 2. Blake rather than the wanderer is capable of the detachment necessary for the effect. The same thing is true of the great compression of meaning in 'mind-forg'd manacles' and in the economy of the images of church façade and palace walls. The control of the poet is felt in the imagery, the rhythm and the compactness of thought.

The word 'hearse' occurs at the very end of the poem and it carries all the force of the rest of the poem—the beings who are insubstantially presented to the wanderer are spectral, figures from the grave. To the wanderer life is death-like, a lugubrious ceremony to be gone through. But 'hearse'

18

carries Blake's vigour as well as the gloom of the speaker and gives a new dimension of meaning to the last stanza. Without the word the stanza might be an attack on prostitution as a disease, but its addition turns the weight of the attack on to the condition of lovelessness, on to the fundamental wrong, on to prostitution as symptom. If Blake's persona is aware of love, it is as an unrealized possibility and the reader feels that he speaks the word 'hearse' without realizing its full implication—that Blake adds the vigour of the new twist at the end, emphasizing the alternative of love, but as an alternative reality and not a fiction. Blake is positively aware of the alternative while his speaker is negatively aware of it. The writer of the poem believes in love though his persona does not.

Blake is critical of the influence of social organization upon any man (including Blake himself), and we can associate Blake and the wanderer, but we cannot fully identify them. Blake holds off from the wanderer because he has a larger purpose, critical of the frame of mind of his speaker. The wanderer has arrived at a statement of truth, but it is not the only truth. Another truth is presented in those *Songs of Innocence* that correspond to the experienced 'London'—one which allows for self-fulfilment and expansion. The contracted and starved condition of the wanderer is a tragic state, men do become like this, but it is not the only state of the soul. In nearly all the *Songs of Experience* there is to be detected a tone of reservation on the part of the poet. The truths of Experience are widespread and they seem, sometimes, inevitable. Innocence is avid to abandon its state to embrace that of Experience. Experience seems wise and necessary. Nevertheless, Experience owes its power of control and its self-assurance, even its level-headed common sense to something it has lost, and not to something won. It has limited itself in order to gain a limited end. The bitterness of the wanderer is due to a realization of his limitations, though not due to a positive knowledge of his lost potential. The positive knowledge of love, contact and enthusiasm which counter-points his bitterness is supplied by the reserved vigour of the poet. Blake's reservations are even more strongly felt when we set the poem against the *Songs of Innocence* where the lost faculties are possessed by the speakers.

As far as the subject of social relationships is concerned, Burke puts the case for Experience magnificently. He is self-assured, intelligent and penetrating. The case put by Paine, on the other hand, is sketchy, inconsistent, and, in its tone, often unpleasant. It may be supposed from what we know of Blake's life that he followed the argument between the two men with unusual interest, and it may be supposed that he saw the excellences of Burke's work and was conscious of the deficiencies in Paine's. The *Songs* give us the reasons why, despite this, he could always retain his radical sympathies.

Godwin, Burke and the wanderer all describe men in the experienced state only, and Burke's description is the most steadily hopeful one for that state, though Godwin is more (unduly) optimistic. Burke does see fitfully beyond the state, and talks of institutions as the 'products of enthusiasm', but he never examines this enthusiasm, and his account is, for the most part, of unenthusiastic man, patiently doing a job he is obliged to do. It is true of Burke and of the wanderer that they see, with each birth, the advent of another individual who must fashion himself to the community and its institutions. Paine, on the other hand, gives every man unlimited scope for choice and self-determination. He claims the right for every generation to refashion its institutions, and with that right goes the ability to assume a character which is, at once, developed and original. The idea is an absurd one. What Paine has seen, or sensed, however, is the need of the individual to fashion for himself. He misunderstands the manner in which individual creation is possible, his reasoning is confused and he loses his altercation with Burke. Nevertheless Blake saw something in the spirit of Paine's poor argument that went far to meet the excellences of Burke's good one.

The Poet as Social Critic

Blake's idea of Innocence is quite different from Paine's idea of an 'original nature', but the two notions may be recognized, all the same, as having a common root. Both wish to make more of the role of the individual than Burke, who has no such ideas, would allow.\ Innocence implies that with each new birth the world does gain a new individual to build it up in freedom, from impulse, and by choice and discrimination.ˈThe institutions of man are created by every human being because he has the wish to do so, and is capable of the effort. Individual election and imagination are the sources of strength of institutions, and not vice versa, and a society that offered theoretically perfect institutions but was composed of supine individuals would collapse immediately. On the other hand, make-shift and imperfect institutions will work admirably where individual initiative flourishes. In the innocent 'Chimney Sweeper' Blake depicts his sweeps giving a meaningful content to catch-phrases and down-at-heel myth. They make the best of the world as they find it, not because they are helpless but because they have the vitality to do so.[1] In that poem, as in many of the *Songs of Innocence*, Blake is concerned with what is important to him: the vigorous human soul transforming shabby materials. Burke is deceived by the trappings and coverings into supposing them the substantial human reality. He sees shoddy human ability carried by institution, where Blake sees shoddy, though necessary, institution revivified by human energy. That is what happens in Innocence, at all events. Burke is not wrong in his enumeration of the factors of the human situation. There is the soul, and there is the material through which it must find expression. It must take what comes to hand. But Burke is wrong in the relationship he sees between these factors. He sees institution, not as means, but as end, and he sees the individual as the subordinate factor. Excellent though his analysis may be, it is only excellent in a situation in which individuals (and, in the best sense, institutions) do not

[1] See below, pp. 38 ff.

fully realize themselves. Unfortunately, such situations do exist. They are the commonplace of Experience.

Through the rags of Paine's argument, Blake perhaps saw a more sympathetic spirit than Burke's. No individual has the transcendent knowledge enabling him to act with god-like freedom in the assurance of absolute principles that one would suppose possible from reading Paine. But his mistake is a generous one. He assumes that anything is possible to humanity. This is not so. We must assume the second-hand tatters or the second-hand furs that society and tradition offer us. Blake's Innocents do not stand above their experience (on Paine's pattern), nor are they the tools of dead circumstances (as Burke's argument tends to suggest we are at best). They take their circumstances seriously and transform them, not wilfully, but by knowing them. There is a difference between being shaped by one's life and entering into one's life. Paine never explores this distinction and it could not occur to him to do so. Fundamentally he, too, is a creature of the world of Experience, but he does leave possibilities open that are closed by Burke. Paine's assessment of the abilities of man is muddled, but he insists on the potency of the individual. That is, perhaps, one of the reasons why we find Blake keeping republican company, and not conservative, at the time that the *Songs* were written.

A number of the *Songs of Innocence* form a contrast to 'London'. The 'Introduction', 'Nurse's Song', 'Laughing Song', 'The Shepherd', 'The Lamb', 'Spring' all have a rural setting and describe simple or young folk enjoying themselves in a spontaneous way. Blake's purpose in the *Songs of Innocence*, however, is not to enthuse over the circumstances of rustic life. Although 'London' and its innocent counterpart, 'The Ecchoing Green', illustrate psychological trends fostered by urban industrial and rural agricultural conditions, the innocent and experienced states are not necessarily associated with a particular environment.

The innocent Chimney Sweeper knows nothing but the city, and the setting for most of the *Songs* is not specified. 'The Ecchoing Green' has a rural setting, but the significance of the poem lies in the qualities of the soul that are depicted.

THE ECCHOING GREEN

The Sun does arise,
And make happy the skies;
The merry bells ring
To welcome the Spring;
The skylark and thrush,
The birds of the bush,
Sing louder around
To the bells' chearful sound,
While our sports shall be seen
On the Ecchoing Green.

Old John, with white hair,
Does laugh away care,
Sitting under the oak,
Among the old folk.
They laugh at our play,
And soon they all say:
'Such, such were the joys
'When we all, girls & boys,
'In our youth time were seen
'On the Ecchoing Green.'

Till the little ones, weary,
No more can be merry;
The sun does descend,
And our sports have an end.
Round the laps of their mothers
Many sisters and brothers,
Like birds in their nest,
Are ready for rest,
And sport no more seen
On the darkening Green.[1]

The young people who sport on the green during their Spring holiday enter wholeheartedly into their activities and are

[1] Blake takes the thread of the poem from *L'Allegro*, lines 91–9.

fulfilled and content in each phase of the day. The activities flow from each other and from the wider setting in which they take place. Sport gives way to weariness, to the desire for comfort from the mother, and to sleep. The day is one to 'laugh away care' but occurs amid the labouring days. The enjoyment of the Spring day is entered into fully as it comes in the round of the year. The sense of present enjoyment and of regular movement are given simultaneously, for the villagers make the most of the day and the season, but both are part of a progression: into Spring and then to Summer, into play and then to rest. The movement of the sun accompanies these progressions. It rises in the first line and descends during the third stanza, to leave twilight deepening at the very end of the poem. Like the other times of the day, the twilight has its own qualities and, as it is presented, gives a sense of intensification. The Green is more itself as it takes on the deeper colour, and activity no longer distracts attention from it. It, too, is at a rest of quietness and sufficiency until morning brings another change.

The poem gives, in a number of ways, then, a sense of satisfaction in the present, and simultaneously a sense of a movement of time giving significance to that present. Nothing is strained after, though it is taken exuberantly, and, once enjoyed, each activity is let go because a new condition has supervened. The changes of the day, of the year and of occupation are accompanied by references to the changing seasons of man's life. The speaker is youthful and the poem races along to accompany him in his sport, but he is primarily engaged in telling us about the day in the first stanza, the 'old folk' in the second stanza, and the 'little ones' in the third. The children, 'like birds', turn instinctively to their mothers to find warmth and security. The old folk take a benevolent interest in the sports of the young without envy or any desire to interfere. They are quite content with their time of life, and being fulfilled themselves, can look on other sorts of fulfilment with pleasure, and remember the past without regret. Blake's poem refers us to states of sufficiency: sufficiencies of racing activity and repose, of gaiety and contemplation, of sunshine and darkness, youth and age. But these sufficiencies gain their support from each other, seasonally developing from the contentment that has gone before.

This flow is celebrated, in the first stanza, by an outburst that is harmonious because wholehearted. Sunlight and bells convey the exuberance of 'merriment', but the exuberance is sustained by the inward quiet of 'happiness' and the communicative sharing of 'chearfulness'. The rejoicing is a letting go, not in wild abandonment, but in the harmony of participation and contribution. The celebration is joined by the birds which:

> Sing louder around
> To the bells' chearful sound.

At the end of the poem, the little children:

> Like birds in their nest,
> Are ready for rest.

The villagers are not unthinking beings, but, like the birds, they can be spontaneous, they respond to the time, and the time elicits a full-bodied response of their powers.

Blake has made the sufficiencies in the poem, its energetic contentments, look beyond the person who enjoys. He employs several devices to achieve this, which may be best seen if we compare the poem with its experienced counterpart. 'London' is written in the present tense, the perpetual present of the wanderer's meditation, which can be disturbed, but not interrupted. In other *Songs of Experience* we find persons who carry about with them a perpetual sense of the future (in 'Ah! Sun-Flower') or of the past (in 'The Garden of Love'). The country folk of 'The Ecchoing Green' are free of such bondage. The last two lines of each stanza of the poem constitute an irregular refrain. In the first stanza they look forward:

> While our sports shall be seen
> On the Ecchoing Green.

They cast back in the second stanza:

> 'In our youth time were seen'
> 'On the Ecchoing Green.'

In the third stanza we are given the period of twilight when time seems suspended:

> And sport no more seen
> On the darkening Green.

The rest of the poem sets off the refrains and is in the present tense. These people can be self-forgetful, and so they are free to anticipate, to recollect or to be relaxed in their sense of time, while their present is being continually encountered, though it comes as a gift and not a burden they must carry.

In 'London', the self was emphasized by the subjectivity of the poem. The cries and sights that disturbed the wanderer's musings were immediately interpreted in terms of his thought. The folk of 'The Ecchoing Green' are capable of being absorbed in their activities and of looking beyond themselves, for their mood is sensitive to times and seasons. In 'London', people impinged upon one another. They communicated nothing, merely noting each other's 'marks', signs to be arbitrarily evaluated. The young speaker in 'The Ecchoing Green' is very much engaged in the sports, but he can be sensitively aware of others. There are no 'bans' here (none that obtrude themselves) for we are presented with a community and not an organization. Institutions, in this poem, are complementary to personal relationships. They do not regulate an impersonal intercourse.

In 'London', the infant sheds tears at the feel of the world where he will not be loved. The little ones of 'The Ecchoing Green' can run off to play by themselves because their mother, their 'sisters and brothers' secure them. The persons in this community may be individual and independent and not, as is the wanderer's case, singular and isolated.

In 'London', the sounds that are heard break painfully into the poem to interrupt the reverie. 'The Ecchoing Green' describes activities, not a brooding inward condition, and we are out among the sounds, which do not force themselves, therefore, but reverberate and connect in an echo. The sound of the bells is responded to by the songs of the birds. The merriment of the first stanza is continued by the laughter in the second. The refrain at the end of each stanza partially repeats the others. Words, phrases and whole lines are picked up again later in the poem, perhaps in an altered form. In the two poems Blake makes us hear two quite different worlds of sound to correspond with the modes of attention of his different persons.

The illustrations to the poems demonstrate these mental states in a more obvious way. One of the illustrations to 'London' shows an old man, blind and on crutches, being guided along the street by a child. His senses, his avenues of communication, are gone. The wanderer is not blind but one notices that the evidence of his ears comes to him with a shock as to a blind man, particularly in the second stanza. In the first stanza, the sights that the wanderer sees come to him without depth as would the evidence of his eyes to a deaf man. The second illustration to the poem shows a child kneeling before a fire in the open with hands stretched out to take the warmth. The gratification being taken in a cold world is, necessarily, a private one. The gratifications depicted in the illustrations to 'The Ecchoing Green' are not secret. There are boys with hoops, bats and kites. Some play a game together. A group of young persons listens to directions being given by a man. Children cluster about their mothers. Here is a world of affections and shared activities.

CHAPTER 2

THE POET'S DETACHMENT

In writing the *Songs of Innocence and of Experience* Blake
answers, in his own way, the question: what is man? The
answer he gives is a complex one, embraces the simpler
answers of Paine and Burke that we have examined, and
attempts to show that these simpler answers are partially
true. Paine suggests that right reasoning is inherent in man,
who needs only consult his consciousness and apply the
faculty he finds there to circumstances. Burke, on the other
hand, suggests that, to reason rightly, man must appeal to
precedent and tradition. Blake, as we shall see, could adopt
neither of these positions, which being advanced in
opposition to each other at the time that the *Songs* were being
written, although in order to appreciate the poet's resolution
of the problem we shall have to go more deeply into the
genesis of the controversy. We will defer the main discussion of this, the historical aspect, to the next chapter,
however, concentrating attention in the present chapter on
certain crucial characteristics of Blake's manner of writing.
In order to appreciate what Blake achieves in the *Songs* it is
necessary to understand his attitude towards the persons he
creates in composing them.

Blake's own ideas about the capacities of the human mind
find their expression through the *Songs*. Indeed, it would
seem at a first glance, that the verses are far too theoretical
to succeed as poetry at all. This is to be observed not only in
poems like 'The Divine Image' or 'The Human Abstract',
which present us with the conceptual ingredients of human
nature (Mercy, Pity, Peace and Love; Fear, Cruelty,
Mystery and Deceit), but in those which purport to give a
description of a place or of persons, such as 'London' or 'The

Ecchoing Green'. Lyrical poetry is frequently the vehicle for a state of mind or of feeling in the writer called up by a particular circumstance or by a particular person. In judging the poem it is usual to take into consideration the adequacy of the writer's feeling, and the liveliness with which we are made to realize the cause of that feeling. In Wordsworth's 'Upon Westminster Bridge' we are attentive simultaneously to the emotion and to the scene depicted when we read: 'And all that mighty heart is lying still!' Those of Blake's *Songs* which come closest to fulfilling this sort of expectation of lyrical verse are the most popular. People look for what they are used to, and 'The Tyger' is Blake's best known poem because Blake seems carried away by a subject that is vividly portrayed. None of Blake's poems fulfils the expectation very well, however. 'London' as we saw, is partly dramatic monologue, partly a revelation of the poet's mind. But the thing described in the poem, the world of the wanderer, is a less substantial and less specific thing than lyric poetry often presents. It is a state of mind, and it is not a state of mind appertaining to a particular man but to all men. It is a possible mentality, and so the poem has, as its subject, something hypothetical. And in describing his hypothesis Blake does not reveal himself openly, but must be 'discovered' as the strategist behind the poem. 'The Ecchoing Green' too, invites the reader to look further than the details of the poem to the intention of the writer. As in 'London' Blake does not attempt to describe a particular scene or particular persons, or attempt to create the illusion that he is doing so. The Green itself and the villagers gathered there (Old John, the young folk and the old folk) are types of place or person. Even the day and the season, with their conventional birds, bells and sunshine, are generalized in the same way. It would not be too much to say, indeed, that the poem is composed of stereotypes, though one must immediately add that the poem as a whole combines those elements into a whole that is highly original.

Blake never used anything but stereotypes and is the only major English poet always to have limited himself in so stringent a way. The success of the *Songs* does not depend on the liveliness of the particulars depicted—they are rather artificial—but on the liveliness of the organization to which they are subordinated. We are not presented with the emotions of a poet responding delicately to a given situation but with an atmosphere of judicious arrangement and contrivance directed by a conscious intention, and this gives the poems their theoretical air. 'London' and 'The Ecchoing Green', for instance, illustrate the place of man in society as considered from different viewpoints. But while the word 'theoretical' stresses the feeling of conscious purpose and calculated effect in the *Songs*, it is inadequate to represent the nature of that purpose.\They appear theoretical in that they present us with a jig-saw in which each piece gives some view of man's situation./Although many of these views contradict each other we have the sense that all the pieces fit together. But if Blake had some master theory that resolved the contradictions, and that was capable of abstract statement, he would, presumably, have given it. He was a man with a fine logical mind, and he falls naturally into an aphoristic and dialectic manner. Nevertheless, he expresses contempt for abstract systems, using them only as counters indicative of some facet of the mind or some aspect of human possibility. One feels very strongly that Blake had an integrated purpose in writing the *Songs* and was conscious of what that purpose was, but that it resisted abstract modes of statement. For our part, we would be unwise to attempt to find any easy formula for it, though we are invited to become consciously aware of what Blake is doing.

Blake denies himself the use of 'characters' and 'realism' in his verse, and relies heavily, for depth of meaning, on the resources of poetry. In 'London', for instance, we are forced to attend to the controlled meanings given to such words as 'mark' or 'black'ning', and the single word 'hearse' guides us to a further dimension of the poem. In 'The Ecchoing Green' the broken refrains are our guide to the changes of tense which are an important aspect of the poem. In such poems as 'Cradle Song' Blake indicates, by poetical means, relationships that it would be most difficult to state in any other way.

There is one sense in which Blake's poetry deals with particulars and not with stereotypes. His figures are stylized or generalized, but they are not associated with a vague or unoriginal purpose. The right generalization must be sought for, and it requires the reader's close attention to find it, especially as the author stands rather behind than among his creations. Blake's apparently conventional Lambs and Angels, his abstract Mercy and Cruelty invite the reader to ransack his own experience and the varieties of his own possible response in order to produce the exact 'thought' (call it) required by the poem. Blake had definite ideas in mind when he wrote his poems, and we are expected to respond with a similar particularity.

We are asked to explore different possibilities of response in reading the two 'Nurse's Songs', one from the *Songs of Innocence* and the other from *Songs of Experience*. In assenting to the truth of each nurse's attitude (in acknowledging the likelihood of her thinking as she does), responsive chords in our own nature are struck, and Blake's very lack of character depiction and realism makes it even more incumbent on the reader to contribute. There can be no temptation to become lost in the action, and intelligent thought (contemplation, recognition, building up) and re-examination of one's standards are an inevitable part of reading the poems. The demand for comparison, for reading the *Songs of Innocence* and *Songs of Experience* together, and allowing the one set to strike off the other is more apparent in the two 'Nurse's Songs' than in the case of any other pair that suggest themselves. Very much the same situation is depicted. The two

poems have whole lines in common. So close are these songs
that the reader even entertains the possibility of the two
nurses being the same person on different occasions, or of
the two poems illustrating different responses striving for
utterance in one person on a single occasion. The latter view
is certainly consistent with the way in which the *Songs*
challenge the reader to assess his own possibilities of
response.

NURSE'S SONG

When the voices of children are heard on the green
And laughing is heard on the hill,
My heart is at rest within my breast
And everything else is still.

'Then come home, my children, the sun is gone down
'And the dews of night arise;
'Come, come, leave off play, and let us away
'Till the morning appears in the skies.'

'No, no, let us play, for it is yet day
'And we cannot go to sleep;
'Besides, in the sky the little birds fly
'And the hills are all cover'd with sheep.'

'Well, well, go & play till the light fades away
'And then go home to bed.'
The little ones leaped & shouted & laugh'd
And all the hills ecchoed.

NURSE'S SONG

When the voices of children are heard on the green
And whisp'rings are in the dale,
The days of my youth rise fresh in my mind,
My face turns green and pale.

Then come home, my children, the sun is gone down,
And the dews of night arise;
Your spring & your day are wasted in play,
And your winter and night in disguise.

The Poet's Detachment

Blake limits himself in the *Songs* to a very restricted vocabulary, and the reader is struck by the commonplace words that are used, by the preponderance of monosyllabic and disyllabic words, and by the frequent repetitions. The 'Nurse's Songs' have lines 1, 5 and 6 in common, and this suggests a degree of identification between the situation of the two nurses, but emphasizes simultaneously the radical dissimilarity of the two states depicted, as the lines held in common have very different meanings. The comment on language is implicit: words, no less than human beings, derive their only true life from what they are in association with others, which is not to deny their individual force in that association. This is most apparent in lines 5 and 6:

> Then come home, my children, the sun is gone down,
> And the dews of night arise . . .

In one poem the dews are life-giving, similar to the silver dew scattered by the Evening Star in the *Poetical Sketches*:

> On every flower that shuts its sweet eyes
> In timely sleep.

The dew in the experienced poem, on the other hand, is dank and detrimental to health. In the one poem there is a promise that the sun which has gone down will rise again, but in the other it has worn quite away, just as youth has worn away from the nurse. Her spring and her day are gone.

The common first line is taken differently into the two poems. The innocent poem repeats the word 'heard':

> When the voices of children are heard on the green
> And laughing is heard on the hill . . .

What is to be heard clearly, what is bold and honest presents itself to the nurse, who receives the sounds as unpremeditated laughter from the open hill. The same sounds come to the experienced nurse as 'whisperings' from the 'dale'. They are hidden, signs of furtive and indecent 'goings on'. She immediately thinks with sick disgust of the 'goings on' of her

own past, though she has, presumably, a history very like
that of her innocent counterpart. She is bound by her suspicions and misgivings and sense of futility. She believes that
no satisfaction may be found in life, for in childhood one is
incapable of being serious about important things, and in
mature life one is so twisted by making pretences to other
persons and by hiding things from oneself that one's notions
of seriousness and importance are wrong. Life is an aimless
wearing away in which the seasons ('spring and day',
'winter and night') are opposed and empty, unlike the
seasons and times of 'The Ecchoing Green' which are full-
bodied but integrated. She regards man as an unpleasant
creature who doesn't know what is good for him at any stage
of his life and who must be kept in order. She probably does
her job as nurse very well, as she understands it, and her
charges are sent off to bed without argument, for like all
bad administrators she must have continuous control. Blake's
illustration to the poem shows her being very conscientious.
Her charges are under her eye, and the boy is having his hair
put into place.

The innocent nurse has much more freedom. Blake's
illustration shows her sitting aside reading a book while her
charges play their game. She does not fret them or herself,
and she is content:

> My heart is at rest within my breast
> And everything else is still.

The lines convey the sense of the quiet time of day, the peace
of the 'darkening Green', but also her capacity to take
pleasure in the present moment and to let be. She describes the
state, not of a 'mind' sickened by regrets and anxieties, but
of a 'heart', a complete being, at peace and in balance. She
assumes that the children, like the birds and sheep of the
third stanza, know what is best for them, and that if they are
left alone they will seek their own good. The children are
free to make their wishes known, and are to '*go* home to bed'

when they know the time is right. Unlike the experienced nurse she assumes that one finds satisfaction all through one's life in obeying one's impulses, and the less man is ordered about, the better he will behave.

The title-page of Blake's work reads: *Songs of Innocence and Of Experience: Shewing the Two Contrary States of the Human Soul.* It is quite plain, in the case of the two 'Nurse's Songs' that Blake is not talking simply in his own person, but that he presents us with the contrary states referred to. The two poems demonstrate poles of tension—there is the possibility, in any circumstance, of being moved towards the sort of response made by the one nurse or by the other. Both types of response are realities in this sense, though there is no doubt, in the case of these two songs, as to which reality Blake supposes it better to attain. The attitude taken by the experienced nurse is quite right in a worldly-wise way, for what that way is worth. Life is a series of completed disappointments when looked at in a certain mood, although another occasion might discover a different interpretation. In the two 'Nurse's Songs' there is no evidence that different sorts of experience are available to the two women—the correspondences between the poems invite us to imagine them in as much the same position as could possibly be—and the character of their observations is determined by their respective attitudes.

The poems do not present us with two subjective interpretations of a situation that are equally valid, however, and it is obvious that objectivity lies with the innocent nurse. Her observations and the unspoken and unformulated principles, which are implicit in her actions, have a validity which is not shared by those of her experienced sister, for the latter is, like the wanderer, in an isolated condition. The experienced song is a monologue conveying impressions and statements highly coloured by a personal mood, and it is interrupted only in order to give a command to the children. The innocent nurse, on the other hand, is less restricted—she is attentive, easy-going and receptive, and she is not the only person to speak in her poem. Her senses, too, act as a vehicle of communication, not as instruments of assertion. Although the quiet of the evening brings a state of contentment to her, a personal mood, it is induced by what is present about her as well as by her inward being. She is in touch. Her experienced sister regulates everything, even the evidence of her senses being an excuse for perceiving in her world what she is disposed to put there.

As has been remarked before, Blake does not present us with rounded characters or with carefully elaborated depictions. But he does, most decidedly, present us with depth of poetic effect to carry out his design. The type of perception that his two nurses are capable of is reinforced by his manner of depiction, and particularly, as we noticed in 'London' and 'The Ecchoing Green', in the presentation of sounds. This is an amazing fact of poems so deliberately restricted in their basic verse patterns and vocabulary as Blake's are. The innocent nurse has the full use of her senses, and the sounds of the poem amplify our knowledge of this by being sharp and vivid: shouts, laughter and echoes. Their sharpness is brought out against the stillness of the evening and the boldness is repeated in the clarity of the things seen. Throughout the poem we are invited to cast our eyes above the horizontal: to the afterglow of sunset, the skies, the hillside covered with sheep, the little birds still on the wing. Clear sound, bold shapes and vigorous movement are brought together in the last two lines of the poem:

> The little ones leaped & shouted & laugh'd
> And all the hills ecchoed.

The innocent nurse is fully alive, her 'rest' is one of participation and of sufficiency, and the vigour of her impressions is a part of her completeness. The experienced song presents us with indistinct whispers and vague, hidden outlines, with conjectural happenings in the valley after dark, and the secrets of disguise. Like the wanderer, the nurse knows the worst, and like the wanderer she finds it in the recesses of her own mind. Her senses act to confirm her suspicions of a world she tyrannizes over, but does not communicate with. This is indicated by the lack of clarity of things heard and seen in the poem.

The two nurses of the *Songs* are administrators, givers of civil laws in a small way, using very different methods. The one is interfering and dictatorial, while the other is tolerant and permissive. The nurses do not tell us, in so many words, the principles of their moral philosophies, but it is clear that they have different intuitions as to the nature of man. The one supposes that man's instincts need to be guarded against by placing him under authority, while the other assumes that man is best left to be guided by his instincts. There is an opposition here, similar in some respects to that we have seen between Burke and Paine, whose political notions are based on opposed psychologies. During the eighteenth century much discussion of moral topics had centred on the 'natural man': a hypothetical being who was supposed to exhibit those characteristics deemed essentially human. Hobbes had postulated a beastly proto-man who was to be brought to a decent state of civilization by observance of the statutes and customs imposed by the community, while thinkers such as Bolingbroke[1] postulated a virtuous 'natural man' who was debased by the 'artificial' conditions of society. Burke's view of man is a balanced one but, broadly speaking, we can align him with Hobbes (who supposes that man needs control), and align Paine with such men as Bolingbroke (who supposes that man is benign by instinct).

In the *Songs of Innocence* and the *Songs of Experience* Blake presents us with opposed notions of man's nature, apparently similar to those just mentioned, and presents them in such a

[1] The victim of an attack made by Burke in his first published work: *A Vindication of Natural Society*, 1756.

way that we must ask what the opposition is due to. It is not suggested, however, that the opposition can be resolved. In the 'Nurse's Songs' man is what the nurse, in each case, is capable of making him. There is no 'man' but as he may be conceived on the basis of some human reality—just as we can abstract different conceptions from the humanity of the two nurses. Blake presents us with his opposed implicit notions of man. He leaves us in no doubt as to which notion is the better conceived, but we are left with both notions as true, because both the contrary states that support the notions are realities. Blake, unlike his predecessors, does not aim at psychological finality.

Blake does not aim at political finality either. 'London' contradicts 'The Ecchoing Green' in its view of the effect of communal life. Does living in developed society, being able to rely on institutions for one's responses and on written and unwritten law for one's actions, diminish responsibility, converting man into an unhappy automaton? On the other hand, does living in developed society, having adequate channels for the release of one's energy, being able to come to a fulfilment that can only be got by participation, does only that make individuality possible? Again, Blake leaves us in no doubt as to which is the happier possible outcome, but both alternatives are true in that both describe a reality. There is no social life except that lived by men, and its character is that realized by particular men. Despite the general cast he gives his poems, Blake asserts, by their means, the importance of the individual, who gives specificity and significance to any situation. This is well illustrated in the songs, one innocent and the other experienced, each called 'The Chimney Sweeper'.

THE CHIMNEY SWEEPER

When my mother died I was very young,
And my Father sold me while yet my tongue
Could scarcely cry ''weep! 'weep! 'weep! 'weep!'
So your chimneys I sweep, & in soot I sleep.

38

The Poet's Detachment

There's little Tom Dacre, who cried when his head, *5*
That curl'd like a lamb's back, was shav'd: so I said
'Hush, Tom! never mind it, for when your head's bare
'You know that the soot cannot spoil your white hair.'

And so he was quiet, & that very night
As Tom was a-sleeping, he had such a sight! *10*
That thousands of sweepers, Dick, Joe, Ned, & Jack,
Were all of them lock'd up in coffins of black.

And by came an Angel who had a bright key,
And he open'd the coffins & set them all free;
Then down a green plain leaping, laughing, they run, *15*
And wash in a river, and shine in the Sun.

Then naked & white, all their bags left behind,
They rise upon clouds and sport in the wind;
And the Angel told Tom, if he'd be a good boy,
He'd have God for his father, & never want joy. *20*

And so Tom awoke; and we rose in the dark,
And got with our bags & our brushes to work.
Tho' the morning was cold, Tom was happy & warm;
So if all do their duty they need not fear harm.

For Blake, the state of Innocence is a state, not of ignorance
but of knowledge, though not a state of being 'knowing'
(which is characteristic of Experience). The first line of the
innocent sweeper's poem is written in the rhythm of explanatory prose and immediately sets the tone of the boy's factual
account of his situation:

When my mother died I was very young . . .

He knows that his life is an exceedingly wretched one and we
are asked to pity him, but it is by Blake that we are asked, not
by the boy. The distortion of his tradesman's cry to ''weep!
'weep! 'weep! 'weep!' is what may, in fact, be heard, and the
distortion suits the pity that may be felt towards the victim of
evil circumstances. The boy knows of the evil—he tells us
that he was sold and he describes very briefly how he lives:

So your chimneys I sweep, & in soot I sleep.

His circumstances could not be more wretched, but he is patient and explicit with his auditor, even rather kindly. The detachment he shows excludes self-pity on the one hand, and is sufficiently unselfconscious to exclude also any form of self-effacement on the other. Blake manages, in the first stanza, to convey to us the sympathy due to the boy without making him in any way appeal for it. The boy's attitude is given by the dignified, patient (and 'unpoetic') first line, the explanatory 'So' that introduces the fourth line, the emphatic, monosyllabic rhyming words and the positive straightforward nature of the rest of the poem. There isn't a complaint in the whole account.

The sweep repeats his boyishly factual 'so' several times in the course of the poem. These 'so's' together with his 'and so's' and 'and's', which occur frequently, as they do in all stories told by small boys, give the poem the authority of a logic that is familiar enough to children perhaps, but often overlooked by adults. What, after all, is more easily taken into account than inescapable fact or more consequential than the course of events. No adult, and certainly no outsider (no person not in the same plight) could offer little Tom Dacre the comfort given by the sweep:

> 'Hush, Tom! never mind it, for when your head's bare
> 'You know that the soot cannot spoil your white hair.'

Only a sweep could offer such comfort. A sense of injustice, dismay, would keep other persons dumb, unable to say anything to the point. Not that the older sweep is unaware of the grounds for such feelings, but his sense of reality outweighs any sense of injustice, and his need for resolute action outweighs dismay. He knows well enough that if the soot cannot spoil Tom's hair it is because the hair is no longer there, but if Tom, more naïve, can allow the one fact to cover the other, if Tom can become resigned for a while (as the sweep is not) until he becomes stronger (as the sweep is stronger) then the logic of the statement is proved by the event:

> And so he was quiet . . .

The reason given little Tom, taken by itself, is a horrifying one, not because it is untrue, but because of what it cynically leaves out. But in the sweep's mouth, cynical truth is no more than fact, and the purpose of the statement, which is to console, allows no place for cynicism in the truth. Fellow-feeling is its main content and that has had its effect. The truth of the statement is proved by its consequence, and the considerations it leaves out of account are rendered subordinate.

In stanzas 3, 4 and 5 Tom's dream is described and in the context of the poem it is fresh and exciting. The ability of the poet to condense is apparent. The 'coffin of black' refers us to the miseries of a sweep's existence, to the chimney in which he works, and to the abbreviation of his span of life. This is contrasted with the movement and light of the world into which the boys are liberated by the 'bright key'. The reader accepts, even, the words of the Angel to Tom that if he'd be good, 'He'd have God for his father, & never want joy.' But these words are the part of the dream that lead the reader to make a second examination and to find that its contents are unpleasant. The details of the dream are beautiful in the sweeper's mouth, but taken out of context they are just as ugly as the comfort offered Tom for the loss of his hair, also taken out of context. One can imagine Tom being told, in all seriousness, that God would compensate him for his present pains in a future Heaven, the condition being that he must 'be a good boy', which means, presumably, that he must do as he is told, and take what comes his way without complaint. Such advice (and Tom has picked it up somewhere) in nearly any mouth could only be callous, the result of folly or hypocrisy.

The truth of Tom's dream, however, is a subordinate consideration in the poem, both as it affects Tom (who believes it) and as it affects the sweep (who neither believes nor disbelieves it). For the latter, the factual truth does not lie in the existence or non-existence of a place where children can live as they ought, but in the effect that the belief in such a place has on his companion. The sweep is pleased that Tom is now 'happy and warm' in his belief. He would not think of upsetting the comfort by questioning it, though not because Tom has found a fool's paradise, but because he has come to a source of strength similar to that shown by the sweep himself.

The sweep's comfort to Tom in stanza 2, and the contents of Tom's dream, looked at apart from the setting in which they occur, are very shabby statements, and they are followed by an equally shabby pronouncement at the end of the poem:

> So if all do their duty they need not fear harm.

In the first place, it isn't true—harm has come to the sweeps —and in the second place, as a cliché, its idea of duty is a deplorable one. It asks men to be sheep. In the sweep's mouth, however, these words do not present us with a catch-phrase. He does not speak them in approbation of himself, nor is he acquiescing in the idea that the world will go well if we perform our tasks in that state to which it has pleased God to call us. He applies it to Tom equally with himself and applies it to their state of mind. Despite the triteness and wrongness of the words, they do really mean something in his mouth. One's duty in the sweeper's sense does not refer to sweeping chimneys well (though he probably does do so), nor does it refer to the building up of a proper credit balance so as to get into Tom's heaven (towards which he is, if not sceptical, indifferent). One's duty lies in doing what must be done, and it happens that this is, for him, an exercise of fellow-feeling. We have seen him demonstrate this towards Tom. If Tom 'catches' the feeling by having a vision which shows a world ordered to the extent of everyone being cared for somewhere at some time, then though the form in which he sees differs from the sweep's form, he has seen the same essential thing: a world in which care and fellow-feeling do matter, a world which sympathy may give order to. Without sympathy it is a chaos. Tom's Sunday-school story has acquired meaning for him through the support he has received from his older companion and can give in return, and the sweep has satisfaction in his friendly act of comfort done for its own sake. One need fear harm only if one neglects one's duty, for then one must undergo isolation in a meaningless world, the misery of being self-centred.

Ignorance and naïveté are not the conditions for Blake's Innocence and the sweep of this poem is neither ignorant nor naïve. He knows that the reason he offers to Tom to comfort him for the loss of his hair doesn't justify the loss, but he is not concerned with the justice of the matter. He is non-committal about the content of Tom's dream. If it were put to him, he might reluctantly agree that the dream was a way of finding compensation, but as we see him he is not engaged in thinking of the motive for the dream, only of the purpose it serves. He is engaged in looking at fact and consequence, and it would not occur to him to explain the dream in terms that are irrelevant.

Someone less wise than the sweep would allow irrelevant considerations to colour his answers to little Tom, or would be left by such considerations with no answer at all. The purpose of the dream might be lost sight of in favour of examining the decency of its message or the propriety of believing it. The most likely reaction from a sympathetic observer would be shock and silence. In 'London' we read:

> How the Chimney-sweeper's cry
> Every black'ning Church appals . . .

The Church here is in the position of regarding the sweep with pity, and the pity is very strongly felt. But the very concern of the Church seems to paralyse it. It is appalled, shocked into immobility. What can be done? Remove the evil? Two thousand years of effort have not done so. Comfort the wretched? With what words? The words of the dream perhaps (though that is to evade the issue), but not with the sweep's words:

> '. . . for when your head's bare
> 'You know that the soot cannot spoil your white hair.'

Only a fellow-sufferer could dare to say such a thing, for only to a fellow-sufferer are the words the plain truth of hard fact. For an outsider concerned by Tom's plight the truth is this: 'Your condition is one of abject misery and men should not tolerate its continuance for one moment.' To make the sweep's answer would, for an outsider, be to lie, because it suppresses that truth. So the outsider is left with no words of comfort. His truths offer none, and he must be callous in order to lie. The sweep can help because his truths comfort, while the outsider can only stand dumb and horrified, miserable in the consciousness of another's woe which he can do nothing to console.

Blake illuminated the innocent 'Chimney Sweeper', and at the bottom drew a frieze showing the little sweeps laughing and running in their green meadow. The Angel assists one of them to rise. The experienced counterpart of the poem is illustrated, and we are shown a sweeper carrying his bags along a street while the snow falls. The text of the poem reads:

THE CHIMNEY SWEEPER

A little black thing among the snow,
Crying ''weep! 'weep!' in notes of woe!
'Where are thy father & mother? say?'
'They are both gone up to the church to pray.

'Because I was happy upon the heath,
'And smil'd among the winter's snow,
'They clothed me in the clothes of death,
'And taught me to sing the notes of woe.

'And because I am happy & dance & sing,
'They think they have done me no injury,
'And are gone to praise God & his Priest & King,
'Who make up a heaven of our misery.'

If naïveté, being unaware of things and leaving them out of account, is a sign of Innocence, then the parents in this poem are more innocent than little Tom. Tom's Sunday-school myth is made of inferior material but he has turned it to good account. These parents have turned their religion, as they turn everything else, to a paltry end. They have exploited their child for the little he will bring in, and their church-going, presumably, has the same nominal aim as Tom's dream:

> And the Angel told Tom, if he'd be a good boy,
> He'd have God for his father, & never want joy.

Where Tom derived from this covenant a notion of the paramount importance of mutual care, of love and so joy, the parents attribute to God the meanness of their own minds, and have struck a bargain with Him. The last two lines of the poem bring out the implications of the parent's church-going in a manner very characteristic of Blake:

> 'And are gone to praise God & his Priest & King,
> 'Who make up a heaven of our misery.'

The linking together of God, priest and king on equal terms, the present existence of heaven, and its foundation on misery imply a great deal. The attack made by these words is directed at the shameful mentality of the parents and also at institutions which, it is suggested, connive at their way of behaving. Joy is postponed, for the parents, to a future life, but meanwhile they occupy a 'heaven' that is very much of this world —a place where self-satisfied and insensitive people may make themselves secure and be comfortable. One 'comfort' for the parents is that they may fulfil their responsibilities by making gestures of piety and another 'comfort' is the convenient fiction that they have 'done no injury' to their child. God is seen as collaborator with 'Priest' and 'King' in these worldly interests. The sweeper has seen that God and Divine Law may become very much what man cares to distort them to, and that practically anything may be done in their name. This pessimism, which belongs to the sweep, not Blake, is carried to too great a length, however. No 'Priest' is likely to view indifferently the misuse of children, especially by the parents, even when the Church feels itself powerless to take vigorous steps in remedy.

The attack on the Church in the experienced sweeper's song is a gross one, and by means of the over-statement Blake is saying something about the sweep himself. He is experienced not innocent, and like all experienced persons he is not quite straight with himself or with others. He lives in disguise, and the poem's explicit comment on parents, State and Church (too crude for Blake) is accompanied by an implicit comment on the speaker. The innocent poem opened with a very matter-of-fact statement by the sweep. Here, we are presented with a pathetic picture:

> A little black thing among the snow,
> Crying ''weep! 'weep!' in notes of woe!

Undoubtedly the conditions of the sweep are most miserable and we are expected to feel that this is so, but we are made to feel also that poverty and maltreatment do not allow people to appear at their best. There is a self-pitying note in the sweeper's cry of woe. He is conscious of ill-usage in a way that the innocent sweep is not. He looks for special consideration on this account, and has his answer (in the form of a hidden accusation) ready for the kindly passer-by who questions him:

> 'Where are thy father & mother? say?'
> 'They are both gone up to the church to pray.'

The story told us by the innocent sweep was punctuated by his 'and's', 'and so's', 'so's', all meaning 'the consequence was'. Here too, we have the childish recurrence of 'and' linked, however, not with 'so', but with 'because'. Where the innocent sweep looked forward in his story to results, the experienced sweep looks backward to motives. He has a complete picture, no doubt a fairly accurate one from his point of view, of a world of self-seeking and indifference, extending from his parents, through society to the Deity, and his tone is one of premature cynicism. The degree of sophistication shown by the urchin is sufficiently great to allow him to point to his apparent innocence in describing his position:

> 'And because I am happy & dance & sing,
> 'They think they have done me no injury . . .'

It is true that if one wishes to find apparent light-heartedness one must look among the less comfortably situated inhabitants of the earth, but the sweep's recognition of this is rather 'knowing'. If he can be light-hearted we don't see it here, and the fact is overlaid for us by his sense of injury and his glib insight into the motives of his parents:

> 'Because I was happy upon the heath,
> 'And smil'd among the winter's snow,
> 'They clothed me in the clothes of death,
> 'And taught me to sing the notes of woe.'

The sweep has been wronged, but he is also unpleasant. There is no reason why we should disbelieve his account of his treatment, yet there is a false ring to it, not in the facts related but in the manner of his relation. There is something self-satisfied in the child, just as there is in the parents he describes. If one is badly off then one can nurse one's grievances and even gain a sense of self-righteousness from the circumstance. One can make a pose, even out of one's real position (it is not necessary to assume a false one), and even out of an appallingly bad position.

None of this argues that we should fail to assist the sweep or his counterparts that we meet or hear of daily. Self-righteous distress stands in need of help. But apart from considerations of relief we are asked in the two sweeper's songs to consider the qualities of two minds giving an account of the same condition. The experienced sweep gives us an explanation. He judges and he fixes motives, but he does not display any freedom, being bound by his idea of himself, his prejudices and his cynicism. Perhaps his prejudices are 'right' and his cynicism 'justified', but they limit his humanity. We do not trust the experienced sweep to see anything very much because he is too much involved in interpretation—he is an 'and because' thinker, immediately finding motive and reason. The innocent sweep with his 'and so' is not concerned with the same sort of interpretation but with consequence. In place of motive and reason he is interested in purpose and outcome, in the way things take their significance from each other, in the meaning Tom's dream has in terms of Tom's situation. The reader is invited to imitate the innocent sweeper and to find the meaning of his statements and the significance of the dream in the fellow-feeling they are intended to convey.

CHAPTER 3

BLAKE'S CRITICISM OF 'NATURE'

IN presenting his account of the states of the human soul in the *Songs* Blake makes, quite deliberately, an attack on the psychologies of his day. His purpose is not an academic one, and the attack is made, not because the psychologies describe inaccurately but because the truths they describe are only half-truths regarded as the whole. Such half-truths are the outcome of half-living, and if subscribed to, encourage the adoption of a half-life. We have already seen that Blake dislikes Burke's opinion that man simply owes his especial being to the institutions that humanize him. On the other hand, he does not accept Paine's negligent view of the effects of institution. Both Burke and Paine attempt to explain the organic whole of man in society in terms of only one part or another, so distorting the picture. Burke is more convincing, but Blake prefers Paine's account for the reason that it lays stress on the importance of the individual, even though the argument put forward is a poor one. Blake's main attack is directed against the view of man that was in the ascendancy during the eighteenth century and, in England, was expressed and developed to the near exclusion of any other, reaching its most developed form in Hume. Burke's view may be seen as influenced by this trend.

In making his annotations to Sir Joshua Reynolds's *Discourses* in 1808 Blake wrote:

Burke's Treatise on the Sublime & Beautiful is founded on the Opinions of Newton & Locke; on this Treatise Reynolds has grounded many of his assertions in all his Discourses. I read Burke's Treatise when very Young; at the same time I read Locke on Human Understanding & Bacon's Advancement of Learning; on Every one of these Books I wrote my Opinions, & on looking them over find that my Notes on Reynolds in this Book are exactly Similar. I felt the Same Contempt & Abhorrence then that I do now. They mock Inspiration & Vision.[1]

The line traced by Blake is from Bacon, through Newton and Locke and so to Burke. The first three men, the early giants of empiricism, are frequently the victims of Blake's ridicule.

It is probable that Blake never read Hobbes. He never mentions his name. Hobbes could hardly fail to have an impact, and Blake was in the habit of commenting on what had affected him. Nevertheless, it is convenient, for the present, to make an examination of the trend of thinking so much disliked by Blake, not through Bacon or Locke, whom he read, but through Hobbes whom he did not. Hobbes is eminently suitable, for a number of reasons. In the first place, he is more wide-ranging than Bacon, and less astringently philosophical than Locke, though, as a philosopher, he is a model of style. As a result, his effect on non-philosophical or quasi-philosophical thought is probably greater than that of Locke, for where Locke received the judicious acquiescence due to a man of his respectable utterances, Hobbes touched, and still touches his readers 'on the raw'. Bolingbroke, for instance, is angered by Hobbes and yet, as we shall see, accepts him completely after giving his ideas a more comfortable shape. Hobbes is one of the earliest empirical thinkers, he follows his reasoning further than his successors care to go, and is clinically inquisitive and impartial to a degree that they find outrageous. The eighteenth century disliked Hobbes and they tried to hide from themselves the fact that their thoughts were basically his. It is not until we come to Blake's *Songs of Experience* that we find a thinker equally prepared, with Hobbes, to look without self-deception on the meaner aspects of man. Blake's view, however, is not confined to that aspect, as Hobbes's is. Hobbes is far-ranging, penetrating, and capable of taking his logic to an extreme without loss of subtlety. He presents, without confusion, the viewpoint of the

[1] Annotation to 'Discourse VIII', p. 244. In *Complete Writings* (1957), p. 476.

empirical eighteenth century to which Blake reacted, and he will bear a direct comparison with Blake. Although Blake may not have read Hobbes, he saw the logical need of a Hobbes to take further the ideas of the writers he did read. His own *Songs of Experience* go towards filling the need he saw, for they mercilessly push the more half-hearted elements of thought of the age of enlightenment to their conclusion.

Hobbes's idea of natural law stands at the centre of his account of man given in *Leviathan*. Natural law is usually thought of as the statement of a higher justice, which is inherent in the universe or implanted in the reason of man, is antecedent to positive law, and should guide the making of positive laws. Hobbes looks at both positive and natural law from a practical viewpoint, and, in doing so, manages to subordinate the natural to the positive. His positive law, it is true, flows from his natural law. Natural law is always there to be appealed to but it seeks its fulfilment in positive law, and its existence is discernible only in its outcome in positive law. Natural laws, for Hobbes, are devices, all contractual, such as:

That a man be willing, when others are so too, as farre-forth, as for Peace, and defence of himselfe he shall think it necessary, to lay down this right to all things; and be contented with so much liberty against other men, as he would allow other men against himselfe.[1]

These devices are, indeed, not properly to be understood as laws at all until they can be compelled:

For the Lawes of Nature (as *Justice, Equity, Modesty, Mercy*, and (in summe) *doing to others, as wee would be done to*,) of themselves, without the terrour of some Power, to cause them to be observed, are contrary to our naturall Passions, that carry us to Partiality, Pride, Revenge, and the like. And Covenants, without the Sword, are but Words, and of no strength to secure a man at all. Therefore notwithstanding the Lawes of Nature, (which every one hath then kept, when he has the will to keep them, when he can do it safely,) if there be no Power erected, or not great enough for our security; every man will, and may lawfully rely on his own strength and art, for caution against all other men.[2]

[1] *Leviathan*, XIV (Everyman edn., p. 67.)   [2] *Ibid.* XVII; p. 87.

Hobbes shifts his natural laws away from everything that is usually made to act as their basis, away from human nature and divine provision, and attaches them instead to positive law and to organized civil society. He retains a connexion of a sort with human nature:

A LAW OF NATURE, (*Lex Naturalis,*) is a Precept, or generall Rule, found out by Reason, by which a man is forbidden to do, that, which is destructive of his life, or taketh away the means of preserving the same; and to omit, that, by which he thinketh it may be best preserved.[1]

The laws are described as the outcome of an instinct for self-preservation, but they do not take their form from the instinct—they must be found out. By search, man discovers the devices that we may call natural laws, and though instinct impels him to the search it does not provide any answers. Justice, equity, mercy, modesty, the moral virtues or natural laws are what man may impose on himself in order to preserve himself, but they are no part of his impulses for his being merely man. He does not search his soul to find them for they are working devices and not innate qualities. They may not be spoken of as faculties or be accounted part of our being. Hobbes is specific on this point:

To this warre of every man against every man [to man in a state of mere nature], this also is consequent; that nothing can be Unjust. The notions of Right and Wrong, Justice and Injustice have there no place. Where there is no common Power, there is no Law: where no Law, no Injustice. Force, and Fraud, are in warre the two Cardinall vertues. Justice, and Injustice are none of the Faculties neither of the Body, nor Mind. If they were, they might be in a man that were alone in the world, as well as his Senses, and Passions. They are Qualities, that relate to men in Society, not in Solitude. It is consequent also to the same condition, that there be no Propriety, no Dominion, no *Mine* and *Thine* distinct; but onely that to be every mans, that he can get; and for so long, as he can keep it. And thus much for the ill condition, which man by meer Nature is actually placed in; though with a possibility to come out of it, consisting partly in the Passions, partly in his Reason.[2]

---

[1] *Leviathan*, XIV; p. 66   [2] *Ibid.* XIII; p. 66.

We may take Hobbes a stage further, even, than this. Not only are there no moral virtues except those that relate to men in society—without society there are not even any men, properly speaking. Hobbes states that the notion of man in a condition of mere nature is hypothetical, is a postulate given likelihood by what can be observed of the behaviour of savages, and of man deprived of civil restraint.[1] The point of evolving the theory of the natural is that it accounts for the observable, for developed man and positive law. Hobbes's natural law is to be seen as the unwritten part of positive law rather than as a source for it.

In Hobbes the connexion between natural law and God also disappears. He seldom contemplates the notion that natural laws are prescribed by divine authority, and he never considers the possibility of their having the authority of some knowledge divinely implanted in our nature. No polemic directed against the notion of such authorities could be more devastating than Hobbes's passing them ignorantly by. He refuses to make any genuflexion of reverence towards naked human impulses or alliances, and when he brings the divine into his system it is subordinated to civil order:

It is a question much disputed between the divers sects of Christian Religion, *From whence the Scriptures derive their Authority*;. . .it is manifest, that none can know they are Gods Word, (though all true Christians beleeve it,) but those to whom God himself hath revealed it supernaturally . . . He therefore, to whom God hath not supernaturally revealed, that they are his, nor that those that published them, were sent by him, is not obliged to obey them, by any Authority, but his, whose Commands have already the force of Laws; that is to say, by any other Authority, then that of the Common-wealth, residing in the Soveraign, who only has the Legislative power.[2]

It had become customary to suppose that if man had any fine qualities they were to be attributed to the influence of the supernatural. The idea of goodness in man was inextricably tied up with theological considerations of the most speculative

---

[1] *Ibid.* XIII; p. 65.   [2] *Ibid.* XXXIII; p. 208.

sort, and Hobbes simply avoids these complications by assuming that the basic characteristics of man are his most unpleasant ones. He makes an apparently healthy response to a tangle of metaphysical considerations by throwing them out, and takes man flatly at his worst. As a result, he was attacked. His readers were outraged by his directness. They called the fear and selfishness which he set up as the basic qualities of man and as the drives to all man's achievements by more respectable names, but they kept Hobbes's fundamental assumptions intact. Hobbes bade an effective farewell to a divine influence which had pervaded the world, and towards which man's chief responsibilities lay. He did not deny the divine, but moved it off to where it could not interfere in practical matters. He is one of the precursors of deism, and deism gives way, in turn, to agnosticism and atheism. Hobbes's God can be seen by man only through the mediation of the state, through authority. Next, He is established as a 'Great Original' only, and by the twentieth century most speculative disciplines have ceased to concern themselves in any way with theological and metaphysical matters. Any contemporary treatise which puts itself forward as being scientific assumes a universe without a resident God, and takes for granted Hobbes's assessment of man.

Hobbesian social, political and psychological ideas have been successful because they describe a materialistic world in which power and money are deemed the greatest goods. There are other worlds with different desires. Other thinkers have fructified the period since *Leviathan*, but there is an attractiveness to Hobbes's thought, even for those who disagree with his assumptions. He is clear, open and thorough. He makes many writers who are more hopeful, more comfortable, more Christian, appear clumsy by comparison, for they often show some degree of muddle-headedness, self-deception and even self-seeking, which is absent in Hobbes. 'If you agree with me', he seems to say, 'that money and power are the things that count, then let us admit it and see

what follows from the admission.' What follows is that law
and justice, honesty and kindliness, tolerance and decency are
all important to man if he is to achieve his full stature. Man
must live in society, and only when these things are respected
can society confer the benefits it should. However, they can
only be respected when they can be enforced:

... before the names of Just, and Unjust can have place, there must
be some coercive Power, to compell men equally to the performance
of their Covenants . . .[1]

Only when there is compulsion can any man be sure that his
endeavours to live well will be matched by his fellows, and if
it were not for this assurance one would have no incentive to
just behaviour. But more is implied: if it were not for the
assurance, one would have no sense of justice at all, for
knowledge of compulsion is a part of the reasoning which
evolves the notion of justice in the first place. The point is a
subtler one than appears at first sight, and is, indeed, typical
of the penetration Hobbes achieves. He is not saying: men
have a sense of justice which they will allow to assert itself
when the fear of the sword assures that it will get a fair
chance. He is saying that the fear of the sword is a part of the
circumstance which allows men to reason about justice.

Hobbes can talk in this way because he is perfectly clear
about his terms, and here the term at issue is 'reason':

Justice therefore, that is to say, Keeping of Covenant, is a Rule of
Reason, by which we are forbidden to do any thing destructive to
our life; and consequently a Law of Nature.[2]

Hobbes's 'reason', like his natural law (which is a part of
reason) is a faculty for calculation, and the issue is never
made more complicated than that. His man in a state of 'mere
nature' trails no clouds of glory, has no alliances, has few
attributes (none of which are human), is (from a point of
view that examines man) a nothing. And that part of man
which we call his reason is a nothing until it has a realm in
which to work. Just as man becomes man only in society, so

[1] *Leviathan*, xv; p. 74. [2] *Ibid.* xv; p. 76.

reason becomes reason only in the eliciting of consequence. Only a fool, given the opportunity of peace on condition of behaving in the ways that we call 'just' (because they prove acceptable), would refuse the offer. It would be unreasonable to refuse the conditions because that would be a declaration of war, a throwing away of one's life. One's reason, which foresees, declines injury to oneself. One's reason, which foresees, declines to allow one to circumvent the covenants which are the outcome of natural law, for the consequences are likely to be prejudicial to oneself:

> He therefore that breaketh his Covenant, and consequently declareth that he thinks he may with reason do so, cannot be received into any Society, that unite themselves for Peace and Defence, but by the errour of them that receive him; nor when he is received, be retayned in it, without seeing the danger of their errour; which errours a man cannot reasonably reckon upon as the means of his security. . .[1]

Coleridge makes a distinction between the 'reason' and the 'understanding' and shows how, from each of these notions distinct systems of political justice may be evolved. The 'reason', he says, is an inward eye acquainting itself with spiritual objects, the eternal and archetypal verities which, it may be supposed, man has knowledge of as a birthright. The 'understanding', on the other hand, is an empirical organ, an eye looking outward to learn its truths from the facts and occurrences of the world. Political theories based on the idea of the efficacy of 'reason' attribute to man an 'original character' by means of which man may rejuvenate his political life at any time. We carry within us, it is supposed, original laws and principles to which we may refer in making the decisions which affect the course of civil society. Coleridge says of this theory that, 'To state it nakedly is to confute it satisfactorily. So at least it should seem.' Nevertheless:

> . . . in how tempting and dangerous a manner it may be represented to the populace, has been made too evident in our own country by the temporary effects of Paine's Rights of Man.[2]

---

[1] *Leviathan*. xv; p. 76.   [2] *The Friend*, First Section, Essay III.

To Paine's variety of Platonism may be opposed the 'understanding' and political systems based on the notion of the efficacy of the 'understanding'. Such systems, Coleridge says, affirm that

... the human mind consists of nothing but the manifold modifications of passive sensation ... The assertors of this system consequently ascribe the origin and continuance of government to fear, or the power of the stronger, aided by the force of custom. This is the system of Hobbes.[1]

In the sense that Coleridge uses the word 'reason' Hobbes takes no account of it. It simply does not exist, because the 'reason' which Hobbes makes the source of his natural law is the power of the mind to calculate eventualities, aided by the memory. It is the understanding of normal consequences. Hobbes is wonderfully clear-minded about this. The products of 'reason': justice, equity, modesty, mercy, are all products of the sphere of their application, of society. They come into being by making a survey of the conditions of their application, and compulsion is seen as one of those conditions. Hobbes's man has understanding only, as Coleridge points out.

The eighteenth century is a period of reliance on systems based on the 'understanding' and the complete success of the Hobbesian way of thinking is nowhere shown more clearly than in the attacks on Hobbes made by such men as Bolingbroke, attacks which accept the very principles they suppose themselves to refute. In addressing Pope, Bolingbroke states:

It seems then to me, that civil societies could not have been formed, nor the distinction of just and unjust, nor the honesty and decorum of life have been established, if there had not been antecedently, such a law of nature as HOBBES denies, and directly opposite to that which he supposes. Your [Pope's] great predecessors, AMPHION and ORPHEUS, would have strung their lyres to little purpose, if there had not been a corresponding unison in the human condition.[2]

[1] *Ibid.* First Section, Essay I. Coleridge adheres to Reason as the superior faculty, but develops the idea of Prudence as guide in practical matters.
[2] 'Fragment III', *Works* (1777 edn.), v, 52.

Amphion, the law-giver, according to Bolingbroke, can persuade men not merely because their understanding shows them the practicability of his proposals, but because they have an innate inclination to the suggestions. The suggestions themselves, presumably, are an outcome of the inclination.

Bolingbroke is presenting us with a quality in man similar to Paine's 'original character'. He does not maintain the idea, however, and in developing his argument he moves unwittingly into the position he supposes himself to be attacking. It is ridiculous, he says,

> . . . to say with HOBBES, that when men distinguished between just and unjust, and made laws and institutions on that distinction, they made that to be just or unjust which was indifferent before. The natural obligation to exercise benevolence, to administer justice, and to keep compacts, is as evident to human reason, as the desire of happiness is agreeable to human instinct. We desire by instinct, we acquire by reason. The natural desire leads us necessarily to the natural obligation: and we proceed, in this case, from intuitive to demonstrative knowledge, by the same sure steps by which we proceed from the knowledge of our own, to that of GOD's existence. The law of nature, or of right reason, is the real original of all positive laws.[1]

Despite Bolingbroke's apparent opposition, there is not a word here that Hobbes would not agree with and the passage may be fairly paraphrased as follows: 'The desire for happiness, which we can't help having, leads us necessarily to ascertain the conditions we must fulfil in our relationships with others to obtain that happiness. And we proceed, in this case, from a wish for satisfactions to finding out the mode of ensuring them.'

Hobbes too, shows that there is what Bolingbroke describes as a 'natural obligation to exercise benevolence, to administer justice, and to keep compacts . . . as evident to human reason, as the desire of happiness is agreeable to human instinct'. If compacts are not kept, Hobbes suggests, one endangers one's liberty, and as that is destructive of

---

[1] 'Fragment III', *Works* (1777 edn.), v, 54.

happiness it is unreasonable to court the danger. If, by
'natural obligation', Bolingbroke means anything other than
what Hobbes describes, he gives us no substantial idea of
what it might be. When Bolingbroke says 'We desire by
instinct, we acquire by reason', he echoes Hobbes who sees
man emerging from a bestial state by virtue of his 'passions'
(fear and desire), assisted by the 'reason' which suggests
convenient articles of peace. By his 'law of nature, or of right
reason, (which) is the real original of all positive laws'
Bolingbroke would like to mean something different to
Hobbes. He would like to imply some divine, non-empirical
function of reason that could provide answers endowed with a
more solid authority than that of their being solutions to the
questions posed. He would like induction to be based on
something better than principles gained from deduction. But
the more Bolingbroke struggles, the more entangled he
becomes in what he wants to get away from. Hobbes's
scepticism is as thorough as it could well be, and veins of
atheism and of cynicism lie very close to the surface of his
arguments. Plainly, he goes too far for Bolingbroke, who
makes up his mind to disagree, but is so much of Hobbes's
mind himself that he cannot establish a difference.

This is most apparent when we consider that Bolingbroke's
'reason', like Hobbes's, requires a principle (instinct or
passion) to urge it to its work. An innate 'pure reason'
would, presumably, discover itself without any prompting at
all. Hobbes describes his urging principle as a 'Feare of
Death' and a 'Desire of such things as are necessary to
commodious living'. Bolingbroke's driving principle is an
optimistic version of Hobbes's. He says, euphemistically, that
reason would come all too slowly:

... if the all-wise creator had not implanted in us another
principle, that of self-love, which is the original spring of human
actions, under the direction of instinct first, and of reason after-
wards.[1]

---

[1] 'Fragment VI', *ibid.* p. 74.

This self-love leads at last to social love, and here too, the argument falls into step with that of Hobbes, though Bolingbroke's terms are slippery and formless. He casts a vapid sense of satisfaction over his argument:

> ... men are led, by a chain of necessary consequences, from the instinctive to the rational law of nature if I may speak so. Self-love operates in all these stages. We love ourselves, we love our families, we love the particular societies, to which we belong, and our benevolence extends at last to the whole race of mankind.[1]

If one does not care for Hobbes's account of humanity and society, then one is invited by his plainly stated argument and spare, supple style to oppose him. Whether he is right or wrong, Hobbes invites appraisal and clarity of thought from his reader, and is conducive to health. Bolingbroke's 'self-love' and 'reason' are the same principles as those of Hobbes, but the comfortable slovenly attempt to view them optimistically shows confusion and a lack of moral discrimination.

In writing the *Songs*, Blake does not attack Hobbes, whom he never read, but he does attack a debased form of Hobbesian thought which, by giving reassuring names to Hobbes's attributes of man, supposes that it is controverting his ideas. Hobbes might have been surprised if he had seen the changes put on his thinking by the eighteenth century. Superstition and self-satisfaction, the two elements that might be supposed incompatible with his system, on a reading of Hobbes alone, had entered it. Nature and nature's laws had been hypostatized and the harsh summary of human tendencies and capabilities given by Hobbes had been adopted as true—not, however, with any sense of shame, but with equanimity and even with pride. Bolingbroke gives Hobbes's selfishness the name of self-love and, like Hobbes, derives the moral virtues from this passion. Unlike Hobbes, however, he is quite complacent about this, and does not use the assumption for a

---

[1] 'Fragment vi', *Works* (1777 edn.), v, 81.

purpose: the derivation of a full and intricate account of social behaviour. His account ends with his statement of the connexion between his psychological principles and his social virtues, so that, while taking exception to Hobbes, he concurs with his basic tenets, restates them in a pleasant form, adds nothing to Hobbes's account, and deprives his own statement of any point it might have had if he had used it to develop practical conclusions. Hobbes's science is limited because it does not describe enough. His account is a magnificent one, but it is an account only of the world of Experience, and a fuller account, as Blake's account is a fuller one, must consider other possible worlds. Bolingbroke's 'science' is not only limited but it is false as well. Hobbes posits his theory of man in order to give an account of his observations. The same theory is simply a dogma in Bolingbroke, who makes no observations, but has a propagandist's interest in passing his theory on to his reader. Proposition in Hobbes (made seriously enough and, as it gathers together the observed 'facts', taken as true) has become an article of faith in Bolingbroke, and its truth is the truth, not of proposition, but of mystery: it rests on mere acceptance, and it convinces, not by the presentation of evidence, but of zeal. It pretends realism but relies on prejudice and man's desire to think well of himself. Its effect on the reader is to destroy clarity of thought, and to entice him into the moral tangle of the writer. Blake describes the tangle in his epitome of this sort of reasoning:

THE HUMAN ABSTRACT

Pity would be no more
If we did not make somebody Poor;
And Mercy no more could be
If all were as happy as we.

And mutual fear brings peace,
Till the selfish loves increase:
Then Cruelty knits a snare,
And spreads his baits with care

He sits down with holy fears,
And waters the ground with tears;
Then Humility takes its root
Underneath his foot.

Soon spreads the dismal shade
Of Mystery over his head;
And the Catterpiller and Fly
Feed on the Mystery.

And it bears the fruit of Deceit,
Ruddy and sweet to eat;
And the Raven his nest has made
In its thickest shade.

The Gods of the earth and sea
Sought thro' Nature to find this Tree;
But their search was all in vain:
There grows one in the Human Brain.

The poem differs from those we have examined in that there is no persona, though there is a shift in the tone of the poem, which indicates that the speaker, Blake, is expounding a view that he holds in contempt. The first stanza sounds very reasonable, and one can assent to the propositions made there:

> . . . Mercy no more could be
> If all were as happy as we.

Pity and mercy can be extended only to beings that require them. Also, we must accept the fact that any society contains men who are more fortunate than their fellows. What is the point of making such trite observations? Plainly the speaker is attempting to make himself easy. The first two lines, in particular, sound as though they might be uttered by someone attempting to justify his playing a role in which he imposes on others, and which he does not feel quite comfortable about:

> Pity would be no more
> If we did not make somebody Poor . . .

Although the first stanza sounds innocuous enough, on the surface, some self-suspicion is being hidden, and the speaker's dishonesty must grow as he continues to live his lie. Blake gives the lines with an apparent show of reasonableness, presumably in order to show how easily the lie is entered upon, but his description of the later development of the liar is scathing.

Verbally, the lie isn't one at all, but an inappropriate truth stated with an unhealthy emphasis. Poverty and unhappiness call out pity and mercy, but the speaker's attention is directed towards the qualities *he* must show, and towards his own comfortable position of advantage. Primarily he is thinking of himself, despite the generalized form he gives his truisms. In the next stanza a third proposition is stated in the same general way:

> And mutual fear brings peace,
> Till the selfish loves increase . . .

There is no need to cite Hobbes to demonstrate the existence of this law. It is a commonplace of thought on civil and international affairs. The axioms of stanza 1 are self-evident on the implicit acceptance of the notion that society is necessarily competitive. The third axiom carries the same hidden acceptance, but the irony with which it is stated is more apparent. 'Mutual' refers, not to a working together but a separate working to compatible private ends—regulated by an 'esteem' based on mistrust. The 'love' is dictated by policy, is 'selfish' and so is not love or any other positive emotion. One's neighbour is an obstacle in one's path to which one must accommodate one's movements. A sufficient increase in these accommodations makes communal life possible, though the condition is one of 'cold war' rather than of peace. So 'peace' and 'love' here describe impulses the very opposite of what we usually take them to mean. Our acts of generosity are really acts of meanness.

The two axioms of the first stanza were 'truths' told with a wrong emphasis, designed to make men easy about exploitation. The third axiom goes further. It suggests that one may now feel quite easy about advantage and exploitation for it insists on the necessity of 'mutual fear' in communal life.

Not only is the disposition to exploit each other creative of the tensions that make civil life possible, but the 'selfish loves' ('mercy' and 'pity') are based on the fear of the consequences of their being withheld. So the form of selfishness we call fear is the efficient cause of these virtues.

The rhythm of the first six lines has a rather trite, expected movement to correspond with the pat statements of the formula they contain, while the remainder of the poem changes to a complex broken rhythm in keeping with its satirical content. The corresponding change of tone occurs at the word 'selfish' which manages to embrace the two sections. The first six lines have referred us in a general way to selfist theories of society. It is true that such exponents of this view as Bolingbroke or Pope would prefer to use the term 'self-love' to 'selfish loves', and there are other euphemistic synonyms and circumlocutions. Perhaps only Hobbes, amongst the exponents of the theory, would accept the bald 'selfish' as being the apt word. The word also anticipates Blake's condemnation of the theory, developed in the stanzas that follow. Blake's voice is plainer in this poem than in, say, 'London'. His insight now takes over and he makes a direct attack on the distorted thinking and hypocritical concealments consequent on the lies of the first six lines. 'Pity', 'mercy', 'peace' and 'love' of the sort we have been presented with may be seen for what they are by their results: 'cruelty', false 'humility', 'mystery' and 'deceit'. Once men have accepted the implications of the selfist theory the way has been opened for complacent feelings in respect to any callous or greedy impulse, for one has rejected the notion of personal responsibility. If the human virtues: mercy, pity, peace and love are not energies of one's own, then their simulated counterparts are a reaction of fear, a display of what society forces one to be. The attempt at self-justification in the opening lines of the poem is a deceit that must blunt the ability to criticize one's motives, and 'Cruelty' is seen as setting a snare and laying baits (semblances of the wholesome) in order to entice to further self-deception, encouraging the worst propensities to be practised with the best of intentions. The illustration to the poem depicts this trap. An old man (the figure of Experience, so often seen in the *Songs*) is crouched grotesquely down in the toils of the net described by Berkeley as the 'fine and subtile net of *abstract ideas*, which has so miserably perplexed and entangled the minds of men'.[1]

In the remainder of the poem Blake uses the image of the growth of a tree to describe the advanced stages of deception. True virtue is unselfish ('charity vaunteth not itself . . .') and the growth, then, commences in the nearest thing to unselfishness that is possible to the being we have been shown, in self-abasement (which remembers the self all the while) and advances to the full fruition of deceitful pride. We distinguish between a proper sense of duty or reverence and an unnatural and distorted dedication. Blake refers to the latter sort of submission, which is always self-centred while it pretends not to be, and the growth starts with the liar on the ground in 'holy fears', 'tears' and 'Humility'. As the tree develops, it converts religious piety into fanaticism, patriotism into nationalistic fervour, partisanship into a bigoted dogmatism. In its most alarming forms it shows us the zealot prepared to lynch or proscribe, in the name of the cause to which he is 'devoted'.

The root of the tree is in a form of self-deception. The denial of the importance of the self is a way of escaping personal responsibility, because the making of decisions may be posted off to something greater than the self. All -isms provide a creed and a body of orthodox thought which are guides to satisfactory conduct. They provide, also, men versed in the tradition, explaining it and providing commentaries. The commencement of mystery is in hidden motives and unexplored beliefs, and the tree luxuriates into a cumbersome superstructure of theories which must continually be added to

---

[1] 'Introduction', *Principles of Human Knowledge* (Everyman edn.), p. 109.

as flaws threaten to reveal themselves. A continuous patch-work of rationalization must go on to keep beliefs alive that have lost contact with the realities of existence and have degenerated into a dogma. Instead of demonstration and critical appraisal, mystery offers persuasion, asseveration, superstition and thickets of argument so dense that the sophistries are hidden. On the leaves of the tree feed those who thrive on the elaboration of mystery: the priest, the politician, the journalist, the scholar. The fruit borne by the tree looks healthy enough—the virtues and values found out by the processes of 'selfish love', 'Humility' and 'Mystery', seem like the real thing, although they are a 'Deceit'. The fruit is an ill one and grows in an ill place, funereally gloomy, fit home for a bird which is songless and joyless. The calcula-ted virtues and qualities of Experience, with their accompany-ing elaboration of reasonings and justifications are heavy, deliberate and without pleasure.

The liar of the poem lives in a state of increasing misery and carries with him a burden of contradictions and hypo-critical solutions. The poem implements this sense of a growing burden in a number of ways. Abstract noun is added to abstract noun: 'Pity . . . Cruelty . . . Humility', etc. The image of the tree emphasizes the slow but inexorable growth, ponderous immobility and gloomy complexity that accom-panies these spiritual elaborations. The atmosphere of the poem is deliberate and silent. The 'selfish loves increase' inevitably, the knitting of the snare and the spreading of baits are nice processes of time, and the 'Catterpiller and Fly' go intently and quietly about their activities. There is not a human word heard in the poem and the abstractions refer to mute internal processes. The vegetable growth of the tree, like the knitting of the snare and the laying of the bait is a secretive movement. The misery and the burden of the liar is emphasized by his posture. He is bowed to the ground which he 'waters . . . with his tears', and he is as fixed there as the tree which casts its shroud of darkness around him.

Blake's Criticism of 'Nature'

The final stanza is written in the rather wintry vein of humour Blake sometimes uses in the *Songs of Experience*. After a consideration of 'Nature' we are returned to the 'Human Brain', and so to the title, 'The Human Abstract'. 'Abstract' is ambiguous, referring to an epitome of what is to be found in the nature of man, and also to the essentially conceptual or theoretical basis of this natural history. Three lines of the stanza are devoted to the difficulty of the search undertaken and the failure to locate the tree of mystery, and only one line to the explanation of the difficulty. The emphasis falls on the blank result of the search through nature because Blake is aware that the moral theory which is epitomized and caricatured in his poem is commonly described as 'natural' by its exponents and he wishes to call the description to account. He has mockingly been considering the development of a 'natural' society all along, and in four stanzas Blake pursues the image of the tree (what object could be more natural?) to mock those who regard society as a 'natural' growth of selfish appetites. The last stanza completes the mockery. Who is better qualified to recognize a natural object than the 'Gods of the earth and sea'? They search hard but they fail to identify this tree as belonging to nature. Blake's manuscript version of the stanza reads:

> The Gods of the Earth & Sea
> Sought thro' nature to find this tree;
> But their search was all in vain:
> (Till they sought in the human brain. *deleted*)
> There grows one in the human brain.[1]

The final version, unlike the deleted one, assumes that the human brain (where the tree grows) is a province beyond the reach of these Gods. There can be no doubt that the 'natural' is, for man, contrived by his mind.

Hobbes describes both his 'Morall Vertues' and their contrary vices as natural. Both are an outcome of the appetite for power and of fear, but the understanding (in the Coleridgean

---

[1] *Complete Writings* (1957), p. 174.

sense) finds conditions in which these appetites may take a virtuous form (that is, a socially practicable form) instead of a vicious (inefficient) form. The moral sense is an outcome of the understanding and moral criteria are utilitarian. Hobbes is remarkably consistent in applying understanding and utility in every field he deals with, and he uses the word 'natural' (natural forces, natural law, natural vices and virtues) to indicate that he can explain the phenomena he observes in those fields. He does not find it necessary to refer to supernatural agencies to fill in any gaps in his account. No doubt he regards his explanation as adequate, and so 'natural' also means, for him, 'substantially existent' or 'demonstrably real', but primarily he means, by 'natural', explicable.

Writers like Bolingbroke, Pope, and others whom we shall have occasion to examine, were content to allow Hobbes to guide their interpretation of the phenomena of man and society, and Hobbes sets the tone of thought on the subject for the whole of the eighteenth century. It will already have been recognized that 'The Human Abstract' epitomizes this trend while it throws it into Blake's perspective. Hobbes regarded man, so envisaged, with a slight distaste. Bolingbroke and Pope were delighted by the same prospect, and it is the Popeian view that Blake's sarcasm is intent on unmasking. It was a mistake of the eighteenth century (as it is of the twentieth century) to consider Hobbes's explanation of the facts to be the correct one. However, most thinkers of the time were not content, like Hobbes, to regard the 'natural' as referring, primarily, to an explanation of the observed, but as meaning something real in itself. In other words, they wished to give a greater degree of authority to an account than its status as a mere explanation allowed it. They equated 'explanation' with 'fact', the mental construction with the reality. 'The Human Abstract' ridicules this uncritical use of the word 'nature', which assumes that knowledge is perfect and pure: that nature provides, not only the data, but the explanation as well.

Blake's Criticism of 'Nature'

A form of self-deception may be practised by invoking 'nature'. Hobbes has listened to nature (his experience of the world) and can speak with a natural authority (the authority of a lively grasp on experience). The later advocates of selfism say that their theory is natural, but their claim lacks the authority of observation or experience. Nature reveals herself (and reveals herself again) to patient study, but that this has not been undertaken, a complete lack of originality sufficiently shows. Blake exposes the concealed claim made by the mystery-mongers of 'nature' that their suppositions have a basis in fact, that their views have an objective validity. Their 'humility' is to assume that they are passive recipients of their knowledge. As they have made no effort of observation or interpretation, however, they are possessed of 'mystery', not knowledge.

'The Human Abstract' derives the 'virtues' of 'love', 'mercy', 'pity', and 'peace' from 'natural' conditions, from man's need to restrain his selfish instincts if he is to survive. Another view of the human virtues is possible, and Blake states it in 'The Divine Image' of the *Songs of Innocence*. The poem attempts no explanations of the virtues, but asserts that they are sympathetic, the assertion being perfectly sure and calm, just because it carries with it no trace of final explanation. There is no dogma in the poem, no implicit complete theory about either the natural or the supernatural. Indeed, any rigid distinction between natural and supernatural is absent.

THE DIVINE IMAGE

To Mercy, Pity, Peace, and Love
All pray in their distress;
And to these virtues of delight
Return their thankfulness.

For Mercy, Pity, Peace, and Love
Is God, our father dear,
And Mercy, Pity, Peace, and Love
Is Man, his child and care.

For Mercy has a human heart,
Pity a human face,
And Love, the human form divine,
And Peace, the human dress.

Then every man, of every clime,
That prays in his distress,
Prays to the human form divine,
Love, Mercy, Pity, Peace.

And all must love the human form,
In heathen, turk, or jew;
Where Mercy, Love, & Pity dwell
There God is dwelling too.

The poem has a clear, precise and logical manner. The statements made are, each of them, quite straightforward, and hide nothing, unlike the axioms of 'The Human Abstract'. The first stanza makes its observations. The second stanza starts with 'for' and explains what is observed. The third stanza (also a 'for' stanza) goes deeper into the explanation. However, these two stanzas do not 'explain' in the same sense that 'The Human Abstract' does. Behind that poem stood a definite theory, while the present verses explain by unfolding the matter: by presenting the observation in new aspects which, again, demand interpretation. Nevertheless, something is resolved, and the last two stanzas, introduced by 'then', state positive conclusions.

The poem is a remarkably delicate and suggestive piece of reasoning or, to use a term Blake might have chosen, of intellect. It must, then, comprehend everything it may understand and it must refuse to attempt anything beyond that. It is too serious for conjecture. The propositions of 'The Human Abstract', it will be remembered, accounted for the four virtues in terms of their social origin and utility. The first stanza of 'The Divine Image' is, apparently, more ambitious, for it talks of man who is sensible, not of the social but of the divine, of man at prayer—intercession and thanksgiving. The prayer is associated, however, very much with personal sensations and knowledge and not with estab-

70

lishing an external relationship. The 'virtues' in the experienced song were made to account for phenomena but here they are described as 'virtues of delight', an intensification of inward awareness and (in the context of the rather isolated states of 'distress' and 'thankfulness') a very specific and incommunicable awareness. Also, the prayer is inward because of what it is 'to'. (How emphatically Blake's 'to's' are placed, implying an orientation, a set direction.) Prayers are to God, but can they afford communication between the creature (who knows distress, delight and gratitude, but little beyond his own state, his own settings towards) and the Creator (some larger influence who has His own secrets)? The communication can be made because the man who prays knows of the divine in himself. His set towards the virtues is indicative of this. Others are set similarly:

> To Mercy, Pity, Peace, and Love
> All pray . . .

There is no need to wonder about God's secrets when every individual feels the force of what is not secret. A man's sense of what is in himself (of what he is 'to') will indicate what is in God, of whom he is the image. What other knowledge can he have? What other revelation is necessary?

What other revelation is possible or so sure? Transmitted revelation comes by chance and is subject to distortion, being soon absorbed in mystery. It relegates the pagan to a condition of ignorance of God and suggests that the unlettered know Him more dimly than the learned. Surely God would be revealed to every man!—and so the song passes mystery ignorantly by. God's secrets are a part of His privacy and dignity, and the poem deals only with what God displays, what it can be quite sure of:

> For Mercy, Pity, Peace, and Love
> Is God . . .

But how can we know that each of these virtues 'is God' as the poem so emphatically says? The knowledge is quite certain if one looks at the only part of God's creation one knows, at oneself, instead of trying to explain Him by supernature or by nature, by one's own abstract creation. If God is good we know it, and we know what sort of goodness He has, by looking at our own goodness:

> And Mercy, Pity, Peace, and Love
> Is Man . . .

There is certainly no other place to look for a knowledge of God than into oneself, not without being presumptuous, not without pretending to know what one can not.

Despite its giving the direction where one may look, the poem does not jumble God and man together. The second stanza enumerates the virtues for God, and then carefully re-enumerates them for man. It says what it can about each being, but has every respect for the individuality of each, and acknowledges in man the same privacy and dignity accorded to God. The virtues are called 'virtues of delight' in the first stanza for they are, as 'delight' implies, very specific to whoever enjoys them. The full sense of the word comes out if one bears in mind the connotations of 'pleasure' which, like 'delight', is associated with satisfactions, but with satisfactions that are understood by all, standard feelings, connected in their several varieties with standard experiences. 'Delight' has no varieties but is specific and never repeated, so it is undefinable, incommunicable and fleeting. One knows where one is with 'pleasure', just as one knows where one is with the social 'virtues' of 'The Human Abstract'. It falls into categories, may be measured, defined and compared and so can be used as the key-stone of an aesthetic system. The virtues of 'The Divine Image' are 'of delight', are sublime, are in their nature unexpected, refreshing and unique.

The double enumeration of the second stanza, then, refuses confusion of God and man, and it also refuses the standardization of God or man. God and man are divine, and, therefore, unique in their being. Their virtues are delightful and so unique in every moment of their manifestation. Although delight is so personal, however, it is generous, feels itself too good to be contained within, and yearns to make itself known by another. Even the double enumeration, the strict identification, insists, while it is made, on the relationship of sympathy between 'God, our father dear', and 'Man, his child and care'. God is Himself, but the next breath of the poem defines Him as He is to man, in terms of man's yearning of affection towards Him. Similarly, man is himself, but immediately the poem sees him as God must yearn to him, and defines man in terms of the solicitude felt by the Father. The orientation of these unique individuals, the set towards each other of the virtues of delight, the yearning between God and man (and between man and man) is emphasized by the character of the delights. They are 'Mercy, Pity, Peace, and Love', and in themselves movements towards another. All relate individual to individual. However much the virtues are themselves they look beyond the self they compose. The virtues hang together and Blake turns them about, altering their order, testing their harmony. They are beautiful as a self, though they are, essentially, an awareness of what is not the self, expressed in intercession and gratitude, affection and concern, respect and sympathy.

'The Divine Image' is as lucidly precise in what it stops short of saying as in what it definitely asserts. The first two stanzas discuss God with the least possible meddling or dogmatism, and the third relates the virtues to man without asserting any theory of the relationship. The virtues are known because they manifest the human, and they are related to what is unseen and inward in man and to the outward and expressive:

> For Mercy has a human heart,
> Pity a human face.

We distinguish between the virtues. Mercy, like the heart, is more hidden, is a disposition seen through gestures and acts, through pity. Pity, like the face, faithfully indicates the disposition within. But the distinction is merely between modes of virtue, just as the expression on the countenance and the motion felt in the soul are modes of working, manifestations of a complete human movement. The complete movement expresses itself through all its 'parts': the heart, the countenance, the body, and even the dress which man adopts as part of himself. The first two stanzas of the poem refused to divide human awareness into parts. What we know of God we know by looking at our own being and we may be content with that knowledge. There is no special religious awareness, but our normal awareness, if informed by our full humanity, embraces the mode. The third stanza, amplifying this refusal to make unreal distinctions, calls the human body divine, and relates it to love, the most sublime of the virtues. Love is between one person and another, and all the attributes of the personality are brought to a focus and find their expression through the body. All that we can know of another is what their body presents in one form or another, and our only knowledge of another is given to our body. All that is within us and all that is without us comes to a resolution in the flesh.

The fourth virtue Peace, like the dress, is more formal and assumed. It appears added to man, and it refers, perhaps, to the social virtues which are acquired by a greater degree of practice, are more conventional, differing in unimportant respects from one society to another, though recognizably taking their origin with, and being a part of, the other virtues. Blake's hint, given by his reference to 'dress', to the deliberately assumed, is a most important one. It indicates, as do his references to prayer (to receiving and gratitude) together with the outward-looking as well as the delighted nature of the virtues, that he avoids regarding his virtues as innate. They are an outcome of man, but of man in action, of man in the body and in the world. The poem studiously avoids assuming, on the one hand, that the virtues are natural in the sense that they are acquired because the world demands them. On the other hand it avoids the assumption that the virtues are natural (or supernatural), in the sense that they are engrafted on the soul. The heart, which is secret and spontaneous, and the dress, which is public and conventional, are modes of virtue, but they are comprised in the divine image. What is without and what is within (what is learned, and what is implanted in the soul) bring each other to a realization perhaps, but even this statement is too much of an abstraction. (It explains the living reality of the whole man in terms of factors that go to make him up (as the writers we have contrasted with Blake all do), instead of doing what 'The Divine Image' does, which is to keep its eye on the living reality, glancing, only, at modes of its expression.

The third stanza, then, does not commit itself to any psychology. The four virtues are enumerated separately, and they are separately attributed to different parts of the divine image for reasons that are sensible enough. But these separations of the virtues, of the parts of man, and the separation between virtue and man are a matter of convenience only and every part implies every other part. Blake suggests this in a subtle manner: 'Mercy has a human heart.' Then 'Mercy' must be a human being. He is not talking of an abstract mercy but of one that *is* man, as he states in the second stanza. We know mercy as we know man—as a complex whole. Mercy, love, pity and peace, the movements of the heart and the countenance, the actions of the body, and even the things that the body attaches to itself are modes of the divine image and not its elements.

'The Divine Image' does not deal with abstract components of the human but with man, and shows that human awareness has a religious mode which, like the dress of man, like the countenance of man, may find its expression in many ways. We recognize our friends by their peculiarities of face and figure, but we recognize their individuality as a mode of the peculiarly human. The costumes of the different races are modes of the seemly according to the idiosyncrasies of the individual or the community. The many religions of man, far from being antagonistic, are all expressions of the religious mode of the virtues. They are all true to the degree that they are not intolerant dogmatic theorizings, but complete a sense of something needed, giving individual point to the mind of the believer. 'The Divine Image' recognizes all religions as being at one, because every man is a perfectly unique centre for religious awareness. In making this assertion the poem cuts away much theology, much metaphysic, and an enormous amount of belief about ritual, right observance and behaviour, but even in cutting away it shows reverence. Heathen, Turk and Jew are human but, like God, they are alien. In terms of the poem, however, every man is alien. We recognize others as lovable by their humanity, but what do we know of that except its appearance in physical action and body?

> And all must love the human form . . .

We know the mode of the divine that one man may display to another, the body and its acts, and even that is different in each individual. What the whole complex of the divine in any single individual may be we can never know and they can never tell. We cannot fathom the complexity of our own self, though we may pretend to do so by making superficial statements, usually of a conventional nature. What can we say of another man, then, without superficiality? Very little. All men are 'heathen, turk, or jew', and like God, their privacy must be respected. We may be aware of the divinity in them through the physical mode of the virtues, just as we are aware of the divinity in ourselves through the presence of the modes there. We cannot account for other men, any more than we may account for God, for ourselves, or for a complex musical line. But we respond to the musical when it presents itself to us.

According to 'The Divine Image' God resides in the human being, though not because He is an artifact of the understanding. Perhaps we must think God, but we don't think Him up. The consciousness of the play of our own energies brings us to a full knowledge of the divine. This may be true of Innocence but is not so with Experience, and 'The Human Abstract' depicts the fabrication of mystery, including religious mystery. The mystery is not seen, it operates beyond us in a manner to be taken on trust, and while innocent belief is based on what it apprehends, experienced belief is credulous, superstitiously emphasizing the unknown.

Hobbes is doubtful about all religious notions, but he contents himself with being openly contemptuous of pagan beliefs only. As it touches Christianity, his analysis of religion brings more into doubt than the administration of Christian institutions, but he makes no statements that might lay him open to a charge of atheism. Indeed, Hobbes's explanations leave very little room for confidence in any religious belief, which he plainly regards as an illusion, though he looks on illusion as a great convenience to the administrator. The 'seed of Religion is onely in man' but, as it is described, the seed is a natural (scientifically explicable) one, an outcome of human limitations: fear, ignorance, servility and silliness, and certainly not an issue of 'divine virtues':

And in these foure things, Opinion of Ghosts, Ignorance of second causes, Devotion towards what men fear, and Taking of things Casuall for Prognostiques, consisteth the Naturall seed of *Religion*; which by reason of the different Fancies, Judgements, and Passions of severall men, hath grown up into ceremonies so different, that those which are used by one man, are for the most part ridiculous to another.[1]

Hobbes's concern is political, and to the degree that God is a political force He falls within Hobbes's purview. Men's beliefs are elements that the political theorist must take into account, and Hobbes is interested in them as phenomena. His interest is a 'natural' one, and in respect of the ethical or theological standing of any belief, Hobbes is indifferent, or,

[1] *Leviathan*, xii; p. 56.

perhaps, regards such considerations as rather childish. The 'natural' seeds of religion are used to impose discipline, on the one hand by an unscrupulous Numa Pompilius and, on the other hand, by 'Abraham, Moses, and our Blessed Saviour'.[1] These men are agents of 'humane Politiques' or of 'Divine Politiques', but this distinction is made for form's sake. Hobbes's 'Politiques' are all 'natural', the product of an 'intellectuall faculty' (into which faith, imagination, 'enthusiasme', 'supernaturall inspiration', do not enter), for experience enforces the knowledge.

There is an affinity between Hobbes and Blake, despite the fact that Blake probably had no knowledge of Hobbes's writings at first hand. Both men are prepared to press their insights to their extreme point, both are thorough and both are capable of handling the most complex material. In addition to this, Blake is, perhaps, the first thinker since Hobbes who is able to assimilate Hobbes's conclusions without being half afraid of them, apologetic, apparently hostile to them, watering them down, or distorting them. Blake, as it were, takes Hobbesian thought (which he understands very well, whether he read Hobbes or not) and says of it: how perfectly accurate, then proceeds to set that thought in perspective against other ways of thinking. Blake's range as a thinker is much wider than Hobbes's, but he penetrates fearlessly into the Hobbesian field. Hobbes describes without delusion, sentimentality, apologetics or falsity one way of meeting life, which finds its echo in the *Songs of Experience*. But there is another dimension to human experience, shown in the *Songs of Innocence*, and Blake's addition of the dimension establishes him as a truly original thinker. It also allows him to come to grips with the Hobbesian method of thinking, to define the limits of the circumstances under which it has validity, and to strip from the method what it had acquired from Hobbes's successors: a layer of sentimentality and satisfaction, disguising descriptions essentially Hobbesian, though Hobbes's

[1] *Leviathan*, XII; p. 57.

influence might be denied or unacknowledged. The account that Hobbes presents bleakly as a piece of unpleasant realism, we find Bolingbroke and Pope embracing as the happy truth; we find Locke and Hume presenting as a judiciously adequate and satisfying account. Not until we come to Blake do we find the Hobbesian man regarded with the same cold stare of disapproval that Hobbes gave him, but, in addition, Blake has another man to contrast him with.

The psychological factors that lead man to religion, according to Hobbes, are fear, ignorance, servility and foolishness. In 'The Human Abstract' they are fear, cruelty, false humility and self-deceit. Blake's poem puts forward an analysis of the same sort as Hobbes's, though there is a shift in any condemnation made. There is a tinge of distaste in Hobbes's tone, and, as his account is presented as generally true, it is man in general that he finds distasteful. In 'The Human Abstract', Blake presents a natural or psychological account similar to that of Hobbes, making it quite clear that he finds the man described by the psychology most distasteful. In the last stanza of the poem he questions whether the growth he has depicted is natural (as Hobbes asserts). As the tree grows in the human brain it represents the way man may go and not the way he must go. In the first place, then, the description need not be generally true. Secondly, the 'growth in the human brain' calls into question the 'natural' method of accounting for man; the abstract method that explains him in terms of determinate factors.

'The Divine Image' presents an alternative description of man, so denying the general applicability of the experienced account. In addition, because we are shown the four virtues, not as determinate factors, but as modes of expression of an unknowable, ever-changing complexity (because of the assumption that we cannot explain God, man or the self, but can only respond to some of the manifestations of these unexplored entities), the poem brings into question the method that 'The Human Abstract' uses to depict its subject.

The innocent poem makes no attempt to analyse or explain man.

In the case of these two songs, the method of accounting for the mind is suited to the mind that is being described. In 'The Human Abstract' a limited and self-centred mentality is shown, intent on getting its own way in a world that opposes it. It is prepared to deceive itself and others to achieve its very set purposes, also its purposes are best served by living in a world that is analysable and predictable, even if it must distort that world and itself to achieve the desired simplicity. It is most comfortably off among 'natural' or fully explained phenomena, its method of handling these phenomena is 'scientific', and it has undertaken the labour of converting itself into a natural and explicable organization. 'The Divine Image', on the other hand, makes no attempt to give an inventory of man. Its careful enumerations emphasize the infinite variety of the mind, and one is aware that the man who speaks the poem can attempt no easy explanation because he is aware of resources in himself, yet unexplored.

CHAPTER 4

THE CHILD AND 'NATURE'

ON Hobbes's view, the impetus to religious observance is a natural inclination to superstition. This is a constant element in men's minds, so that one religion replaces another, and he attributes the failure of any particular religion to 'unpleasing priests'. It is a source of wonder to a modern reader that a writer who can think along these lines should also regard himself as a faithful son of the Church. To be cynical is to deny that the religious impulse has any basis except fear and ignorance—that is an attitude we are familiar with—but it seems the very refinement of cynicism when one whose rationalism reduces the greater part of religion to superstition subscribes to a particular doctrinal system. It is as if Hobbes says: there is nothing sacred about this, except as a convention we accept. Religion is a game we play and the rules at present in vogue make up the game.

Hobbes is perfectly consistent, though, and, given his assumptions, his cynicism cannot be viewed as trivially inclined. He has shown that we owe everything we possess, materially and spiritually—our outward manner of expression, and, inwardly, our reason and human nature, to society, the sword, institution, order. Our very being is composed by conventions, by the rules of the game to which we must accommodate ourselves, and it is a game we have no choice but to take seriously. Remove the conventionally instilled part of man and nothing whatever of a recognizable human being is left. If convention and institution make us human that is enough to establish them as sacred. If people wish additional authority (if they wish to take their superstitions seriously) and suppose that the sacred character of any institution depends on some mystical sanction, that only goes to show that they have not reached the stage where they can give a reasonable account of things to themselves. Hobbes leaves them to be devout in their own way.

No doubt it was difficult for a seventeenth-century Englishman to think of himself as anything but a confessing member of some church, whatever the nature of his privately conceived scepticism. Things have altered since, the churches have lost their institutional importance and when the superstitious part of religion fails in any man then his religion fails altogether in most cases. One can imagine the surprise of a Hobbes if it were suggested that loss of faith were a reason for estrangement from the church. He would point out that, on the same argument, if one should doubt the abilities of a king or the honesty of his ministers one should estrange oneself from the commonwealth. As it is manifestly impossible to cut oneself off from either church or commonwealth then faith is a matter best left to those to whom it is granted and to those whose occupation it is to promote it.

What is it that is promoted, though? If any church saw itself as dedicated to the furtherance of an impulse to religion in man, an impulse regarded as divine, not 'natural', not a form of credulity and ignorance, then the dogmatic part of religion would always give way, after representing itself fully, to the conscience of the individual. It would give way gladly as to its proper guide. If, however, a church did not see itself as a servant, albeit a well-informed and wise one, to the individual conscience; if the position it adopts is authoritarian and it regards the acceptance of its tenets as necessary to salvation, then it regards man as essentially unregenerate, fallen and 'natural'. As a 'natural' phenomenon, the soul may be viewed as inclined to religion, but it must be brought to the correct religion by education and discipline.

As all churches see themselves in the latter of these two ways, it is quite clear that Hobbes's way of looking at religion comes very close to that adopted by any priesthood. Hobbes differs only in his clear view of the matter. There is no place for mystery in Hobbes if he is properly understood, whereas most priesthoods, even Christian ones, must locate the source of their religion in the unknown (the supernatural) as they dare not locate it in man. We have seen Blake refusing to accept the mysterious and supernatural part of religion in 'The Divine Image', where he finds that religious knowledge is a form of awareness properly (though not 'naturally') possessed by the individual. In 'A Little Boy Lost' of the *Songs of Experience*, Blake depicts the priest, whose religion has its source in mystery, and a little boy who has an insight akin to that contained in 'The Divine Image'.

A LITTLE BOY LOST

'Nought loves another as itself,
'Nor venerates another so,
'Nor is it possible to Thought
'A greater than itself to know:

'And Father, how can I love you
'Or any of my brothers more?
'I love you like the little bird
'That picks up crumbs around the door.'

The Priest sat by and heard the child,
In trembling zeal he siez'd his hair:
He led him by his little coat,
And all admir'd the Priestly care.

And standing on the altar high,
'Lo! what a fiend is here!' said he,
'One who sets reason up for judge
'Of our most holy Mystery.'

The weeping child could not be heard,
The weeping parents wept in vain;
They strip'd him to his little shirt,
And bound him in an iron chain;

And burn'd him in a holy place,
Where many had been burn'd before:
The weeping parents wept in vain.
Are such things done on Albion's shore?

When Christ gave the two great commandments, the scribe answered:

> Well, Master, thou hast said the truth: for there is one God; and there is none other but he: And to love him with all the heart, and with all the understanding, and with all the soul, and with all the strength, and to love his neighbour as himself, is more than all whole burnt-offerings and sacrifices.[1]

The professional priest of the Gospel account sees that Christ has gone to the essence of worship, passing by a great deal of Old Testament legal elaboration and ritual. Christ's words have come to the little boy, however, in the spirit of the pronouncements against which Christ was reacting when He spoke them. He gave a new and lively form to an automatic and so meaningless code, but His 'love' has been preached to the child in a mechanical way as the code of a later day. The child now questions the doctrine of love which has, in its turn, become the vehicle of dogmatism and mystery:

> 'And Father, how can I love you
> 'Or any of my brothers more?'

As is the case here, it is often difficult to know when a child is being forward. He may have a problem that stems from some contradiction of the adult world. At the catechism class he is told that God is love, that it is sinful not to love God, that love must govern all his relations with his fellows, that love is quite unselfish, and so on, until eventually love must lose all meaning it might ever have been felt to have. In the drawing-room, on the other hand, the child hears a conversational version of

> God loves from Whole to Parts: but human soul
> Must rise from Individual to the Whole.[2]

Love, Pope argues, originates in self-love. It is small wonder that when a child asks to have such diverse statements explained he should be found annoying, even if the request should be made in all innocence.

---

[1] Mark xii. 32.   [2] *Essay on Man*, iv, 361.

In the poem, the priest overhears a prayer, but has no doubt that he is being 'got at', and he has been waiting to make an example of someone. The boy's forwardness in questioning the iron law of love is bad, but he goes on to a worse impertinence in making a statement which throws a doubt on the authority of the priest to speak on religious matters. The priest has told the child about God and is insulted when the child doubts whether God can be known:

> 'Nor is it possible to Thought
> 'A greater than itself to know . . .'

The insult is in no way lessened by the fact that the boy has gleaned his queries when listening to adult conversations of a Deistic tendency—echoes of Hobbes, perhaps:

. . . men that by their own meditation, arrive to the acknowledgement of one Infinite, Omnipotent, and Eternall God, choose . . . to confesse he is Incomprehensible . . .[1]

Echoes of Pope:

> Know thy own point: This kind, this due degree
> Of blindness, weakness, Heav'n bestows on thee.[2]

Echoes of Locke:

. . . it may be of use to prevail with the busy mind of man to be more cautious in meddling with things exceeding its comprehension; to stop when it is at the utmost end of its tether; and to sit down in a quiet ignorance of those things which upon examination are found to be beyond the reach of our capacities.[3]

In place of the indirectly revealed mystery of love the child apparently sets up the unrevealable mystery beyond nature. Pope likens the relationship between God and man to that between man and the steed he bestrides.[4] The horse is aware of man, but cannot know anything of his purposes—cannot comprehend him. The little boy uses the analogy of a bird:

> 'I love you like the little bird
> 'That picks up crumbs around the door.'

[1] *Leviathan*, xii; p. 55.
[2] *Essay on Man*, i, 283.
[3] *Human Understanding*, i, i, 4.
[4] *Essay on Man*, i, 61.

The bird thinks in terms of crumbs and can't understand the human motives involved in putting them out. In speaking of God's gifts and love we think in terms of human motive, but can't understand the divine nature, if God can be said to have a nature. The child seems to imply this, and that is what the priest assumes him to intend saying.

In fact, the boy intends nothing of the sort. He is paraphrasing, parrot-wise, something he has heard, without being aware of the implications of his words. He also speaks with unconscious intent, speaks so that Blake may tell us something of the child in reminding us of 'The Divine Image'.[1] It is not possible for thought to know a greater than itself, and it is not necessary that it should. Locke and Pope suggest that man can know only his own corner of the universe. Blake suggests an alternative meaning to the child's pronouncement: that the universe, for man, is sufficiently contained in man. Nothing is unknown. Any true knowledge of God is to be got from a full awareness as a human being. The comparison with the bird may suggest, in Pope's manner, that man is unfit to know God just as the bird is unfit to know the human, but looked at in another light, it emphasizes man's adequacy just as it emphasizes the bird's. The little bird doesn't even think of the man who put the crumbs out, but in picking them up it is making as complete an acknowledgement of the man as is appropriate to a bird. Blake indirectly suggests that the little boy makes as complete an acknowledgement of God as is appropriate to a little boy by partaking of His creation, without it being necessary that he should understand the priest's nice points of doctrine.

One of the chief absurdities to which the poem points is the fact that the priest burns the little boy for being superficially in agreement with him. The sentiments expressed by the little boy, taken (as the priest takes them) in their Lockeian sense, taken to mean that we can know only our own 'natural' sphere of existence, may deny man's competence to probe the

---

[1] See pp. 69 ff.

unknowable, but they do not deny the unknown. 'Nature' and supernature are not incompatible and both, as we have seen, being abstract, admit of mystery. The more obvious sense of the boy's words, then, grants the priest the existence of his mystery, and the priest is angered by the setting up of reason as the judge of its limits; angered by the fact that the boy seems to point out that the unknowable cannot be expounded. He is roused, presumably, not because the child introduces an element foreign to the practice of priestcraft, but, apparently, insists on one essential to it. The initial source of institutional religion is in divine revelation, but its later practice is nourished by transmitted revelation, speculation and explanation. Faith is a rational and deliberate exertion of the mind for most people, and if, as the priest suspects, the child were making a mock of him it would be by harping on this aspect of belief, one which the priest would rather ignore. It makes his esoteric knowledge into commonplace pedantry, reducing him to a normal human stature, and in order to denounce the 'error' he retreats to the sanctuary and elevates himself once again, 'standing on the altar high'!

Blake's attack on priestcraft in the poem has no finesse about it whatever and his victory is easily taken. The last four stanzas verge on the melodramatic, but they do not want vigour and economy. The priest is avid of power, avid to enforce discipline, and sits by, sadistically waiting for his opportunity:

> In trembling zeal he siez'd his hair:
> He led him by his little coat . . .

By repeating the 'he' Blake emphasizes the vicious single-mindedness of the priest whose obsession does not allow him to know how ridiculous he is made to look by the littleness of the coat he has triumphantly seized.

The priest's flock do not see him as ridiculous, but as 'admirable'. They eagerly take their excuse for a legitimate exercise of cruelty:

> They strip'd him to his little shirt,
> And bound him in an iron chain;
>
> And burn'd him in a holy place,
> Where many had been burn'd before . . .

The littleness of the shirt is now pathetic, set against the iron chain, and there is now nothing ridiculous about the breaking of the butterfly. Even the parents must acquiesce, to a degree, with the fate of the apostate. They do not run frantic with indignation, but 'weep in vain'. They weep for grief, but also in regret that their child should be culpable. They weep in vain because no mercy is to be had, but also because they cannot expect it. Their sense of what is holy, remotely and inexplicably 'true', overbears their sense of what is real, the truth of their affection. The doctrine of love is more powerful than the ties of compassion.

Blake's attack verges on the melodramatic, but it never becomes so. For one thing the poet is too conscious of the ridiculous. The boy's statements taken in their obvious (Lockeian) sense are such that Blake himself would find them obnoxious, though the boy has no idea of what he is saying. Yet the child's words may also be taken in a way that does justice to his innocence. The child gets into trouble for ignorantly extolling the reasoning powers, yet the real crime for which he is made to suffer is that, in doing so, he gives too accurate a description of the priest's own methods. The machine set into motion for the destruction of the child is altogether too weighty for so slight an occasion and the priest and his collaborators are very intent and very 'devoted'— quite incapable of seeing themselves. Even the boy seems to weep because he is guilty. All this is presented in such a way as to emphasize the absurd, and the absurdity is pointed out by the question of the last line. Blake takes his reader aside at the end of the poem for a pointed personal comment, just as he does at the end of the 'Human Abstract' where he sets the gods to searching for a natural phenomenon which (we are taken into his confidence) he has hidden up his sleeve. In that

poem, however, there was the faintest glimmering of a joke
showing through the frost of Blake's humour, whereas here
there is none whatever. The ridiculous is accompanied by the
conspicuous absence of any trace of the amusing.

(In the *Songs of Innocence* Blake avoids mystery, and mocks
at it in the experienced *Songs.* In 'The Divine Image' he
discusses man, God, and virtue without attempting to
account for them, and he suggests in the experienced 'A
Little Boy Lost' that the child, though he is curious about
what he is told about God and love, is being led away from a
genuine knowledge of what these might be, as explanations
are multiplied. A doctrine of love ousts the exercise of love
and even the parents of the boy are at war within themselves,
their compassion held in check by their principles. God, love,
goodness, nature, all themes of mystery for experienced
beings, are very different intuitions for the innocent mind
which works in a less complicated but more responsible
manner. Blake explores the topic in 'The Little Boy lost' and
'found' of the *Songs of Innocence.*

THE LITTLE BOY LOST

'Father! father! where are you going?
'O do not walk so fast.
'Speak, father, speak to your little boy,
'Or else I shall be lost.'

The night was dark, no father was there;
The child was wet with dew;
The mire was deep, & the child did weep,
And away the vapour flew.

THE LITTLE BOY FOUND

The little boy lost in the lonely fen,
Led by the wand'ring light,
Began to cry; but God, ever nigh,
Appear'd like his father in white.

89

He kissed the child & by the hand led
And to his mother brought,
Who in sorrow pale, thro' the lonely dale,
Her little boy weeping sought.

The illustration to 'The Little Boy lost' shows us a child in a wood following a will-o'-the-wisp with outstretched hands. The text of the poem is illustrated with small figures of angels. The second poem shows us the boy, now found, being fondly led by an adult who holds him by the hand. Blake did not invariably print the two poems on successive sheets, but we will treat them as one poem, for it is plain that we are meant to do so. There is a temptation, in these poems, for the reader to introduce will-o'-the-wisps of his own. They are apparently so simple that one feels that Blake must be up to something deep. A little boy is led astray by a vapour which, he supposes, is his father. He is returned to his mother by God who takes on the form of his father. The story sounds rather childish and one looks for something more, though it might be wise to expect as little more as is possible, for fear of adding mysterious elements to a situation deliberately made simple.

The situation is very much simpler for the little boy than it is for the reader and Blake exploits this in order to make us aware of the gulf between one's own experienced mind and the Innocence he wishes to illustrate. We have some acquaintance with this in the case of the innocent 'Chimney Sweeper's Song' where one was made to feel the difference between the sort of comfort that could be offered by a fellow-sufferer and the onlooker's inhibiting despair and inability to find words that would be of effective use. The onlooker cannot grasp the realities, only the principles of the situation, and would be useless to little Tom who is in need of a real comfort that no explanation of principles could provide. To be innocent in respect of any situation, perhaps, is to be a participant in it, while to be experienced is to be an outsider. The outsider is in command of himself, is collected as an observer, and if any emotion is aroused it is an emotion that has reference to himself, though it might go under the same name as a more urgent feeling. Thus the onlooker's pity may have more of dismay in it than compassion, and his joy contain more of amusement than delight. The moral philosophers of the Enlightenment are quite right when they give a selfish cast to the mind they dissect, because the circumstances in which we have leisure to examine our motives—the circumstances of the outsider—permit an interpretation in terms of the self. Psychologies tend to be explanations of the experienced state because only that state observes itself. Innocence is too much involved, too much engaged in experiencing, to account for itself, though its very preoccupation might make it appear self-centred to the eye of Experience. The state of Experience, as we have seen it, is habitually a spectator of its own life, reacting to the circumstances in which it finds itself, but at a remove from them. The innocent state is caught up in its activities.

It requires an effort of the imagination on the part of the reader of 'The Little Boy lost' and 'found' to realize how very differently the child sees the events of the poem. The boy is completely taken in, for while the reader never meets the father at all, knowing that he is impersonated in both poems, the boy's situation is that he is with his father nearly all the time. The result of this gap between the child's knowledge and the reader's knowledge is that a number of irrelevant considerations stand in the way of realizing what the feelings of the child are. Only by an effort can the urgency of the distress of the child be appreciated. The poems present a very painful picture indeed of extreme bewilderment. We know that the real father is absent, and while we feel sympathy with the child for his being lost, probably fail to appreciate the fact that to the child it seems that it is his father (who has supported him) who now behaves in so bewildering a manner, hastening away indifferently in a cruel silence. The cries of the child in the first stanza, his struggles in the second and utter bewilderment in the third stanza present an extremely pathetic condition—more pathetic than one realizes as an outsider. The case is a common one when dealing with children. Their emotions are violent and come and go easily, but though the occasion of the passion might seem illusory and the reaction appear to be excessive there is, for the participant, nothing trivial about a childish crisis. When an adult enjoins a child to control his emotions he advises something that is impossible for the child (except in so far as he is already adult) to do. The very young child is less in control of himself because he is more sensitive, more easily directed by impulses from without. What the adult is saying, really, is not: 'Control your emotions', but: 'Collect your self, be aware as an enclosed being and less sensitive as a vulnerable one, behave less as though you were a manifestation of your world and more like its judge.' The adult has elected to harden himself against circumstances—wisely, no doubt.

Blake exploits our adult mentality by shocking it with a naïve idea, baldly presented in the third stanza:

> . . . but God, ever nigh,
> Appear'd like his father in white.

> He kissed the child & by the hand led
> And to his mother brought . . .

As there is no attempt whatever to explain why or how God should appear we are left feeling rather stupid about the sort of thing (such are our habits of mind) that we like to have some reason for. The little boy has no such complications. God is taken to be his father, and to be as real as his mother. The supernatural, in this poem, is an adult idea. We have seen it presented, also, as an adult idea in its experienced counterpart 'A Little Boy Lost'. There, the child takes God very much as he would a substantial parent, while the priest is the exponent of the supernatural, and burns the child for attempting to bring esoteric accounts down to earth, to apply 'reason' to 'mystery'. The mysterious parts of the poem at present under discussion are provided by Blake, and his lost boy is quite unaware that it is God who comes to his rescue. The reader is free to deepen the mystery by asking such questions as: is it really God?—are we to interpret this appearance in some especial way? We tend to commence in mystery (in speculation about the supernatural) and only from that point of view do we begin to interpret the poem. We see the aspects of the situation that puzzle us and only later come to a realization of the poignant aspects of the verses, the depth of bewilderment of the child, and his relief. When we have penetrated that far into the significance of the poem the mystery has been set aside, for the child knows nothing of mystery, only of the behaviour of his father, his distress, and the lifting of the distress.

We are invited to discard mystery for realities whenever we confront a child, particularly when we attempt to present the child with an idea of God. The less abstruse and elaborate the account is made, the more effective it can be. The child lacks the groundwork for understanding metaphysical and dogmatic subtleties, and if these are to come, as they will come in only too great an abundance, something simple and particular must be referred to first. When we tell a child that God is a father capable of caring for every one of His creatures individually, explain Him as He appears in this poem, we are not descending to a lower level of conception and argument from a higher one, but the reverse. In translating our sophisticated notion of God into the version a child can understand we achieve a greater degree of insight, if we are sincere, just as in moving from the onlooker's to the participating levels of Blake's poem it gains in significance. The God we describe to a young child has a better title to respect than the God who is made intelligible to the reservations and demands for completeness of an adult mind. The former God must be made credible to a being whose habits of knowing and perceiving are not yet clouded, conventional and self-enclosed, and in forcing ourselves to be clear to one who is 'limited' in this way we can get rid of a great deal of our intellectual mumbo-jumbo.

Blake brings together, in 'The Little Boy lost' and 'found', the aloof, querying, sceptical yet superstitious world of his reader, and the world of the child, who is eager to be told but incapable of superstition because he must translate what he is told in terms of the real things he knows. In the experienced world real things have the character of an illusion, while the innocent confers reality, even on the illusory. Blake's poem contains two spirits: the wandering light (a natural spirit) and the spirit of 'God, ever nigh'. The adult is not likely to be led away by the wandering light. He knows that it is an illusion, can be naturally explained. Also, he is unlikely to be carried away by a supernatural light because God, like the will-o'-the-wisp, is part of the furniture of his mind. Both are old familiars. The child, on the other hand, lacks 'knowledge' and 'discrimination' and is likely to confer substance on to the spirits he comes into contact with because neither spirit is part of his mental stock. The experienced mind has explanations for all appearances, and so can keep itself at a distance in any circumstance, observing 'nature' and observing supernature. The innocent mind is so devoid of explanations that it does not even distinguish between the 'natural' and the supernatural and the child enters, instead, into a relationship, finding his father in the lights that come to lead him. A child is entranced by the extraordinary, but his own imagination is not fantastic and the commonplace is sufficiently wonderful to him. God can appear in no more wonderful form than that of the boy's father, and can do no more wonderful thing than return him to the care of his mother. This care is emphasized in the last two lines of the poem. It is the most substantial care that the child knows, and lends support to other, weaker, forms of affection, human and divine. Even God's best care is to return the child to this reality.

Blake took the outline of the incidents in 'The Little Boy lost' and 'found' from a story related in *Elements of*

Morality, for the use of children, translated and adapted from the German of the Rev. C. G. Salzmann by Mary Wollstonecraft, and published in 1790.[1] The illustrations for this book were adapted and etched by Blake, and it seems likely that he was introduced to the work while producing the *Songs of Innocence,* etched in 1789. One of the tales told in the book describes how little Charles wanders in the wood and is lost at nightfall. The child is unable to set about getting out of the wood, for:

He could not reason justly on account of his youth; and wanted his father's advice to teach him how to think, as much as his strong arm to support a poor tired boy, whose legs tottered under him.[2]

In the moonlight Charles imagines that he sees frightful objects, including a death's head and a devil, and is terrified by a tall black figure wearing a white cap and with a white pigeon flying before it. He runs away and falls. The terrifying figure turns out to be the curate of a nearby village who leads him from the wood. The white cap is the curate's wig and the white pigeon a handkerchief. There are two illustrations to the story, one showing little Charles lost and frightened among the trees, while the other shows Charles on the ground being raised by the curate.

The student, going through the books that Blake read (some of which he helped to illustrate) is surprised at the frequent allusions made by the poet. Some of these, such as Biblical references, are obvious, are of importance to the understanding of the verse, and the reader is expected to identify them. Other references are made in a more general way, such as that to 'natural' theories of man in 'The Human Abstract'. These allusions, also, are meant to be recognized, as Blake is using them to make a comment of some sort. There is, also, a very large part of his reading that

---

[1] Wicksteed discusses the relationship of Blake's poem to this work in an article, 'Blake's Songs of Innocence', in the *Times Literary Supplement* of 18 February 1932. The link had been suggested to Wicksteed by Max Plowman.   [2] *Elements of Morality* (1792 edn.), I, 25.

Blake used in order to provide himself with the outlines of plots, fragments of images, suggestions of an action, and often this sort of allusiveness (if it truly is allusion) is obtrusive, and mystifying to the reader. In the earlier poetry, with which we are concerned, this occurs in the form of Ossianic names; in language that is Biblical, Swedenborgian, Spenserian, Shakespearean or even in loose quotations from these sources; images taken from the Greek writings translated by Thomas Taylor; subjects depicted in the paintings or reproductions that Blake studied; occurrences in Blake's daily life; references to books Blake was helping to illustrate, as in the case we are examining at present. It is of interest to be able to identify this sort of 'allusion' but the use to which Blake put this material is so very individual, he subordinated it so very much to his own purposes, that the identification by no means provides the reader with a means of interpreting Blake's verse. Blake, presumably, did not expect such 'allusions' to be recognized. He brings into poetry some of the habits of the pictorial artist, and, like all pictorial artists, expected his depictions to be intelligible without the viewer being obliged to refer to the odds and ends accumulated in the studio.

'The Little Boy lost' and 'found' is quite intelligible as the poem was written. There would be no point in alluding to Mary Wollstonecraft's story of the lost boy and Blake's etchings for the story except as a curiosity, an illustration of the way Blake ground his colours before starting to paint, if it were not that the book from which the story comes illustrates, for us, the sort of thinking that might have helped provide Blake with a clue to his distinction between Innocence and Experience. If it did provide such a clue, it provided it in the negative way in which Blake usually encountered his clues. The book contains ideas that Blake would regard as mistaken, and so, studying it (or something like it) might have assisted him in evolving an unmistaken view. The eighteenth century, the age of reason, provided a one-sided description of man. It described the aspect we have called Experience and Blake was not satisfied that this description was a complete one. Perhaps he was given a hint as to how the account might be filled out when he observed the description being applied, as it is in the *Elements of Morality*, to children, to creatures whom it did not fit. Mary Wollstonecraft's free translation of Salzmann falls within the conventional pattern of thinking of the day. The book appears to have been successful for there were further editions in 1791 and 1792, and the publisher, J. Johnson, brought out Mary Wollstonecraft's *Original Stories*, written on the same lines, in 1791. Blake designed and etched the plates for this work too, and 'alludes to' (uses) it in the *Songs of Experience*.

Blake's 'The Little Boy lost' and 'found' emphasizes the literal and practical manner in which the childish imagination works. This is by no means an inferior mode, for an exploration of realities is difficult to achieve and requires a fresh and vigorous mind. The vitiated imagination evades this labour by escape into speculative and fanciful modes. Salzmann sees something of this difference between the childish and adult modes, although he inverts the values Blake places on them. For him, the child is a being who has not yet developed beyond the stage when it requires particular examples to support the abstract statement:

Teach [a child] that envy is the vexation which is felt at seeing the happiness of others, you will have given him a just idea of it; but shew him its dreadful effects, in the example of Hannah, in chap. 29, Vol. ii, who was so tormented by this corroding passion . . . as to embitter her innocent sister's pleasure: this representation has determined the child's disposition—he will hate envy.[1]

This sounds reasonable enough: let the child draw the obviously right conclusion from something of a practical nature. Salzmann is by no means content, however, merely to tell his stories. Not only are they interspersed with moral injunctions, but the characters seize every occasion they can,

---

[1] *Ed. cit.* 'Introductory Address', i, vii.

opportune or not, to moralize, and, in doing so, draw the most soul-killing conclusions. After the curate has rescued Charles he takes him to his own home. On the way, he is met by his family and sends them ahead so that he may continue his counsel to the exhausted Charles. He starts with one of his frequent definitions:

Do you know then what joy is? We feel it when something agreeable suddenly occurs. My wife and children rejoiced to see me again, because they love me, and know that I have their good at heart . . . But believe me, my dear child, that even joy when it is too strong, does as much harm as violent fear. It disturbs the operations of the understanding to such a degree, that a man is no longer directed by reason, and in this confusion often hurts himself.[1]

Examples follow, such as that of the peasant who broke his ankle running to meet his son come home from sea. Charles is enjoined to guard against immoderate joy, and when he asks how to do so, is told:

You must often think that the unexpected good is never as great as we at first imagine, and that there is always something disagreeable attached to it.

This sort of chill is cast continually, and the mean-spirited approach of the book is to be seen, not only in the material that is to be read to the children, but in the way in which it is advocated it should be read. In the 'Introductory Address' it is suggested that the reader should break off suddenly and not be prevailed on by the entreaties of the children to continue. This is done 'merely to try their patience'. The children are told that if they behave well, the relation will be continued on the following day.

Mary Wollstonecraft was a 'liberal', an admirer of Paine, and an advocate of the rights of women, including the right to an education befitting the dignity of a human being. Her books for children are not more, but less offensive to the modern reader than similar publications of the period, yet there are two aspects of *Elements of Morality* which it is

[1] *Elements of Morality*, 1, 43.

very difficult to condone. First, the child is seen as no more than a creature exercising the 'natural' understanding, and secondly, the stories corrupt the child (or attempt to corrupt him) by introducing him to vices he may have no knowledge of, in order to claim his mind for the realm of this sort of understanding, and the exercise of the 'virtues' annexed to it—the virtues of 'The Human Abstract'. All this is done with the best of intentions. It is quite taken for granted that the only inducement to virtue that can reasonably be held out to the child is his own advantage, as is usual when putting forward the 'natural' argument. Charles and the curate relieve an injured coachman's anxiety about his family by sending word of his condition, and the curate comments:

... pity, the compassionate feeling I am describing, is very useful, as it impels us to assist our suffering fellow creatures ... And when we have comforted an afflicted man, we are so light, so gay, that every pleasure has a finer relish ... always exercise your compassion, instead of trying to stifle it for present ease ... Then would your heart soon tell you what you ought to do and pity would procure you many such pleasant moments as you now enjoy.[1]

It is easy enough for the modern reader to see this 'pity' as a queer mixture of ideas of function, amenity and profit. We have the advantage of living after such men as Blake. Yet when we consider the fact that this conception of virtue was taken seriously in the eighteenth century, and remember what a limited conception it is, we must also remember that the men of that time took the conception as a basis for action, and conscientiously applied this rather shabby notion of doing good.[2]

It is a pity that such a work as the *Elements* feels obliged to work so hard at justifying decent behaviour as though it were something to be ashamed of. The child James catches a mouse in the fields and wishes to cut its ears and tail off in order, as he says (having caught the natural note), to punish

[1] *Ibid.* I, 131.
[2] See the accounts of the century given in various works by M. Dorothy George. M. G. Jones, *The Charity School Movement in the Eighteenth Century* (1938), is of interest.

it for being destructive.[1] The reader agrees when James is told that 'He who can torment a little helpless animal, has certainly a bad heart'. This method of dissuasion is improved upon, however, by a description of how ingeniously the mouse is made and it is even compared with a watch. James responds at this mechanical level by declaring that the mouse is good for nothing, but he is shown to be insufficiently versed in mechanical theory when he is told that the mouse is eaten by the Raven. Everything is given a use. Rich men set the poor to work.[2] Spiteful men contribute to the happiness of industrious men by bringing their industry to the notice of their employers.[3] Even pain has its function:

life is a blessing . . . because it is a gift from God, who, when He called any creature into existence, designed to communicate some degree of happiness to it; and when it suffers pain, it is to render it better, in order that it may enjoy more pleasure.[4]

All this explanation in terms of function, utility and profit assumes that the childish mind works exactly like the adult's as conceived by the psychology of the Enlightenment. The individual is self-seeking, and very much the onlooker. The child's mind is regarded as unfurnished even though he is capable of being rationally persuaded, and the stories are so arranged as to provide material to support the principles that follow. The peasant broke his ankle when running to meet his returning son. Immoderate joy causes pain. Moderate all feelings. This is added to: the peasant's son had become a thief and if his parent had thought of this possibility, he would not have broken his ankle. The moral seems to be that one must always think the worst. It is fortunate, perhaps, that children are fairly resilient, even more fortunate that they are less rationally persuadable than Salzmann supposes. The child will continue to think the best of people, placing so much faith in their sapience and goodness that he will willingly accept moral precepts out of love of the preceptor. This

---

[1] *Elements of Morality*, III, 37. [2] *Ibid*. III, 93.
[3] *Ibid*. III, 96. [4] *Ibid*. III, 137.

incentive to morality is not considered in the book. Such an approach might be excusable if the book were designed for adults, but it completely overlooks the child and the psychology of a better being. A better being has his ankle broken in running to embrace his son and has no thought of what the son might have become. A better being stands in danger of having his spontaneity injured in running to embrace such precepts as are laid down in *Elements of Morality*, simply for love of the person who enjoins him to accept them.

That is the omission for which the *Elements* is to blame. It sees the folly and the wayward emotional course of the child which makes it necessary that he should be given direction and control, but it ignores the fact that it is just this energy, emotionality, and wholeheartedness that makes him capable of entering into close and vital relationships, capable of love and faith and attachment, capable of accepting the direction and controls suggested to him. The rational arguments of the *Elements* are absurd, and the attempt to reinforce them with illustrative stories almost as absurd. Nevertheless, the book was probably effective, not because of any quality it has but because of the qualities in children which it deplores. The ignorant enthusiasm of the child, his simple-minded desire to please, together with his credulous trustfulness would allow him to accept, not the reasonings of the book or the principles exemplified, but the attitudes of the adult who was telling the stories. Blake sees the importance of this relatedness of the child and, at the end of 'The Little Boy lost' and 'found', the child, who has been with his father nearly all the time (has been making up a relationship), is returned to his mother, the adult most likely to be capable of meeting him on his own close terms of affection. It is to this capacity for affection in children that Salzmann's book must have owed any good effects it might have had.

Salzmann conceives children as rational, but without the experience which would give their reasonings proper direction.

Consequently, they foolishly choose the immediate gratification instead of the solid one, are gluttonous, lazy and unreliable because they do not see that more pleasure may be got by being moderate. It is not necessary to regard children as paragons in order to find fault with Salzmann's approach. Most children need some reformation for the reason that they have already started to be adults, have already started to become the self-enclosed and selfish beings of Experience to whom, one would suppose, the 'natural' arguments of function, utility and profit would have an appeal. But most children are also Innocents, and, to the degree that they are, remain endowed with impulses conducive to virtue, superior to anything 'natural' arguments can instil. The effect of the 'natural' argument is to erode the innocent positive endowment, replacing it with principles designed to suppress errors of selfishness and greed, errors which the 'natural' argument itself suggests. Salzmann's stories, for instance, implant the notion of jealousy in order to encourage the idea of the control of jealousy. Its teachings are negative (repress this, don't do that) and so, in effect, it makes the assumption of positive evil tendencies in the child. In the process of indoctrinating with the negative 'virtues' it must establish the positive vices, even if only by making the child too much aware of himself in the wrong way.

If Blake was stimulated to write 'The Little Boy lost' and 'found' by reading about Salzmann's lost child, he wrote his poem in order to show an altogether different version of childhood, a version based on the conception of Innocence and not on the child as a miniature adult. His little boy thinks, not in terms of natural and supernatural illusions but of affectionate relationships and of realities. Salzmann's children were expected to think in terms of self-interest and consequence and so come to the repressive social virtues. While such thinking might be common enough in Experience, the innocent awareness is directed differently, being capable of sympathy and of dwelling on the present

moment., These virtues, so contrary to Salzmann's, are particularly described in 'On Another's Sorrow', one of the *Songs
of Innocence*:

ON ANOTHER'S SORROW

Can I see another's woe,
And not be in sorrow too?
Can I see another's grief,
And not seek for kind relief?

Can I see a falling tear,
And not feel my sorrow's share?
Can a father see his child
Weep, nor be with sorrow fill'd?

Can a mother sit and hear
An infant groan, an infant fear?
No, no! never can it be!
Never, never can it be!

And can he who smiles on all
Hear the wren with sorrows small,
Hear the small bird's grief & care,
Hear the woes that infants bear,

And not sit beside the nest,
Pouring pity in their breast;
And not sit the cradle near,
Weeping tear on infant's tear;

And not sit both night & day,
Wiping all our tears away?
O! no never can it be!
Never, never can it be!

He doth give his joy to all;
He becomes an infant small;
He becomes a man of woe;
He doth feel the sorrow too.

Think not thou canst sigh a sigh
And thy maker is not by;
Think not thou canst weep a tear
And thy maker is not near.

O! he gives to us his joy
That our grief he may destroy;
Till our grief is fled & gone
He doth sit by us and moan.

The symmetry which is so often found in the *Songs*, and is very conspicuous in 'The Divine Image', is to be observed in this poem. The first three stanzas ask a series of questions about the relationships of human beings to one another and, in the third stanza, return a definite answer. The next three stanzas ask a similar set of questions about God and return the same answer. The final set of three stanzas are cast differently, and make positive statements. Although the poem deals separately with human and divine manifestations of pity in the first and second groups of stanzas, there is no attempt to make any distinction between the sorrows and sympathies of the first three stanzas and those of the second three. They are separately enumerated as the virtues of God and man were in 'The Divine Image', but they are spoken of in exactly the same manner and there is no reason to regard them as different in kind. As in 'The Divine Image', there is a very close correspondence between the three stanzas devoted to man and the three devoted to God. We are invited to think of the two on parallel lines but not to confuse them. God and man are neither confounded nor rigidly distinguished, so that there is a peculiar fitness in the last group of three stanzas which talks of man and of God simultaneously—for it is particularly Christ, both God and man, who is referred to, though not an historical Christ, but one who is a present reality. To emphasize this, the whole poem is written in the present tense. In addition there is no mention of God or Christ by name. We may identify them by their mode of being only.

Although the first six stanzas of the poem are cast in the form of a series of questions it is positive in tone, assertive of truths it has no doubts about whatever. The questions are rhetorical and the speaker puts certain statements as questions to which, he is quite confident, there is only one answer because, by eliciting the answers, he is able to advance his knowledge. We noticed, when examining 'The Divine Image', with which this poem has so much in common, how Blake relies on a clear, logical method of argument, just as he does here. The speaker's manner of exposition is impeccable, and follows the method of Descartes so closely that it is worth quoting that philosopher on the laws of logic he deemed sufficient:

The *first* was never to accept anything for true which I did not clearly know to be such; that is to say, carefully to avoid precipitancy and prejudice, and to comprise nothing more in my judgment than what was presented to my mind so clearly and distinctly as to exclude all ground of doubt.

The *second*, to divide each of the difficulties under examination into as many parts as possible, and as might be necessary for its adequate solution.

The *third*, to conduct my thoughts in such order that, by commencing with objects the simplest and easiest to know, I might ascend by little and little, and, as it were, step by step, to the knowledge of the more complex; assigning in thought a certain order even to those objects which in their own nature do not stand in a relation of antecedence and sequence.

And the *last*, in every case to make enumerations so complete, and reviews so general, that I might be assured that nothing was omitted.[1]

The speaker in Blake's poem follows each of these laws to the letter. He 'divides his examination into parts' and introduces them in such order that the 'simplest and easiest to know' comes first. This is what is presented most immediately in an examination of himself:

> Can I see another's woe,
> And not be in sorrow too?

He continues by enumerating examples that he cannot know so easily, but, nevertheless, examples that are presented to his view so 'clearly and distinctly as to exclude all ground of

[1] *Discourse on Method*, Part II.

doubt'. In making this examination he moves from the 'simplest and easiest to know . . . to the knowledge of the more complex', moves from himself to the father, to the mother, to God, pursuing inquiries, all the while, to which clear answers can be returned:

> No, no! never can it be!
> Never, never can it be!

The considerations of Divine pity and human pity 'do not stand in a relation of antecedence and sequence', but they are 'assigned a certain order in thought', human pity being dealt with first, and the questions settled quite firmly by an answer the speaker is sure of, and a consideration of Divine pity following in the same manner. The third section of the poem indicates the artificiality of the 'relation of sequence' by being obliged to take the human and Divine simultaneously. This simultaneous consideration is necessary in order that the 'enumeration should be complete and the review general', and also provides an opportunity to reinforce the 'clear and distinct' truths of the first two sections by a deductive truth drawn from them:

> Think not thou canst sigh a sigh
> And thy maker is not by;
> Think not thou canst weep a tear
> And thy maker is not near.

The deduction drawn here is stated negatively, just as the answers to the questions in the earlier part of the poem are negatively stated. Despite these negatives, responding to the inquiring nature of the poem, the effect is not one of doubt or need for conviction, but the reverse. It is precisely because the speaker is absolutely sure he is making statements which are evident, orderly and consequential that he can use the method he does. The propositions are not put as questions in order to invite agreement with a point of view, but because there cannot be any disagreement. If, then, we take the poem to be a statement of the efficacy of sympathy, its existence as an active principle, the statement is made, not as one of belief, but of faith (following Coleridge's definition):

> . . . faith is a total act of the soul: it is the whole state of the mind, or it is not at all; and in this consists its power, as well as its exclusive worth.[1]

The logical expository method is an indication of conviction so deep and secure that the speaker can be calm, sure, patient and rational in his disclosure.

The theme of the poem may be summed up in the word 'sympathy', if by this is implied more than an emotion in the breast that acknowledges or understands the emotion of another. The words 'love', or 'sympathetic love', might be better ones to apply, though Blake avoids them, just as he avoids 'sympathy' in the *Songs*. The union between sufferer and 'sympathizer' is a very close one indeed:

> Can I see another's woe,
> And not be in sorrow too?
> Can I see another's grief,
> And not seek for kind relief?

The stanza could be taken to imply: When I see sorrow in another I feel sorrow (of my own) at their sorrow. When I see grief in another I try to find some way of alleviating their misery. The poem continues:

> Can I see a falling tear,
> And not feel my sorrow's share?

The sorrow is shared as if it were one sorrow, and as if the tear were that of the person who sees it fall. Clearly, the first stanza should have been taken differently: The woe of another person is felt also by me; the grief of another is felt by me so that I must seek relief for both of us. The poem does not describe an emotion in the observer that we can designate pity, an emotion with its own nature, different in kind to that responded to. It does not even describe a sympathy or com-

---

[1] *The Friend*, II, Essay XI.

passion taken as an emotion in the onlooker correspondent to that of the sufferer. The relationship to the sufferer is such that, to some degree, the onlooker becomes identified with the sufferer. The third stanza goes on to emphasize such a relationship:

> Can a mother sit and hear
> An infant groan, an infant fear?

We could fill out a meaning: Can a mother sit and hear with equanimity? But plainly Blake's intention is conveyed by the words as they stand in the poem. The mother ceases, in her closeness to her child, to be an auditor but behaves as if the pain or fear were her own. She participates with the child, losing her own immunity in the urgency of her caring.

God's pleasure in created beings is apparent (He smiles) but, like the mother, He ceases to be a mere hearer in His compassionate participation:

> And can he who smiles on all
> Hear the wren with sorrows small,
> Hear the small bird's grief & care,
> Hear the woes that infants bear . . . ?

In the next stanza we are told that He sits 'Pouring pity', but He participates as well:

> Weeping tear on infant's tear . . .

There is the same ambiguity here. God drops a tear for every tear of the infant but, also, the tears that are dropped by the infant are those that God weeps. God has, to some degree, become identified with the infant in his grief, and He enters into all grief.

The last three stanzas of the poem assert a manifold divine activity. The 'maker' gives and the 'maker' pities. He is nearby wherever there is grief or pain. He takes on the human form in incarnation. He takes an identity with the sufferer. There are several levels at which the seventh stanza may be read:

> He doth give his joy to all;
> He becomes an infant small;
> He becomes a man of woe;
> He doth feel the sorrow too.

He instils joy, which offsets grief. He is born in the flesh, and assumes its sorrows. He 'enters into' the feelings of the sufferer. God is seen as the benefactor of man, as the fellow of man and, lastly, as one who accompanies every man in sorrow, participating in his emotion.

'On Another's Sorrow' does not attempt to deal with any matter it has no first-hand knowledge of, or which is not perfectly clear to its understanding. It knows that there is pain and grief in man's life, but it does not wonder how these come to be there, does not attempt to fit them into any cosmic or 'natural' scheme. The function and origin of pain is not considered, and the utmost that is stated resembling a 'natural' argument is that God offsets pain by joy:

> O! he gives to us his joy
> That our grief he may destroy . . .

For the rest, the 'natural' and supernatural mechanics of the universe are ignored, as the protagonist presents us with clear and distinct knowledge, not conjecture.

What the speaker knows is this: that sympathetic love (compare the 'natural love', explained by advantage and utility), while it certainly does not allow one to become another person, does cause one to concentrate one's attention in them. The relationship of sympathizer towards a sufferer is not that of an onlooker but of one disturbed to a degree where his own self becomes less and less attended to and the needs of the other dominate the feelings he has. The focus of the mind is moved to take in something of the awareness of another. The speaker is sure also that God is compassionate in need, moving close and attending every motion of the sufferer. His awareness becomes ours because of His love. The reader of the poem is aware that the speaker knows God, and knows Him so positively not because he has any theoretical or esoteric information (though he is, it happens, in possession of Christian ideas) but because of his actual knowledge of love or sympathy in his own living sense. This latter knowledge is not mental and verbal (a matter of belief) but a function of his whole being, his experience, and so a matter of faith. His faith (clear and certain awareness) informs his Christian belief, giving it significance and substance.

Salzmann sets up a false idea of childhood by resting it prematurely on the pure understanding to the detriment of enthusiasm and affection. He takes no account of the delicate perception on the child's part of the exact state of feeling in others and his ready adoption of those feelings. The child learns his attitudes, including his moral attitudes, not by rational persuasion (which would make him a passive recipient) but by sympathy, by projecting his awareness into that of another or, at all events, by being keenly alive to attitudes in others, so keenly alive that they become his own. On this latter view the child is not passive, but imaginatively and sensitively active. He does not merely imitate but must show the most delicate—though unselfconscious—perception in order to create his attitudes. There is, as a result, always this transformation in the child, that given even the shabbiest models to work from, and though he will work them as exactly as he is able, he cannot help rejuvenating them, giving them some degree of his sense of wonder, confidence and wholeheartedness. Wordsworth recognizes the quality:

> One is there, though the wisest and the best
> Of all mankind, who covets not at times
> Union that cannot be;—who would not give,
> If so he might, to duty and to truth
> The eagerness of infantine desire?[1]

The psychologies of the eighteenth century never glimpse the qualities of sympathy and imaginative intelligence

---

[1] *Prelude*, ii, 22.

ascribed by Blake to the state of Innocence. Even when these qualities are, apparently, given a place in an account of humanity, they are seen, when examined, to be 'natural' components conceived in the rationalist manner. Hume, for instance, accounts for man's moral nature on a principle of the understanding (as Salzmann does), but changes his mind, wishing to find some more elevated basis, something 'laudable and good' which gives a 'just notion both of the generosity and capacity of human nature'. He hits on the principle of sympathy as this basis, but on a very different sympathy to that contained in 'On Another's Sorrow'. Hume's moral philosophy expounded in the third volume of his *Treatise* is basically Hobbesian. According to Hume, the institutions and conventions set up by social man to regulate his behaviour are given direction by his appetites, particularly by his desire for possessions, and our notions of justice spring from an understanding of what rules are most likely to assure each man in his property. We see, also, that we are all likely to make greater advances in the acquiring of possessions under the restraints of law and morality than we possibly could if there were a universal licence, and so we control the cruder forms of self-seeking by a refinement of selfishness embodied in our institutions:

. . . whether the passion of self-interest be esteemed vicious or virtuous, it is all a case, since itself alone restrains it; so that if it be virtuous, men become social by their virtue; if vicious, their vice has the same effect.[1]

It is strange to find an apparent contradiction in Hume at the end of Book III, section ii, where he argues that the ideas of virtue and vice which we attach to justice and injustice are based, not on the self-interest which gave rise to the notion of justice but on the directly contrary principle of benevolent disinterestedness which he derives from the existence of 'sympathy'. An examination of this 'sympathy' as it is expounded in Book III, section iii of the *Treatise* shows the

[1] *Treatise*, III, ii, 2. Everyman edn., II, 197.

sentiment to be a very cerebral activity. Like his 'imagination' in Book I it is an aspect of the intellect, a very busy but
not particularly bright 'daughter of the memory'. It would
not misrepresent Hume's sympathy to define it as follows:
sympathy is an awareness, when any situation is represented
to us, of the advantage and pleasure (or their opposites)
arising to the persons represented, as if to ourselves. Hume
explains also that this must be a matter of an appreciation of
universal or general consequences, for 'such interests and
pleasures touch us more faintly than our own'. All this
establishes the sympathizer very much as a spectator, aware
of what is represented, very much aware of his own interests,
and relating these two conjecturally. No very active understanding of the mind of the person being sympathized with is
necessary. What is of importance is the realization of the
effects (in a general way) of the circumstances to which he is
subjected, and an understanding of what 'pain' or 'pleasure'
such circumstances (generally) involve. The shift of attention
is a subtle one from *this person* to *this sort of eventuality* but it
involves a shift from a going out of the attention and a giving
of the self to a gathering in of attention to consequences
centred on the self. Hume's 'sympathy' is that of 'The
Human Abstract', that of Experience. In Innocence, as is
made clear in 'On Another's Sorrow', sympathy is a movement of the heart towards another, is a source of our divine
humanity, and not an outcome of the 'natural' being.

CHAPTER 5

THE GULF BETWEEN INNOCENCE
AND EXPERIENCE

HENRY CRABB ROBINSON came to know Blake slightly in
1825, two years before the poet died, and it is to this acquaintance that we owe a record of some opinions passed by Blake
on the subject of Wordsworth's writings. On several occasions
Blake expressed his admiration of the poetry though, like
Coleridge, he found Wordsworth's explanations of the verse
unsatisfactory. Also, the admiration was usually accompanied
by a reservation in respect to Wordsworth's veneration of
nature. Robinson writes of one of his talks with Blake:

December 24th.—A call on Blake—my third interview. I read him
Wordsworth's incomparable ode ['Intimations of Immortality'],
which he heartily enjoyed. But he repeated, 'I fear Wordsworth
loves nature, and nature is the work of the Devil. The Devil is in
us as far as we are in nature.'[1]

Blake's condemnation of Wordsworth's 'love of nature' was
recorded in more detail in some very sketchy annotations he
made during the following year in a copy of Wordsworth's
Poems of 1815, lent by Crabb Robinson.[2] The 'Preface' to
that work cannot have made a very good initial impression on
Blake, and must have confirmed him in his suspicion that
Wordsworth was too much committed to a 'natural' way of
explaining things. The first paragraph of the 'Preface'
enumerates the 'powers requisite for the production of
poetry': observation, sensibility, reflexion, imagination,
invention and judgement. This clinical list had no appeal to
Blake who, figuratively speaking, put his pencil through it,

[1] *Diary*, ed. T. Sadler (1869).
[2] Gilchrist prints these annotations in his *Life*, in chap. xxxvi. They appear,
also, in *Complete Writings* (1957), p. 782.

8 113 GB

and wrote down: 'One Power alone makes a Poet: Imagination, The Divine Vision'. Wordsworth had, apparently, gone to a great deal of trouble in making an analysis that was altogether inappropriate. By 'Imagination, The Divine Vision' Blake must have meant to imply the capacity, something of which we have seen in his Innocents, to participate sympathetically and whole-heartedly in an experience of the utmost breadth, a capacity altogether beyond the comprehension of 'natural' philosophies with their insistence on stilted explanations in terms of abstract factors. Wordsworth's factors, his 'requisite powers', do not distinguish poetry from any other mode of writing, being equally necessary in all expression.

Against the 'Preface to the Second Edition of the Lyrical Ballads' with its 'Supplement' Blake writes: 'these Prefaces . . . are very mischievous & direct contrary to Wordsworth's own Practise'. This inconsistency is remarked on frequently:

I see in Wordsworth the Natural Man rising up against the Spiritual Man Continually, & then he is No Poet but a Heathen Philosopher at Enmity against all true Poetry or Inspiration.

Blake objects whenever Wordsworth becomes the 'natural' theorist, both in the prose prefaces and in the poetry. Blake makes his objections to Wordsworth's ideas in large Swedenborgian terms which are by no means fortunately chosen. He is obscure, tends to carp, and is rather obstinate—refusing, even, to acknowledge that Wordsworth's attempt to describe the poetic in a 'natural' and rationalistic convention is a courageous one. If the 'Preface to the Second Edition of the Lyrical Ballads' is a failure, as Blake implies, it is one in which Wordsworth may be admired. He adopts such terms as 'pleasure' and 'sympathy' which belong, properly, to Hume, but is never in bondage to them because he is accompanied, throughout the essay, by a sense of there being something more than his explanation has disclosed. This sense enters the essay in various ways. Near the end it is introduced in the emotion that precedes 'tranquillity'. Tranquillity and order are decidedly manifested in poetry, which exercises control in the highest degree. But the degree is high because it wishes to direct the attention of a human being in all his complexity, so Wordsworth makes his tranquillity supervene upon a state of powerful feelings. A more complete, if less accountable, state gives support to the deliberations and conscious selections of tranquillity.

Near the beginning of the 'Preface' Wordsworth announces that he has chosen themes from humble and rustic life because:

. . . in that condition, the essential passions of the heart find a better soil in which they can attain their maturity . . . our elementary feelings coexist in a state of greater simplicity . . . in that condition the passions of men are incorporated with the beautiful and permanent forms of nature. The language, too, of these men has been adopted . . . because such men hourly communicate with the best objects from which the best part of language is originally derived.

Even if one agrees with Coleridge that Wordsworth's diction is not rustic, and if one doubts whether this description of rustic man is altogether true, this in no way detracts from the truth of Wordsworth's intuition that human awareness is a much more complex and wonderful thing than is normally envisaged, and that it is the business of poetry to explore this complex realm. He puts forward rustic and simple men as being proper subjects for poetry and this suggestion, if it does nothing else, asserts that the mind of sophisticated man, limited by its axioms and definitions, may lose contact with a dimension of awareness that is valuable. Like Blake, Wordsworth knows that the poet must see the significance of Innocence if his account of the soul is to be complete and, like Blake, he finds Innocence well exemplified in the rustic and the child.

A page or two later Wordsworth discusses the ability of the poet to react to a fictitious circumstance as if it were real, and remarks:

. . . whatever portion of this faculty we may suppose even the Greatest Poet to possess, there cannot be a doubt that the language which it will suggest to him, must often, in liveliness and truth, fall short of that which is uttered by men in real life, under the actual pressure of those passions, certain shadows of which the Poet thus produces, or feels to be produced, in himself.

This by no means asserts that under the 'actual pressure of passions' men are very articulate or that they need say anything at all. What Wordsworth implicitly states here is that poetry is to be associated with utterances that are spontaneous and express the deeper impulses of the soul rather than with those that are more consciously controlled to suit some particular purpose. Like Blake, Wordsworth knows that there is an Innocence belonging to the poet.

We use words rationally in a way that limits and focuses the efforts of our mind and so achieve precision in conducting our affairs. Poetically, we use words to extend our awareness and sensibilities. The civilized man uses words in both ways, applying them scientifically in order to be exact, and imaginatively in order to extend the range of his being. There is some confusion in Wordsworth between these two modes— certainly too much for Blake's taste, but the reader is nearly always aware of an intuitive reluctance on Wordsworth's part to commit himself too deeply to a 'natural' manner of explaining himself. In the prose discourses on poetry he is never really satisfied. Some remainder that he cannot fit into his explanation is always left, which sends him off on a further search for the truth. Perhaps this itch in Wordsworth to set it down philosophically is due to the fact that he was so much less capable than a man like Blake of handling theories and abstractions. Blake's grasp of systems is masterly and so he can afford to be contemptuous of them. He turns up his nose at Locke and—so we may infer—at Hume because he has understood and rejected the terms of their explanations. He dismisses Wordsworth's Prefaces because he sees that the method of analysis that they use is a limited one, yet he expressed the greatest respect for the poetry because he sees that Wordsworth has already arrived, poetically, at the position that, mistakenly, he wishes to attain rationally. Blake does not do the Prefaces justice, however. Wordsworth himself senses the limitations of his method of explaining poetry, never really thinks that he has given the final word of explanation, and his expectations of poetry are as high as Blake's and are very similar.

Blake felt compelled to write down his unqualified admiration for only one of Wordsworth's poems: 'To H.C. Six Years Old'.[1] He says:

This is all in the highest degree Imaginative & equal to any Poet, but not Superior. I cannot think that Real Poets have any competition. None are greatest in the Kingdom of Heaven; it is so in Poetry.[2]

No praise could be higher than this. An examination of the poem shows an absence of the 'natural' elements that mar the 'Intimations' ode, but does reveal the sensitivity of Wordsworth when he is most free. It also shows that Wordsworth had an understanding of the importance of the state of Innocence fully equal to Blake's.

TO H.C.

SIX YEARS OLD

O Thou! whose fancies from afar are brought;
Who of thy words dost make a mock apparel,
And fittest to unutterable thought
The breeze-like motion and the self-born carol;
Thou faery voyager! that dost float
In such clear water, that thy boat
May rather seem
To brood on air than on an earthly stream;
Suspended in a stream as clear as sky,
· Where earth and heaven do make one imagery;
O blessed vision! happy child!
Thou art so exquisitely wild,
I think of thee with many fears
For what may be thy lot in future years.

[1] *Poems Referring to the Period of Childhood*, xv (1849–50 edn.).
[2] 'Annotations', *loc. cit.*

I thought of times when Pain might be thy guest,
Lord of thy house and hospitality;
And Grief, uneasy lover! never rest
But when she sate within the touch of thee.
O too industrious folly!
O vain and causeless melancholy!
Nature will either end thee quite;
Or, lengthening out thy season of delight,
Preserve for thee, by individual right,
A young lamb's heart among the full-grown flocks.
What hast thou to do with sorrow,
Or the injuries of to-morrow?
Thou art a dew-drop, which the morn brings forth,
Ill fitted to sustain unkindly shocks,
Or to be trailed along the soiling earth;
A gem that glitters while it lives,
And no forewarning gives;
But, at the touch of wrong, without a strife
Slips in a moment out of life.

The child's lightness and freedom conveyed in the first stanza are contrasted with anxious and heavy tendencies in Wordsworth. The last two lines of the first stanza, so dangerous in tendency, come very glibly into the poem:

> I think of thee with many fears
> For what may be thy lot in future years.

What could be more natural than to cast the mind forward in a kindly concern for the child, yet this kindness is an interference really, is typical of the sort of influence that will cause the H.C. we have seen (the innocent H.C.) to 'slip in a moment out of life' (to lose his Innocence). The child will soon become the anxious and ponderous adult, will soon adopt the 'industrious folly' and 'causeless melancholy' which Wordsworth's preoccupation with future times exemplifies. H.C. will become infected by influences of the sort Wordsworth brings to bear in his kindly but unsympathetic concern for the child's future.

The concern is introduced thoughtlessly at the end of the first stanza, but a few lines later Wordsworth checks the tendency that is potentially destructive of the child's innocent poise, the tendency that threatens to destroy his own innocent pleasure in the child. Until he disturbs himself with his anxious irrelevancy he has delighted in contemplating H.C. for the joy of doing so, without attempting to probe into the child's nature, but he succumbs to the more subtle temptation of probing into a future that it has not yet come to. The destructive preoccupation is drawn back from immediately, but only by a visible effort on Wordsworth's part in bringing himself back to reason.

The difference between the poise of the child and the inertia of the (experienced) adult is brought out by a contrast in the images of the first stanza, on the one hand, and of the first four lines of the second stanza, on the other. In describing his over-anxious mind, Wordsworth says:

> I thought of times when Pain might be thy guest,
> Lord of thy house and hospitality;
> And Grief, uneasy lover! never rest
> But when she sate within the touch of thee.

The relationship between the mature self and its pain is well described by comparing them to an over-solicitous host and an unfamiliar guest. There is something always requiring attention and disruptive of peace, even at times when the visitor is not in evidence. The metaphor introduces, also, the idea of a nagging feeling of responsibility which burdens the experienced mind. This suggestion is reinforced by the compulsion of the uneasy lover, who cannot leave alone and must meddle, in and out of season. These images convey, not only the pain and grief to come to H.C., but also something of the habitual restlessness and anxiety of the future being they are to come to. Both metaphors are drawn from the world of adult experienced relationships of an uncomfortable sort.

The images of the first stanza emphasize the self-sufficiency of the child and suggest that there is something wonderful but alien in his nature. They emphasize, also, Wordsworth's

119

contentment to let the child be. The child is intangible, and enjoyed without the urge to touch:

> Thou faery voyager! that dost float
> In such clear water, that thy boat
> May rather seem
> To brood on air than on an earthly stream;
> Suspended in a stream as clear as sky,
> Where earth and heaven do make one imagery . . .

No clear separation of the elements is apparent and the datum of the horizon is absent, for although the child is made of the human stuff of the poet, and lives in the same world, he is lightly afloat, bright and distant. He is 'faery': apparently human but belonging to some other realm. He is a voyager in transit between strange places, touching on our sphere but with his proper life enjoyed in his own motion.

The lightness of the child has nothing frivolous about it. On the contrary, he seems to have a more proper seriousness than the adult is in possession of. The boat is steady without effort, and is said to 'brood'. This suggests a wholehearted, loving concentration of attention which, while it contrasts with the uncomfortable anxieties of the second stanza, is compatible with the 'exquisite wildness' of the first. Even in his excitement the child shows poise, retains the dignity and seriousness of a being capable of absorption in his doings. The doings are not senselessly wild, though, 'breeze-like', they are strange, fresh and unexpected. Wordsworth depicts his own mind as following more predictable patterns and describes how he slips into a stereotyped way of thinking about the child which is inappropriate to the occasion. The child 'dresses up' in his words, and his thought is 'unutterable' because the 'dressing up' is part of an impulse that expresses his whole being. He dedicates himself to the moment, unlike Wordsworth whose language helps him to conform to a general pattern that thwarts spontaneity, and brings him 'industrious follies' and 'causeless melancholies' in place of a true seriousness.

The Gulf between Innocence and Experience

Wordsworth regains his own poise in the course of the second stanza, regains it in a rather theoretical way, but he is obliged to take the adult means of collecting himself. He must accept, not only that H.C. will experience pain and grief, but also that the pain and grief will destroy the H.C. he sees. An altogether different being will receive the wrongs of the world, and his own concern should be to appreciate the being who confronts him now. Innocent moments are rare in the adult, though such a moment has been instilled in Wordsworth by his contemplation of H.C. and then almost destroyed by the meddling of his 'knowing' self. The adult who retains the innocent habit of mind is an extremely rare person. Wordsworth states the possibility of H.C.'s 'season of delight' being protracted, of the preservation, as the child matures, of a 'young lamb's heart among the full-grown flocks', but it is more likely that 'nature will end him quite', that the innocent being will disappear to be replaced by an experienced one. The image of the dew-drop in the last seven lines of the poem returns us to the view of the child of the first stanza but intensifies the suggestion, implicit even there, of the fragility of the state of Innocence.

The child who delights Wordsworth cannot be contaminated by 'sorrow' or 'injuries', for their effect is to change him immediately into a different being, destroying the present one:

Thou art a dew-drop, which the morn brings forth,
Ill fitted to sustain unkindly shocks,
Or to be trailed along the soiling earth;
A gem that glitters while it lives,
And no forewarning gives;
But, at the touch of wrong, without a strife
Slips in a moment out of life.

The precious morning freshness of H.C. is not a quality that it will be necessary to watch as it slowly decays. If it is touched or meddled with it will immediately disintegrate. How suddenly this occurs is indicated by the abrupt 'slips' of the last line. Innocence trembles always on the brink of extinction and the wrongs of Experience create, immediately, an experienced being to cope with them. The avidity of Innocence to embrace all that may be enjoyed ensures, indeed, that it will find the means of its own destruction.

Wordsworth's anxiety about the future is the sort of contaminating influence that will destroy the child. He brings the boy into contact with a person who wrongs him by reacting without spontaneity, who subordinates delight to assertive anxieties. Wordsworth's own innocent poise in relation to H.C., his expansion into the moment of appreciation, is almost spoiled by the same officious fore-knowledge of what must befall. His own interference succeeds in disturbing his clear sight, and it is only by an effort that shakes and almost destroys the dew-drop of perception that it is preserved. He is obliged to thrust his 'industrious folly' consciously aside.

The tact of 'To H.C.' is apparent if the poem is compared with 'Intimations of Immortality'. Blake 'heartily enjoyed' the 'celebrated ode' when Crabb Robinson read it to him. He must have recognized some fine lines and stanzas, and may have felt sympathy with some of the sentiments expressed. When he comes to read the 'Ode', however, on page 3 of the *Poems* of 1815, he merely makes a brief entry critical of the superscription. He reserves his recognition of the sublime until he encounters 'To H.C.' where he makes the annotation we have seen. 'To H.C.' is a restrained poem that conveys a delight Wordsworth has felt. As the poem unfolds, it shows Wordsworth arriving at a further insight: the fragility of the being who delights him and the precarious nature of his own proper attitude in response to it. The additional insight is arrived at in the course of the poem, and the reader is aware that Wordsworth is conveying something that moved and absorbed him. The experience is related as it developed because that is the only way of conveying the particular satisfaction that the deeper realization has given the poet. The 'Ode' was commenced a year later (in 1803) and has as its subject the child's tenure of its world, but the delicacy of

'To H.C.' is gone. Individual lines and stanzas are convincing, but the poem as a whole is not a sublime one. Wordsworth forces the theme, attempts to say too much, and says it in a way that thrusts his theories at us in place of a living apprehension. The 'Ode' is abstract, rhetorical (as Coleridge points out),[1] and factitious (as F. R. Leavis says).[2]

The factitiousness of the 'Ode' is most evident in the intention to establish a theory of the special qualities of the child, qualities which are contrasted favourably with those of the adult.\Clearly there is something here of the distinction Blake makes in depicting Innocence and Experience, but where Blake is content to draw the distinction, and to allow certain moral implications to emerge from what he has shown, Wordsworth in 'Intimations of Immortality' explains his distinction 'naturally'. He falls back on metaphysical assertions or, at all events, on statements that have a metaphysical ring to them. The difference, poetically speaking, between 'To H.C.' and 'Intimations of Immortality' is not that the one poem deals with a particular experience and that the other is a general statement. It is possible to write imaginative poems without their being descriptive of specific occasions, as Blake's poems show. 'To H.C.' is imaginative (and is innocent) because it shows us the whole intelligence of the poet enlivened, whereas the 'Ode' is inert (is experienced) because the interfering 'natural' mind has taken over the control of its subject and is asserting its abstractions. The same interfering mind nearly upsets Wordsworth's response to H.C., but in the earlier poem he saw his error and checked it. In 'To H.C.' the boat is:

> Suspended in a stream as clear as sky,
> Where earth and heaven do make one imagery . . .

The words convey the lightness and brightness associated with the child and reinforce the impression of intangibility and strangeness. In the 'Ode' the images are much more

[1] *Biographia Literaria*, xxii. [2] *Revaluation* (1936), p. 184.

ponderous, more assertively confident, more inclined to bully us into a sense of proper reverence:

> But trailing clouds of glory do we come
> From God, who is our home:
> Heaven lies about us in our infancy!

The 'heaven' of 'To H.C.' is as much Wordsworth's as the child's and is as much the sky as it is the celestial sphere. We comfortably accept the lack of specificity because the object Wordsworth presents is not for analysis but can only be regarded in its complexity. We are meant, even, to be a little bemused. The 'clouds of glory', 'God' and 'Heaven' of the 'Ode' are mysterious abstractions. As a complete man, showing delight and sympathy (as the man who was absorbed by H.C.) Wordsworth vanishes from the 'Ode' and the 'natural' philosopher takes his place. There is no precarious balance in relation to his subject to be lost here, no dew-drop of appreciation, magically held within its frail and perfect circle. The 'Ode' is built mostly of coarser materials, the poetical-philosophical 'sublimities' which have ensured its popularity.

In his study of Innocence, Blake often puts forward the child for our contemplation, although he shows us innocent adults as well. He must have found 'To H.C.' very pleasing because, as well as indicating the perfect balance of the child, Wordsworth himself maintains, for a time, a perfect balance in his own relationship to H.C. He shows also that nothing short of a perfection of balance will serve to maintain Innocence, and shows this in respect of both the child and himself. Innocence is not seen as peculiar to one time of life, as a stage in a 'natural' development, but as a state: an equilibrium in which the energies proper to the individual may have full expression. The same perfection of balance is required also in poetry, which cannot exist by halves. Blake's praise of 'To H.C.' leads him to add: 'I cannot think that Real Poets have any competition. None are greatest in the Kingdom of Heaven; it is so in Poetry.' If a work may be called a poem it contains everything needful to make it so, in the proper degree, and is itself in perfection. Anything short of this ideal falls altogether out of the category. Perfection of appreciative awareness is one of the themes in Wordsworth's poem, and Blake is reminded by this of the perfect sincerity of insight that all poetry must show.

In 'To H.C.' Innocence is illustrated in persons very different to each other: in the child and the man who contemplates it. Wordsworth's innocence is peculiar to himself and proper to a man, while the child is innocent in a way proper to his age and to the moment in which he finds himself. Blake stipulates that Innocence is a state of wisdom not ignorance,[1] and we can see that this is so in Wordsworth's poem because the child knows everything he needs to know for the balance he strikes, while the poet, untrammelled and receptive at the moment, knows all he needs to. Indeed, it is when the man attempts to force more than he needs that he nearly falls from wisdom. Innocence, as it is presented by Blake, is a state and also an ideal. It is an equipoise, and has no ingredients because it is proper only to the person displaying it. It can be indicated by no formula because it exists as the occasion demands it, and Blake defines it only by presenting us with poems in which we can recognize it. Many of these poems exhibit children, but that is because the childish state attains the ideal more frequently. Children are in reach of the state as their birthright, perhaps, provided this way of putting it does not imply that the state has anything of an 'original character'. There is nothing passive in Innocence, which is a balance, an attained state, even in a being who has never been out of equilibrium. Innocence is not a faculty brought into the child's life at his birth but a quality he may display. A toy top stands quietly on its point while spinning, not because of any original character. Its symmetry comes into its own for the display of balance

---

[1] *Unorganiz'd Innocence: An Impossibility.* Innocence dwells with Wisdom, but never with Ignorance. (Note on a page of 'The Four Zoas', *Complete Writings*, 1957, p. 380.)

only when it takes energy, and at other times the top is grotesquely unstable. For the adult who is so much more complex than the child and in whom so much learning and experience is centred, the attainment of the poise of Innocence is an unlikely occurrence. But it remains as an ideal of a sort very different to the ideals that can be deliberately pursued: ideals of skill or knowledge. Innocence cannot be willed or obtained through any discipline. It can, perhaps, be courted, like grace, in the hope that it will come to one.

Innocence has always appeared to men as a starting condition from which there is a subsequent lapse into Experience. This notion appears in several forms. Wordsworth, for instance, finds Innocence in the child on the threshold of life, and, although his explanations of the source of this innocence are not convincing, his insight into the quality very often is. His theories, which place the child in a special relationship with 'nature' or with supernature do not ring true, but his sympathies are often sincere. Wordsworth also points out the limitations of the adult, who has qualities of a different sort:

> In the faith that looks through death,
> In years that bring the philosophic mind.[1]

These qualities, Wordsworth senses, never quite make up for the simple integrity that has been lost. Blake recognizes this distinction between child and adult, and he makes it, very sharply, in both his 'Little Boy' poems. The child and the priest in the experienced poem are poles apart, and in the innocent poem Blake exhibits two worlds existing within one: a world of 'natural' and supernatural certainties for the adult experienced mind, and a world of affectionate relationships for the Innocent.

Another way in which the notion of a starting condition is entertained is in the idea of the primitive or simple man. This idea was much in vogue during the eighteenth century,[2] and

---

[1] 'Intimations.'

[2] For a detailed account of the popularity of this ideal in the eighteenth century see L. B. Whitney, *Primitivism and the Idea of Progress* (Baltimore, 1934).

may be viewed as an attempt to seize upon the concept of
Innocence. Pope's primitive and virtuous man, described in
his *Essay*, is an animal really, but, like all animals, is an
innocent creature, expressing himself without restraints, yet
admirable. This notion is an irrational intrusion upon Pope's
moral philosophy, which he is, nevertheless, determined to
have. Pope and Bolingbroke have no real place for the noble
savage, for they are committed to a 'natural' explanation of
man[1] which attributes his humanity to the operation of the
understanding. If man must struggle to ascertain what conditions are conducive to peace and justice it is absurd to endow
him with benevolent impulses that would ensure these social
benefits without the struggle taking place. Nevertheless,
these writers are prepared, figuratively speaking, to forswear
themselves in order to hang on to an idea of an original
character of virtue. Even Hume is prepared to betray the Age
of Enlightenment and, with a greater pretence at reason, to
forswear himself as his predecessors did. He does not go to
the lengths Pope and Bolingbroke do in setting up a noble
primitive man, but he goes so far, in his postulation of
'sympathy', towards the advocacy of an original greatness
and goodness as to make his reader gasp at the audacity of his
contradiction.

Wordsworth interests himself in the transition from
Innocence to Experience in the individual, while Bolingbroke
is interested in the transition that takes place in communities
as they grow up. Innocence, he suggests, is possible in
primitive communities but men are not found in the state in
'artificial' societies. Blake's 'London' and 'The Ecchoing
Green' may be taken as acknowledging this distinction. In
London, according to the wanderer, all men are inturned and
solitary, while the inhabitants of the Green are in harmony
with their world.

Bolingbroke, Pope and Hume are obliged to make the

[1] For a restatement of my view of the 'natural' explanation of man and of
the contrasting innocent view, see below, pp. 133–8.

perfections that they attempt to introduce impossible, by mingling them with the imperfect. In order to make a show of consistency they must derive the Innocent from, and explain it in terms of, the 'natural'. There is no dividing line between Hume's 'sympathy' and his self-interest. Pope shows all loves, even love of the divine, spreading from a selfish centre. Blake and Wordsworth do not make this mistake with their 'perfection'. Blake refuses to state the ingredients of Innocence and Wordsworth fails, even to his own satisfaction, to identify them when he tries. Both men regard Innocence as a state, a balance, though Wordsworth's intuition that this is so must often assert itself against the pressure of his philosophic pretensions. Innocence, they see, exists and can be recognized as impossible of improvement. Deterioration, also, is impossible because anything short of perfection is utterly destructive of perfection. Blake insists on the truth, more fitfully grasped by Wordsworth, that it is impossible to say quantitatively and generally what makes for Innocence, but that qualitatively it is set apart from any other state.

A third way in which we set up Innocence as an ideal is in the myth of the Fall and it is here, perhaps, that we manage to keep most clearly in mind the implications of the concept. The state of the beings in the Garden before the lapse was altogether different to anything we can imagine now; yet Adam and Eve were, in all their needs and powers, minds, activities and abilities just as we are. One false awareness, one concealment of aim, and the equilibrium was gone. Innocence 'slipped in a moment out of life'. Blake reminds us of this connotation of Innocence in the 'Introduction' to the *Songs of Experience* and in 'Earth's Answer'. The bard refers to the Fall, and Earth laments her fallen state.

There is another way in which Innocence may be regarded. It is seen as present at all beginnings, at the beginning of the life of man in Eden, of the life of social man in primitive conditions, and in the beginning of each man's life. Also each day and each moment may be viewed as a fresh beginning or, at least, as the possibility of one. In 'To H.C.' we saw Wordsworth accept the invitation proffered by the occasion, and then lapse. In the two 'Nurse's Songs' Blake shows us the invitation accepted by the one nurse and passed over by the second.

One of Blake's poems, 'A Little Girl Lost' of the *Songs of Experience*, depicts the Fall in such a manner as to bring to mind several of the ways of regarding Innocence that have been outlined. As in 'To H.C.', the Fall is sudden and it is complete. It is shown as consequent on a first experience, though not that of a child. It results from eating of the 'tree of the knowledge of good and evil', and we are clearly directed to think of the Biblical account of Paradise.

A LITTLE GIRL LOST

Children of the future Age
Reading this indignant page,
Know that in a former time
Love! sweet Love! was thought a crime.

In the Age of Gold,
Free from winter's cold,
Youth and maiden bright
To the holy light,
Naked in the sunny beams delight.

Once a youthful pair,
Fill'd with softest care,
Met in garden bright
Where the holy light
Had just remov'd the curtains of the night.

There, in rising day
On the grass they play;
Parents were afar,
Strangers came not near,
And the maiden soon forgot her fear.

Tired with kisses sweet,
They agree to meet
When the silent sleep
Waves o'er heaven's deep,
And the weary tired wanderers weep.

To her father white
Came the maiden bright;
But his loving look,
Like the holy book,
All her tender limbs with terror shook.

'Ona! pale and weak!
'To thy father speak:
'O, the trembling fear!
'O, the dismal care!
'That shakes the blossoms of my hoary hair.'

It is not often that Blake talks directly in his own voice in
the *Songs of Experience*, though he does so here. In 'London'
he spoke in a muted voice behind that of the wanderer. In
'The Human Abstract' he sarcastically talks on behalf of the
'natural' moralist until he turns to be humorous with the
reader in the last stanza. In the experienced 'Chimney
Sweeper' and 'Nurse's Song' he stands aside and allows the
speakers to give themselves away. In the present poem we are
told a tale by Blake himself, as in the case of 'A Little Boy
Lost', also of the *Songs of Experience*. It is necessary for him
to take the relation into his own hands in these poems because
he deals with both innocent and experienced persons in each
of them, with the boy and the priest in 'A Little Boy Lost'
and the girl and her father in this poem. In some part of both
songs the reader is directly addressed: in the last line of 'A
Little Boy Lost' ('Are such things done on Albion's shore?'),
and in the introductory verse of 'A Little Girl Lost'.

Here, the reader addressed is the child of a future age of
renewal that has answered the call of the 'Introduction' to the
Songs of Experience, has returned to a state in which men are
innocent, and 'Love, sweet Love' is no longer 'thought a
crime'. The return to this state does not seem imminent and,
though Blake addresses the child of the future as being more
likely to understand his indignation than any present audience
could do, a little reflexion leads one to doubt that such future
beings could form the least notion of the change the girl goes

through on encountering her father. She falls from Innocence, and only a 'child' of the present age could understand what it is to fall. Blake has turned rhetorically away from his real reader, but only in order to provoke that reader into taking bearings on his own position. Blake has us in view in the corner of his eye, for he is, once again, being humorous though with no attempt at being facetious.

The poem assumes that 'children' of a future age will be very like the 'children' of the present time and the story of Ona is told so as to be read as history both in the future and the present. The body of the poem is written in two tenses, the present and the past, alternating with each other, never confused but requiring no effort of transition. In the second stanza, the

> . . . Age of Gold,
> Free from winter's cold . . .

is the classical age of everlasting Spring. It is also the time when, 'they were both naked, the man and his wife, and were not ashamed'. However, this stanza is written pointedly in the present tense, for our own time too, is the Age of Gold. Every generation learns its own sense of shame, and the fall of Ona is told for all times. The third stanza is related in the past tense. We are told of a 'youthful pair' who

> Met in garden bright
> Where the holy light
> Had just remov'd the curtains of the night.

We are in the 'garden' which the Lord God 'planted eastward in Eden' and it is not long after the time when 'God divided the light from the darkness'. But although Blake brings in Adam and Eve by implication he is not specific, for he wishes to refer us to any unspoiled love. Eden is perennial and the holy light is the dawning of sexual love, the possibility of a new day of knowledge.

Blake's use of two tenses simultaneously is so skilful that it might pass unobserved on a first reading of the poem. What does strike the reader is the prominence of the rhymes, the effect of which is to emphasize the repetitions of the poem. Such words as 'care', 'fear', 'holy' and 'love' occur more than once and in such a manner as to mean quite different things in different parts. The youthful pair are 'Fill'd with softest care' and in the next stanza 'the maiden soon forgot her fear'. In the last stanza the key words are repeated when the father says:

> 'Ona! pale and weak!
> 'To thy father speak:
> 'O, the trembling fear!
> 'O, the dismal care!
> 'That shakes the blossoms of my hoary hair.'

By now Ona has lost her innocence. She has 'slipped in a moment out of life', and what has deprived her of her purity is not the encounter with the young man but the knowledge gained from a single 'loving look' from her father. The experienced 'care' which is over-anxious, possessive, secretly destructive, and a misery to those who must exercise it, is contrasted with the 'care' of the one lover towards the other, outgoing and considerate. The 'fear' of the maiden in the earlier stanza is natural enough, is a fear of what is unknown and strange, whereas the 'fear' of the father tortures the mind with artificial and self-imposed doubts, phantoms from within which infect the girl so that

> All her tender limbs with terror shook.

Not a word has passed before what she has so much enjoyed becomes furtive and ugly, the 'brightness' all gone. An act that was 'holy' and God-given in the light of Innocence is now, like the word of God, turned against fallen man, who is subject to the 'holy book', the record of his guilt and the law of what he may not do.

The young couple had agreed to meet again when daylight was gone:

> When the silent sleep
> Waves o'er heaven's deep,
> And the weary tired wanderers weep.

They are aware that life is not all spent in a garden. Later they will be obliged to undergo the griefs and labours of the world, but they will always be able to love one another. They are not aware that the world will take even this consolation away, for it will infect them with its sense of guilt, self-seeking and anguish that will make loving impossible. They will meet, but not to love as they have done. Ironically, the last line of the poem reminds us again of the garden, but the 'blossoms' that shake are those of age and anxiety, linked to the frozen 'whiteness' of the father, the winter of a love lost in 'cares' and 'fears', and not the 'brightness' of the youth and maiden in their spring.

We have considered Blake's poems against a background of some of the writings on moral philosophy of the seventeenth and eighteenth centuries. We might have taken a different selection and seen much the same pattern of thought, though we would have found nothing as thorough, secure and consequential as *Leviathan*. The writers we have examined attempt, in some part of their work, to give an answer to the question: what is the source of virtue in man?—and they find the source in either the 'understanding' or, conversely, in some principle which has the nature of an 'original character'. In 'understanding', man pragmatically determines what conduct is most likely to gratify his appetites. He finds (so the advocates of the 'understanding' aver) that he must be considerate and restrained, and obey the conventions and laws of society which embody the rules of conduct found most conducive to gratification. Man becomes virtuous by studying nature (the world as he finds it) which suggests to his intelligence what right (effective) conduct consists in. Doctrines of an 'original character', on the other hand, assume that men are able to decide on what is right and wrong by reference to principles which are inherent in the mind. These principles are apparent to all men, though not as a result of being found out by an effort of the attention directed at nature. They are a part of man's endowment and they guide the operations of his attention. Virtuous conduct is not conduct that follows society and nature, for these may be in opposition to virtue. If it were not that his 'better nature' suggests what is proper conduct according to an absolute standard that has nothing whatever to do with nature (the world and the flesh), man's virtue might be overthrown by these enemies.

The eighteenth century is a time of reliance on the 'understanding', yet all the thinkers we have examined, with the exceptions of Hobbes and Burke, allow their arguments to become tainted by a confusion of 'understanding' with some more elevated but incompatible principle. Hume, for instance, establishes 'greatness and goodness' in man by postulating an original character of 'sympathy', though when we come to examine the grounds of this goodness we find that Hume has deceived himself. This original character is nothing more than the 'understanding' giving itself airs. Self-interest is as solidly the basis of 'sympathy' as it is of 'justice',[1] and far from one's sense of the greatness of human nature being increased by contemplation of the principle, it is decreased. One turns back to Hobbes's principles with relief because they are without pretence. Hume claims to advance beyond Hobbes in putting forward his principle, but, on the contrary, the fact that he could advocate it shows that he had never fully understood him.

Bolingbroke is much less convincing than Hume. He states that a natural and intuitive knowledge of justice and benevolence leads to a reasonable and 'demonstrative' knowledge. He fails to make this good, however, and the reader soon becomes aware that his 'demonstrative' knowledge is 'naturally' derived.[2] In the *Essay on Man* Pope reflects more sceptically than Bolingbroke, but to no better purpose. He finds the 'god within' by no means infallible, rejects it and is obliged eventually to find virtue in a submission to the order imposed on the universe. The full working of that order is a

---

[1] See pp. 111–12.   [2] See pp. 57–60.

mystery beyond man, but everything works to a proper end which we do not see. This supernature is, like the priest's in 'A Little Boy Lost', a part of nature really. Its very existence is an outcome of the 'understanding' and the idea of divine order is a projection into the 'unknown' of a pattern imposed by scientific man on the known. The 'understanding' attributes functions and a hierarchy to the parts of nature, hypostatizes the notions, and extends them into fields of superstitious creation.

Wherever we turn among our moralists with the question 'In what does virtue lie?' we are confronted with the answer that it is an outcome of the 'understanding'. Hobbes's answer is taken up even by his detractors, and, to the degree that they depart from Hobbes, the departure is into contradictions which amount, sometimes, to a form of self-deception. There is a desperate urge to escape from the position of Hobbes on the part of men who are thoroughly committed to it. They are intent on giving a scientific account of man's behaviour, but are disappointed when they come to the conclusion that the human intelligence is a sufficient key to right conduct and that moral values are conventionally established. Yet their conclusions are consequent on their method. Their science assumes that man may impartially observe an undoubted reality, though it was Hume who pointed out that reality is a chimera given substance only by our habit of association. Blake takes the limits of the method seriously and says implicitly, in the *Songs*, that as the man is, so will he conceive what he 'observes'. If (he seems to say) you are in the habit of behaving well because it is the intelligent thing to do, and for no better reason, then the only way in which you can observe humanity will lead rationally to the conclusion that the 'understanding' is the basis of morality. Furthermore, you will be convinced that the satisfaction of the 'understanding' that this is so, is sufficient proof of the efficacy of the 'understanding'. If there is some better urge active in your soul than the 'understanding' (sympathy, for instance) you will, in sincerity, perceive it at work in the world because your observations of your world must account for what you need to find there. If Hume and Bolingbroke (the *Songs* imply) are not satisfied with their 'natural' accounts of the world the fact might be to their credit, for it argues the presence in them of better impulses than the 'understanding', although their contradictions make one suspect that they are merely being insincere. For a different apprehension of man, Blake invites us to listen to the child, to adults in their visionary moments, to the poet. The child's words may be a patchwork of the sentimentalities adults find it fit to impose on him, yet he believes in them, and his very gullibility is indicative of a principle at work superior to the 'understanding'. The child can show trust.

Blake does not discount the 'understanding' as a principle conducive to virtue—far from it; it is the guide to right conduct in Experience, in the world of affairs, control and institution. It imposes various degrees of moderation and rectitude, presenting us with a Caesar but with Brutus too. Blake takes understanding man quite seriously in the *Songs of Experience* but he does not regard the restrictions suggested by the understanding as the only way to right conduct—a better state needs no restrictions in order to be benign. Blake takes Experience seriously but he does not take it kindly. It has no proper control of its energies, and they are not centred deep in its being. It is regulated superficially by calculation, and the calculations go wildly and absurdly wrong. Blake is intent on pointing this out in such songs as 'A Little Boy Lost' and 'The Human Abstract'. Even when it is doing its duty, apparently harming no one else, Experience is a frustrated and self-destroying condition as in 'London' or the experienced 'Nurse's Song'. Experience puts forward the virtues of loyalty, courage, steadfastness, pity, mercy, but even these are tainted by being shut up too close in the cupboard of the self. Experience can justify these virtues but it does not conceive them, for the state is not a primary and originating one, but secondary, fallen, derivative and conserving.

Innocence has no ideals because it is engaged in imaginatively being and not in fanciful self-examination. Experience can create no ideals because its attention is upon itself and advantage to the self. Its values are pragmatic, but it sets up ideals by remembering its Innocence and putting forward the memories of its innocent qualities as a norm. It is helped in this by the statements of innocent men, the prophet and the poet in their different fields, but the memory of Innocence is a blurred one and the prophetic message ill-understood. The conception of 'pure reason' is an ideal of this sort, a confused memory of the completeness of mind—the wisdom—enjoyed by Innocence, but Experience conceives it as a mental possession, a key to an absolute truth and not as a balance always being energetically won. In its crudest form this notion of the reason implies, not only that man has benevolent inclinations, but that they are accompanied by intuitively known and unquestionably right principles which may be made verbally evident without any distortion whatever. This notion takes one out of the realm of the moral philosopher, however, and into that of the political and religious propagandist.

Experience may account for itself in terms of certain principles. In turning to Innocence, Blake makes no attempt whatever to give an explanation of it. Like Wordsworth in contemplating H.C., Blake is quite content to appreciate, to describe, and, best of all, to sympathize with and so enter into the feelings of the state. He makes no attempt to dogmatize and it never even occurs to him to do so, although he is blatantly dogmatic in the *Songs of Experience* where it is appropriate. The experienced 'Chimney Sweeper's Song' conducts its inquiry in terms of 'and because'. Explanations thrust themselves forward so that we mistrust the impartiality of the speaker, while the modest 'and so's' of the innocent song present us with an observer whose interest in the situation he describes turns in the direction of trying to do it full justice.

Blake's method of depiction in the *Songs of Innocence* is the reverse of the 'natural' one. He is not asking us to look at something to see how it exemplifies a theory, but to look attentively, without prejudice, though with an inclination to be moved. He shows human beings in harmonious balance, exhibiting a grace. We cannot specify the principle of what we see because it has no recipe. It is not an original character and is not an outcome of the understanding. We can go so far into generalization as to indicate some of the qualities that the state displays (we can detect the manifestations of the condition) but we can't find any standard ingredients. Innocence, we can say, uses its senses in order to come alive to, and not to regularize, its world. It is capable of a sympathy which catches up its whole attention. It can let things be, and let things go, having a respect for other creatures and no desire to meddle with them. It acts in a way that exercises its whole self as is appropriate to the occasion, and does not suppose that it can isolate its perceptions, appetites, intelligence or feelings from the rest of its being. We can say all these things of Innocence, and will have occasion to say many things more, but we are not invited to find any set pattern for it. By presenting us with poems that work by implication, however, Blake invites us to become the Innocent, to find Innocence in ourselves. Only by laying aside our dogmatic and unbalanced selves, by using all our knowledge without forcing any; only by being imaginative and disciplined can we be properly critical of, properly sympathetic towards these songs. We are expected to contribute the Innocence proper to a reader in meeting them.

Each song presents us with a study in one of the contrary states, except for three which deal with the transit from a state. Such a topic needs handling from a point of vantage superior to that of the beings who are described. Innocence cannot conceive of the Fall, and Experience cannot recall its Innocence except in a distorted way. Blake uses the imaginative latitude allowed to the poet and speaks in his own voice, that of the bard or prophet. In 'A Little Girl Lost', as we have seen, he tells Ona's story in the capacity of the seer speaking to a future 'guiltless' age. The 'Introduction' to the *Songs of Experience* calls for a renewal of fallen light and addresses us in the 'voice of the Bard'. 'The Little Girl Lost' and 'The Little Girl Found' which were originally placed among the *Songs of Innocence* and are plainly meant to be read as one poem, describe a return to the 'Age of Gold'. As the second line of the poem tells us, this story, also, is told prophetically.

THE LITTLE GIRL LOST

In futurity
I prophetic see
That the earth from sleep
(Grave the sentence deep)

Shall arise and seek
For her maker meek;
And the desart wild
Become a garden mild.

In the southern clime,
Where the summer's prime
Never fades away,
Lovely Lyca lay.

Seven summers old
Lovely Lyca told;
She had wander'd long
Hearing wild birds' song.

'Sweet sleep, come to me
'Underneath this tree.
'Do father, mother weep,
'Where can Lyca sleep?

'Lost in desart wild
'Is your little child.
'How can Lyca sleep
'If her mother weep?

139

'If her heart does ake
'Then let Lyca wake;
'If my mother sleep,
'Lyca shall not weep.

'Frowning, frowning night,
'O'er this desart bright
'Let thy moon arise
'While I close my eyes.'

Sleeping Lyca lay
While the beasts of prey,
Come from caverns deep,
View'd the maid asleep.

The kingly lion stood
And the virgin view'd,
Then he gambol'd round
O'er the hallow'd ground.

Leopards, tygers, play
Round her as she lay,
While the lion old
Bow'd his mane of gold

And her bosom lick,
And upon her neck
From his eyes of flame
Ruby tears there came;

While the lioness
Loos'd her slender dress,
And naked they convey'd
To caves the sleeping maid.

THE LITTLE GIRL FOUND

All the night in woe
Lyca's parents go
Over vallies deep,
While the desarts weep.

Tired and woe-begone,
Hoarse with making moan,
Arm in arm seven days
They trac'd the desart ways.

Seven nights they sleep
Among shadows deep,
And dream they see their child
Starv'd in desart wild.

Pale, thro' pathless ways
The fancied image strays
Famish'd, weeping, weak,
With hollow piteous shriek.

Rising from unrest,
The trembling woman prest
With feet of weary woe:
She could no further go.

In his arms he bore
Her, arm'd with sorrow sore;
Till before their way
A couching lion lay.

Turning back was vain:
Soon his heavy mane
Bore them to the ground.
Then he stalk'd around,

Smelling to his prey;
But their fears allay
When he licks their hands,
And silent by them stands.

They look upon his eyes
Fill'd with deep surprise,
And wondering behold
A Spirit arm'd in gold.

On his head a crown,
On his shoulders down
Flow'd his golden hair.
Gone was all their care.

'Follow me,' he said;
'Weep not for the maid;
'In my palace deep
'Lyca lies asleep.'

Then they followed
Where the vision led,
And saw their sleeping child
Among tygers wild.

To this day they dwell
In a lonely dell;
Nor fear the wolvish howl
Nor the lions' growl.

In the story of Ona it is the girl who undergoes the Fall and she does so in becoming infected by the attitude of her father. The story of Lyca reverses this order. Here, the parents are renewed (though they cannot be said to return to Innocence), and the renewal takes place when they follow in the footsteps of the Innocent, their daughter. In both poems Experience is associated with a negative attitude towards the passions. Ona's innocent acceptance of sexual experience is dispelled, and she lapses. Lyca's parents meet an angel when they encounter the lion, and it seems likely that we are meant to understand by this, and by the contentment they find amongst the beasts, that the parents come to terms with the 'animal' or 'instinctive'.

Some elements of Lyca's story gain significance if we keep Ona's poem in mind. That poem was preceded by an introductory verse, distinguished from the remainder by the use of Roman lettering, addressed to children of a better age. The first two verses of Lyca's story have a similar improved age in mind and they are separated from the remainder of the poem in the plate etched by Blake. We read of the time when

. . . the earth from sleep
(Grave the sentence deep)

Shall arise and seek
For her maker meek;
And the desart wild
Become a garden mild.

As the eye attempts to pass on to the next line it runs into the distended mouth of a snake twined amongst the branches of the decorative surround to the stanza—a reminder, perhaps, that we are fallen, not inhabitants of the garden that we saw Ona leave. Our loss of Innocence is felt in the world because our inhibited enjoyments result in the earth being dead to us or asleep. Blake's parenthesis, 'Grave the sentence deep', is equivocal. It refers to the sentence of death passed on the earth by our lapse into a state of shame at our bodily or earthly manifestations. Also, it exhorts the prophet, graving tool in hand, boldly to set down his message: that in order to seek our 'maker', to qualify for paradise, we must perfect ourselves, transforming the desert we inhabit into a fruitful garden. We must be prepared to pay proper respect to what is of the earth in our being before we can be complete, and so re-generated.

Ona was innocent, an inhabitant of the 'Age of Gold', though she was aware of a future time of struggle and anxiety when 'the weary tired wanderers weep'. In Lyca's song the parents toil and weep in their anxious passage across the desert before meeting the lion, and in the realm of the beasts they find rest. In the lion Blake expected his reader to recognize the dignified representative of the Golden Age, a composite of classical and Biblical allusion, commonly depicted in Baroque art in company with women and children together with a lamb or a hare.

Like Ona, Lyca is identified as an Innocent at the outset of the poem. She is an inhabitant of the 'southern clime',

> Where the summer's prime
> Never fades away. . .

This is equivalent to Ona's

> Age of Gold,
> Free from winter's cold

Lyca has only just emerged from childhood, is at an age when she is no longer dependent on her parents. She is aware of herself now as a responsible being and has advanced beyond innocence of the babyish sort. She has left the garden for the desert of the experienced world:

> She had wander'd long
> Hearing wild birds' song.

Although she wishes to accept the passions that are stirring within herself, although, like 'sleep' these come unbidden and are not to be indefinitely resisted, Lyca is disturbed by her consciousness of parental solicitude:

> 'Do father, mother weep,
> 'Where can Lyca sleep?'

The parents are no longer in Lyca's company, for she has entered their adult world where all men are strangers. All are lost in an unpopulated desert. The child's real bond with its parents has gone, but it is kept anxiously aware of the parents' insistent 'care':

> 'If my mother sleep,
> 'Lyca shall not weep.'

Lyca is not afraid to 'sleep' in the frowning night of the desert, though she is grieved by the fear her parents demonstrate and keeps herself awake until she is overcome by her need and sinks into 'sleep'. In the remainder of the 'Lost' poem she encounters the adult passions.

The passions with which the poem is concerned are, presumably, those which impel the child to make her own way in the world, to enjoy as an independent being. Blake might refer to the desire to know, to test one's powers, but, whatever impulses he does refer to, the sexual is prominent among them. He is not explicit, but we may infer that this is so. The sexual is associated with sleep, causes parents more concern than any other 'vagary' of their children, and brings children more humiliation and distress than any other bugbear set up by their elders. The mode is designated 'animal' and

'beastly' in sweeping terms by persons who should know
better, and is often treated with an inordinate degree of
delicacy by persons who know that there is nothing shameful
about it whatever.

Blake is delicate without being inordinately so. He sends
Lyca off on her adventures, including the sexual adventures,
without accompanying her. When she has addressed her
parents she 'falls asleep' and that is the last we hear from her.
The illustrations to the poem fill out Blake's commentary, or
lack of one. There are four designs. The first shows a young
woman and a naked young man clasped in an embrace. The
second shows Lyca half reclining beneath a tree. In the third a
tiger stands with its head raised. The fourth depicts the Age
of Gold. Beneath the intertwined trunks of a great tree a
young woman lies naked and asleep. Three children of
different ages are amusing themselves by clambering upon
the back of a lioness or by 'making up to' a lion.

In 'The Little Boy lost' and 'found' it was necessary to
make an effort in order to realize what the feelings of the
child could be. His situation, in the imagined care of his
father, was so different to what the reader could immediately
see. A rather similar change in perspective is required of us
in Lyca's song. So much movement of wild beasts goes on
about the girl that it is only with an effort that we can
appreciate that we are not told anything about the girl's
feelings at all, for she is asleep. The passions, the 'animals',
are elements of Blake's world or the reader's. We may make
of them what we like, and Blake awards them dignity,
simplicity and a touching readiness to be compassionate.
Lyca's sleep is her private affair which we can know nothing
about—how can we? By the end of the poem the parents are
prepared to accept her, asleep as she is. The working of the
passions in her breast is something they do not pretend to
be able to violate with mental hands. They abandon the
experienced and 'natural' assumption that all men are
identical psychological units, that they know all about their

daughter's impulses; the assumption under which all growing children are made to smart.

The 'Little Girl' and 'Little Boy' poems have this element in common too, that they both contain an apparition. To the little boy the wandering light and God appear like his father. To the parents tracing 'the desart ways' comes the dream of their starved child:

> Pale, thro' pathless ways
> The fancied image strays
> Famish'd, weeping, weak,
> With hollow piteous shriek.

Blake shows how 'imaginative' the adult is, by comparison with the child. The little boy, in his innocent poem, translates the reality he sees but cannot place, into a reality he can understand. Lyca's parents know no rest because they are disturbed by a spectre made of their fears: what will happen to their daughter in the world?—what is happening to her now that she has entered it and is, in spirit, set apart from themselves? They are troubled by a morbid form of the concern that came to Wordsworth in contemplating H.C. Their wish to keep control of the direction of their child's emotions is understandable but, if they could be successful in maintaining the hold, it would only stunt the child. They demonstrate, also, an illogical lack of faith in the impulse to seek freedom. It was, after all, as a result of their own breaking away from parental love to find a love of their own that they have been able to know the joy of Lyca—a joy that they are turning to ashes for themselves.

Lyca, as we have seen, never meets the animals, and it is impossible for us to know what she does meet. Passions, unlike ideas, cannot be rendered verbally. What the parents have in mind when they think of their daughter, however, is an *idea* of what the passions involve and, like Blake or the reader, they encounter the beasts. In idea, the passions congregated about the sleeping form of Lyca are, first of all, dangerous:

> Soon his heavy mane
> Bore them to the ground.
> Then he stalk'd around,
>
> Smelling to his prey . . .

They are unthinking, violent and destructive—ready to consume the human part of one's being. But the passions may also be viewed as benign. The lion becomes

> A Spirit arm'd in gold.
>
> On his head a crown,
> On his shoulders down
> Flow'd his golden hair.

The passions are regal, chivalric and fine, bringing riches, beauty and power into human life. It is with this latter idea of the fate that has met their daughter that they are re-united with her, though not on the old footing—she remains asleep and absent from them. Their 'care' is abandoned.

Most parents probably undergo a long passage of anxiety about their children, are terrified when their fears are realized and they first see the adult passions manifest themselves, but later see that nothing very dreadful has happened, after all. By the end of the poem the parents have reached a new equilibrium in regard to Lyca, and we could, perhaps, with a slight stretch, regard this as a return to Innocence. The stretch is there because, if their vision of the passions as fit for a cave is an outcome of fear, their new vision of them as inhabitants of an underground palace is equally personal, the projection of a different scene of busy activity about the sleeping Lyca. She sleeps, undergoes changes that are private, incommunicable, unfathomable. It is as much an interference to suppose these private experiences are attended by angels as to assume that they are 'poore, nasty, brutish'. However, the parents must find their equilibrium by what means they are able, and they are less likely to do damage with their new view than with the old. They let the girl be, and Lyca, if she dreams while she sleeps, is likely, now, to have pleasant visions and not disturbing ones.

CHAPTER 6

BLAKE'S CRITICISM OF 'LOVE'

IT is generally agreed that Blake wrote the *Songs of Innocence* and *Songs of Experience* at different periods: in 1789 and 1793, although the evidence that they were written at just this interval is by no means conclusive.[1] Yet even if this interval in composition is accepted, it should be recognized that the two sets, which lend significance to one another, form an artistic whole, and it is as a whole that they must have been conceived. Each series has its own title-page, but in bringing the two series together under the comprehensive title and a third title-page Blake indicated that the work composed of the contraries was now gathered together. The design of the inclusive title-page is significant, for it emphasizes, at once, the grounds for uniting and for separating the *Songs*. Beneath the heading, *Songs Of Innocence and Of Experience, Shewing the Two Contrary States of the Human Soul*, is a depiction of Adam and Eve immediately after the Fall. They have covered their nakedness with tendrils of the grape-vine, and are bowed towards the ground in attitudes of despair. Adam and Eve are the same individuals before and after the Fall and Blake's illustration serves to relate the contrary states, which both act in the same person. But Adam and Eve have altogether different lives before and after the Fall so, in emphasizing the Fall itself, the illustration serves to stress the fact that the two states are set quite apart from one another. There is no overlap or confusion between Innocence and Experience.

Even the task of the poet must differ in writing songs for the two states, and Blake defines the poet's function differently in the first poem of each book. In the *Songs of Innocence* he appears as a piper who tells how he came to set down his songs:

[1] See the Appendix for a fuller discussion of this matter.

INTRODUCTION

Piping down the valleys wild,
Piping songs of pleasant glee,
On a cloud I saw a child,
And he laughing said to me:

'Pipe a song about a Lamb!'
So I piped with merry chear.
'Piper, pipe that song again;'
So I piped: he wept to hear.

'Drop thy pipe, thy happy pipe;
'Sing thy songs of happy chear:'
So I sung the same again,
While he wept with joy to hear.

'Piper, sit thee down and write
'In a book that all may read.'
So he vanish'd from my sight,
And I pluck'd a hollow reed,

And I made a rural pen,
And I stain'd the water clear,
And I wrote my happy songs
Every child may joy to hear.

The bard who introduces the *Songs of Experience* takes on the duty of instructing an erring mankind, like a prophet of the Old Testament. The piper of the introductory song in Innocence has no duty. He makes music, sings and writes because he feels inclined to, he enjoys the music for its own sake and he takes an additional pleasure in the delight it gives the child. As the child is described by the piper it is a very vivid and positive presence, and yet a very insubstantial one. It appears on a cloud, and it vanishes abruptly, leaving the piper to his more solitary task. Wordsworth saw H.C. as a

> . . . faery voyager! that dost float
> In such clear water, that thy boat
> May rather seem
> To brood on air than on an earthly stream . . .[1]

[1] See p. 117.

We are meant to see the child as a strange being with whom Wordsworth does not wish to meddle. When he clutches at H.C. with mental fingers he destroys his pleasure. The piper does not have to contend with a clumsy, grasping self, has no impulse to pull the child from its cloud and put it on earth where it should be, and has so much enjoyment in the child because he takes it exactly as it comes. When the child leaves, the piper turns his attention without regret to writing down how much he liked being with it.

Blake etched two plates showing the piper, and placed them immediately before the title-pages of *Innocence* and *Experience*. In the first engraving the piper holds his pipe at his side and gazes upward at the child who has interrupted his 'songs of pleasant glee'. Young trees grow on either side of the piper, and in the background a flock of sheep is grazing. The child half reclines on a cloud and half floats in the air, its arms outspread as it addresses the piper. The significance of this picture, and so of the imagery in the poem, is brought out by a comparison with the companion plate in the *Songs of Experience*. Here the piper has no instrument and he carries the child (who now has the wings of a cherub) on his head. The piper's arms are raised so that he may hold the child's hands to support it as it sits. Both these illustrations contain the same elements: childhood and rustic simplicity together in a 'valley wild', entertaining one another. In the first illustration, however, the piper and child are shown as simultaneously meeting and parting. Each has been arrested momentarily by the attraction of the other, and their movements in their separate spheres (valley and cloud) are half checked, and half being carried forward. They gaze full into each other's face, although the gaze is a passing one. In the second illustration the pair are placed in a closer and more lasting relationship but have lost contact with each other. Placed as they are, with the child on the head of the piper, neither can see the other, the child is a burden on the piper, who cannot even use his arms and, as the child has wings, the piper is a hindrance to its freedom.

Blake's Criticism of 'Love'

In his *Notebook*, Blake wrote a poem which says very much the same thing as his etchings of piper and child:

> He who bends to himself a joy
> Does the winged life destroy;
> But he who kisses the joy as it flies
> Lives in eternity's sun rise.[1]

The poem states the paradox that it is only the man relaxed enough to be careless of his gains who can give his attention and so obtain from any situation of delight the benefits that are offered. Any attempt to snatch at what may be got or to give the joy a lasting form perverts the experience. The innocent piper can allow others their own freedom and life. He appreciates the child but has no desire to seize it. He passes with gusto from one activity to another, and in each phase 'kisses the joy as it flies'.

In the course of the game played by the piper and child, the former is gleefully ordered about, being told, first, to pipe his song, then to sing it, and lastly to write it down. With the last injunction, the child disappears. It has played the game out now, and abandons it. We are left at the end of the poem with the piper writing his happy songs 'Every child may joy to hear', and on the way to assuming this task he has stepped across the gap between music and speech as though it did not exist. As we first encounter the piper he is quite alone and he is making music, making sounds that are wordless but certainly not mindless. Whatever beauty the sounds may have is the result of organization and a sense of harmony within the piper. He uses his pipe, we can say, for self-expression, but by that we do not mean that he explains himself or makes precise statements of what goes on within. By the end of the poem the piper is using words instead, but the tenor of the 'Introduction' is to place these verbal songs on the same footing as the wordless ones. They are the same songs because, although

---

[1] *Notebook*, pp. 99, 105. Given in *Complete Writings* (1957), pp. 179, 184. Blake illustrates Oothoon kissing a joy as it flies in the *Visions of the Daughters of Albion*, plate iii.

their medium is a different one, they express the same piper, and they do not express only the sense that the piper has put consciously into them. They have a richer content than mere statement, and do not tell us only about the lamb.

The experienced person stands in the relationship of onlooker even in regard to himself. If he knows anything about himself he does so by finding the words that describe the self he sees. The piper, on the other hand, is uttered by his song, he does not stand back from himself, and he does not have to be consciously aware of a movement within himself for that movement to have its expression. Thus his songs, when he writes them down, though we may expect them to make statements, please us because the statements reveal the life of the being who makes them. The piper we leave at the end of the poem using his rural pen, made from a reed, is doing basically the same thing as he was when he played his pipe. Innocent poetry uses words, the 'Introduction' implies, in such a way as to carry meaning into the poem from the whole being of the singer, not merely to make deliberate reference. A similar view is put by D. W. Harding when discussing poetry in general:

When we speak or write, experience in some way merges with, and emerges in the form of, patterns of language. But in some minds the language processes reflect not only the main experience, in statements that could be more or less paraphrased, but also much subtler features of the preverbal experience, and features of which the writer may have no awareness except through the overtones of what he finds himself writing. Even then he may well fail to notice what he has said.[1]

The expression of these 'subtler features' of experience, Harding suggests, is characteristic of poetry, where they manifest themselves as 'complexity' (not 'confusion') and are indicative of the mind working in a higher, not lower, way. Blake, too, sees that a piper who writes his songs from the

---

[1] 'The Hinterland of Thought' in *Metaphor and Symbol, Colston Papers*, XII, ed. Knights and Cottle (1960), p. 16; reprinted in D. W. Harding, *Experience into Words* (1963), p. 187.

fullness of his heart, not from the mind alone, is not a limited person. On the contrary, the piper displays intelligence in a most important sense of the word.[1]

It is a remarkable feat on Blake's part, in writing the innocent 'Introduction', to comprehend, by an intellectual stretch, the spontaneous depths of poetry. It is a stretch for Blake because, although he insists in all his writings on the importance of inspiration, no poet shows a more careful control of his utterances. He is a poet of the intellect, but of an intellect so good that he can put the intellect in perspective and come forward as an advocate of the unpremeditated. The *Songs of Innocence* present beings who do not precisely define or fully verbalize what they are aware of, but though this is true of the piper, Blake himself has clear and definite ideas.

The piper's songs are simply a form of self-expression, but this manner of composition is possible only for the innocent. In Experience, the poet has lost the gift of spontaneity, and poetry has a different end. In the 'Introduction' to *Songs of Experience* the singer has a precise purpose to fulfil and, far from being immersed in the moment, stands clearly viewing 'Present, Past, & Future':

INTRODUCTION

Hear the voice of the Bard!
Who Present, Past, & Future, sees;
Whose ears have heard
The Holy Word
That walk'd among the ancient trees,

Calling the lapsed Soul,
And weeping in the evening dew;
That might controll
The starry pole,
And fallen, fallen light renew!

[1] For a fuller discussion of this aspect of poetry see: L. C. Knights, 'Poetry as Discovery', *Reality and Creative Vision in German Lyric Poetry, Colston Papers*, xv, ed. A. Closs (1963).

'O Earth, O Earth, return!
'Arise from out the dewy grass;
'Night is worn,
'And the morn
'Rises from the slumberous mass.

'Turn away no more;
'Why wilt thou turn away?
'The starry floor,
'The wat'ry shore,
'Is giv'n thee till the break of day.'

EARTH'S ANSWER

Earth rais'd up her head
From the darkness dread & drear.
Her light fled,
Stony dread!
And her locks cover'd with grey despair.

'Prison'd on wat'ry shore,
'Starry Jealousy does keep my den:
'Cold and hoar,
'Weeping o'er,
'I hear the Father of the ancient men.

'Selfish father of men!
'Cruel, jealous, selfish fear!
'Can delight,
'Chain'd in night,
'The virgins of youth and morning bear?

'Does spring hide its joy
'When buds and blossoms grow?
'Does the sower
'Sow by night,
'Or the plowman in darkness plow?

'Break this heavy chain
'That does freeze my bones around.
'Selfish! vain!
'Eternal bane!
'That free Love with bondage bound.'

Blake's Criticism of 'Love'

In the 'Introduction' to the *Songs of Innocence* we listened to a dialogue between the piper and the child, but in these two poems Earth does not understand what the bard says, no communication takes place, and the introductory poem is replaced by two related monologues. The bard announces himself as prophet and messenger. He commands attention imperiously in the first line of the poem and presents his credentials in the remainder of the stanza. In the second half of the poem he announces his message, starting off with the flourish of:

'O Earth, O Earth, return!'

Then he breaks into the appealing mode of the last stanza:

'Turn away no more;
'Why wilt thou turn away?'

The tone of the poem in general is a mixture of these elements, being official and important in the first and third stanzas and more pathetic and compassionate in the second and fourth. The Bard speaks as the representative of a greater power, but breaks into an urgency which indicates that the message from that power is felt as a message of his own.

Appreciation of this complex tone helps to solve the ambiguities in the poem which have been the cause of much comment.[1] Who is it that calls the 'lapsed Soul' and weeps in the evening dew? It seems to be the Word, but Blake's own punctuation (never very helpful) might indicate that it is the bard. Also, it has been pointed out, God walked in the garden in the cool of the day (when Adam and his wife hid themselves among the trees) not to weep but in order to curse the creation, so it must be the bard who weeps. Further, who is it that might control 'the starry pole' and renew fallen light— Word, bard or lapsed soul?

These ambiguities cease to be confusing when we remember that, in the *Songs*, Blake is interested in the psychology of

---

[1] See: A. E. Housman, *The Name and Nature of Poetry* (1933), pp. 41–2; Stanley Gardner, *Infinity on the Anvil*, pp. 118–19; René Wellek, *Scrutiny*, v (1937), 377; F. R. Leavis, *Revaluation* (1936), pp. 140–2; and *The Common Pursuit* (1958), p. 216; R. F. Gleckner, *The Piper and the Bard*, pp. 232–7.

religion but not in the least concerned with theological verities or with the correctness of religious mythology. In the 'Introduction' Blake is not interested in God, whoever He (in an absolute sense) may be, but is most interested in the God that the bard can utter. This is made clear by the way in which the bard alternates between the tone of the nuncio and that of a man pleading on his own behalf. The bard speaks God's word, but only by speaking as himself in pity of Earth. What is the alternative? The alternative, as in 'A Little Boy Lost', is to speak as the priest does who makes pronouncements on behalf of a mysterious being beyond himself and succeeds only in placing himself upon the altar, for his mysterious God is a superstitious fiction. The bard's speaking, unlike the priest's, is not an arrogant seizing of power. The God he speaks for is known by the virtues of man, the Divine virtues which yearn towards another.

In the first stanza the warrant to speak is presented. The bard sees 'Present, Past, & Future', not because of any mysterious omniscience but because his ears have heard

> The Holy Word
> That walk'd among the ancient trees.

The bard has glimpsed Innocence as a state of perfection in the garden, but also as the perfection of God (and of man) in Christ or the Holy Word. His ears do not hear the terrible being who put temptation in man's way and then cursed him for disobedience. Instead he hears a God who weeps over man's departure. Fallen man, such is his mind, hears the word of God as the curse of a frustrated tyrant, and in the next poem Earth makes answer to that being, for when the bard makes his announcement, the Earth hears her God speak, not his.

What the bard hears is the voice of the Holy Word, of Christic,

> Calling the lapsed Soul,
> And weeping in the evening dew;
> That might controll
> The starry pole,
> And fallen, fallen light renew!

This is the LORD God of Genesis, but He is heard as Jesus in the Garden who asked His disciples to watch with Him. Christ might control the earth and raise man up, but not in the way of being omnipotent or, indeed, of having any power whatever except that of eliciting a response to love.[1] Man's mind exhibits the contraries and in calling on God he calls on Him in contrary forms although, just as Experience is a departure and a lapse, Nobodaddy is a debased and externalized notion of God that succeeds the collapse of the Divine Image. It is not surprising that men know diverse Gods, seeing that they conceive even their simpler notions in more than one way. The idea of control, for instance, in the stanza just quoted may involve either participation with, or imposition upon. The bard, talking for the Saviour, justifies the ambiguity of the last three lines of the stanza (who controls?) for he indicates that it is both Word and Soul who are in control, and are renewed when they are together. Being together in mutual participation is to control and be controlled. But control may also imply isolation of will and the eliciting of obedience, control by the Deity alone. It is that meaning of the word 'control' that Earth hears—and very rightly turns away from in loathing.

Whatever the bard says is inevitably misinterpreted by Earth. In the last two stanzas the call to return may be taken as inviting Earth's reunion with Nobodaddy through a renunciation of the 'starry floor' and the 'wat'ry shore' (by which we may understand the firmament amidst the waters and so the creation we know). Earth, and so her creature man, has an idea of life in the body as a degradation and this conforms to her idea of God as the being who curses man and

---

[1] Blake's religious ideas are very much in advance of his time, but are confirmed by the best thought now current. Dietrich Bonhoeffer, for example, says: 'This is the decisive difference between Christianity and all religions. Man's religiosity makes him look in his distress to the power of God in the world; he uses God as a *Deus ex machina*. The Bible, however, directs him to the powerlessness and suffering of God; only a suffering God can help.' ('Letter of July 16th 1944', *Letters and Papers from Prison*, 1953, p. 122.)

curses the earth with him. The Earth supposes that the bard is calling upon her to return to the Creator by leaving the 'slumberous mass' of creation and by rising to better things. He seems to say that what is of the earth (the body, the passions) must be purged away for the transformed creation (the spiritual body[1]) to be fit for its transcendental life when a new day breaks in a celestial sphere. If we listen to what the bard is saying instead of to what (so Earth supposes) he should be saying we can hear that he calls Earth to life, not death. True, Earth is asleep or dead in life but that is because she has miscreated it, just as she has miscreated God. The bard is not concerned with any after-life, just as he is not concerned with any mysterious God, and the day he speaks of is one that breaks *on* earth, not away from it. The bard, in short, is not concerned with the transcendental aspects of religion, and the new day he announces suffuses the present darkness:

> 'Night is worn,
> 'And the morn
> 'Rises from the slumberous mass.'

This is not the end of time, but a rejuvenation within it. The Earth is told to 'Arise from out the dewy grass', but this is no suggestion that she leave the flesh. Rather, she is to awaken to the flesh, to realize it for what it is. What is of the earth is a gift:

> 'The starry floor,
> 'The wat'ry shore,
> 'Is giv'n thee till the break of day.'

This firmament, the lines imply, is a gift and, most important, it is beautiful. The lines convey the idea of a place that is splendid and precious, just as the earlier reference to 'dewy grass' is not merely a symbol interchangeable with 'physical body' but carries the association of something growing, vigorous and refreshed. The last two stanzas convey the bard's feeling for Earth as something wonderful and very dear which can become more splendid, not by changing into

---

[1] Cf. 'To Tirzah', analysed on pp. 232 ff.

something different or as a result of anything being added to her, but by the onset of light which will show the beauty which is hers by right.

Commentators on the 'Introduction' remark on its difficulty, but overlook the tone which supplies the solution to the difficulty. The bard does not speak on behalf of some absolute being, calling from beyond time. He must speak on his own behalf if he is to say anything worth paying attention to. Also, his appeal to Earth is not that she should leave her present state for a dimly conceived immaterial heaven, but turn towards a knowledge of her own beauty, and a realization of joy. Again, the bard must call to her on his own behalf, as a lover would, to be saying anything worthwhile. Earth may come to a knowledge of her beauty through feeling the desire of the bard. Bard and Earth may 'control' each other in the sense of the word that we have discussed, that of mutual participation.

There are hints of sexual desire in the imagery of the last two stanzas. These are brought out in 'Earth's Answer', and in anticipation of this the 'Introduction' is illustrated by a representation of Earth as a naked woman who lies on one side and turned away. The couch or bed on which she reclines is set among clouds and stars, the 'wat'ry shore' and 'starry floor'. The illuminations to the text of 'Earth's Answer', on the other hand, refer back to the 'Introduction'. They illustrate the Fall which the bard wants undone. Amongst the foliage which extends between the lines is a tendril of the grape-vine, and at the foot of the page a serpent writhes along the ground.

In her fallen state, in the isolation of Experience, Earth cannot speak in the role of God as the bard does. To do so would be blasphemous because she can only conceive of God in a superstitious way as a supernatural being who controls the universe. The religions of Experience, even Christianity, are inclined to degenerate into notions of control, prohibition and power. Christianity, however, allows its followers both experienced and innocent religious modes, for while it takes its inspiration from a God of love it also sees Him as the jealous tyrant of the Old Testament. The bard speaks for the former God, 'weeping in the evening dew', but Earth replies to the 'Father of the ancient men'. She hears nothing of the regret of the Word or of the possible beauty of 'wat'ry shore' and 'starry floor'. She knows only of a vale of tears where the stars are not beauties of the firmament, but, in their endless circling, signs of the law of the universe. The God she hears, if He weeps, does so in frustration. He is so powerful that He could force man to be happy and virtuous just by willing it. He could control all the motions of earth and renew all who fell from His dominion, both in the case of men who are cast out of the Garden and of those angels who were cast down and 'delivered into chains of darkness'.[1] It is probably an inevitable outcome of the creation of God in fallen man's image that such a creature as this should be the result. God must be the epitome of power, must be all-knowing and capable of complete control. But if He were to exercise this power, if He were rigidly to 'control the starry pole', there would be no sense of power. The tyrant always wants to be loved for himself, and this means that his creatures must appear to submit voluntarily to him. The result, in the Old Testament, is a God who is continually giving His creatures too much latitude, and continually punishing them for not using their freedom as He wishes them to.

The 'Father of the ancient men' is a God imposed on the Earth by man, and, like experienced man, He wants impossible things. He is a solitary, selfish and wilful creature who is incapable of love but insists that Earth love Him. Like experienced man He secretly loathes the self-gratification which goes under the name of love and so has come to regard all kinds of physical loving as shameful and guilty. The prison into which Earth is cast is one of being degraded by this sense of shame. Instead of being able to contemplate her naked

[1] 2 Pet. ii. 4.

beauty in the light, as the bard hopes she will be able to, the Earth (the body, the passions) is slighted by being approached only guiltily in the secrecy of darkness:

> 'Does the sower
> 'Sow by night
> 'Or the plowman in darkness plow?'

She is enchained in the humiliation of prudish laws and customs which imply that the flesh is indecent and ugly. Life is poisoned and constricted by the effect of prohibitions and distortions imposed on its energies.

In the 'Introduction' and 'Earth's Answer' God's call is received in different ways. In the first poem the call itself comes from the being who hears it, he hears because he loves the Earth to whom he must deliver it, and he delivers it half prophetically, half as the plea of a lover. In the second poem the call is heard as a demand for love, and the Earth answers half in defiance and half in pleading for the freedom which might make love possible—for 'free Love with bondage bound' is an absurdity.

As in all the contrasts he makes in the *Songs* Blake shows great delicacy in his use of language. The Word whom we hear 'weeping in the evening dew' is disconsolate at his loss, and the sense of loss is heightened by the repetition in the last line of the stanza: 'And fallen, fallen light renew!' There is a brooding over the event, which is so final. Also, there is the implication that the fall goes on, the breach ever widened. Like the 'Word', 'Starry Jealousy' also weeps:

> 'Cold and hoar,
> 'Weeping o'er,
> 'I hear the Father of the ancient men.'

The weeping is now the result of a much more selfish emotion. The use of the word 'o'er' gives the impression of a grief being nursed. The word 'Father', which may carry associations of care and responsibility, here refers only to the severe patriarch. With him is associated a mother Earth who is blind, grey and barren, tyrannized over by the Father, and alternating between pity for herself and abuse of the tyrant.

The two contrary states of the soul are presented in 'Introduction' and 'Answer', and so there are two values to the things depicted. Earth is a desirable young woman and a shrewish and disappointed old one. God is the Man of Sorrows and He is Jehovah. Sexual attraction and meeting is delightful (the budding and blossoming of Spring) and it is a furtive and cruel self-satisfaction (a chaining down in darkness). Blake presents the theme of love between Creator and creation in terms of sexual love, and can do so most convincingly because at both these levels love is a term that means contrary things. Both sorts are powerless to bind anyone against their will, but the selfish variety insists on outward submission and so comes to know love as ugly. The love of the Word, on the other hand, knows the beauty of its partner without any thought of making demands, and love itself is beautiful.

The theme of sexual love is never very far below the surface in the *Songs*, probably because Blake, engaged in discussing crucial differences, could use the aspect of life where they were most apparent to keep clear his view of an extraordinarily difficult subject. There is such a resemblance in appearance between Innocence and Experience that we describe the states by means of the same words. 'Mercy', 'pity', 'peace' and 'love' are the virtues of both states. In 'A Little Girl Lost' both the youth and the 'father white' show their 'care' or love for Ona. The innocent sweeper and the parents of the experienced sweeper refer themselves to the same 'God', or suppose they do. Both nurses utter the same words when calling their charges to 'come home'. Our lives are shot through and through with such resemblances, so close that we are often puzzled to know the exact spirit in which anything is done. In Innocence and Experience, Blake insists, apparent resemblances may hide a world of difference in underlying spirit. We are most sensitive to these differences in the persons who are most close to us, our associates and then our friends. The relationship in which we are most sensitive of all, and the relationship in which we have the best chance of achieving an innocent perfection is, perhaps, the sexual one. Sympathy, unaffected admiration, self-forgetfulness and delight are the characteristics of sexual love or it is not love at all, and these are the qualities of Innocence. Blake helps steady himself in his description of Innocence by keeping in mind the perfection of sexual love, so that sexual overtones appear in songs in the most unlikely places. It is not always necessary to recognize these overtones, which appear irrelevant in some poems (in 'Night' and 'On Another's Sorrow' for instance). Often, however, the recognition adds significance to the poem.

Blake does not confine his sexual references to the background of his poems, but also meets the topic directly. However, he keeps to the convention (announced in the innocent 'Introduction') that his poems are such that 'every child may joy to hear'. He takes up a suggestion made by Salzmann that infants be told all about sex, but uses a tact in the telling altogether beyond that worthy man. Blake's sexual poems are ambiguous to such a degree that one may find in them only what one brings to them. He goes into considerable detail in presenting the sexual act and the sexual parts, as in 'The Blossom' and 'The Sick Rose', but the reader must provide the detail from his or her own experience.[1]

---

[1] In the second part of the *Botanic Garden* (issued in its complete form in 1791), a work for which Blake engraved a number of plates, Erasmus Darwin describes the sexual parts of flowers allegorically in terms of human beings. An anther overtopped by six stamens might be a queen guarded by six tall warriors, and so on. Here a harmless topic is harmlessly represented, and it must have afforded Blake some amusement to reverse this order so as harmlessly to represent the unmentionable.

THE BLOSSOM

Merry, Merry Sparrow!
Under leaves so green
A happy Blossom
Sees you swift as arrow
Seek your cradle narrow
Near my Bosom.

Pretty, Pretty Robin!
Under leaves so green
A happy Blossom
Hears you sobbing, sobbing
Pretty, Pretty Robin,
Near my Bosom.

THE SICK ROSE

O Rose, thou art sick!
The invisible worm
That flies in the night,
In the howling storm,

Has found out thy bed
Of crimson joy:
And his dark secret love
Does thy life destroy.

'The Blossom' is a *Song of Innocence*, and the attitude taken towards sexual intercourse (the subject of the poem) is profoundly different to that found in the experienced 'Sick Rose'. There is no hidden suffering here, for the blossom sees her companion with pleasure in the first stanza, even with pride at his jaunty confidence and the sureness with which he finds his destination. In the second stanza, the blossom, still happy, feels tender towards a bird who has changed. The 'sobbing' is not necessarily in grief, but in fullness of emotion. Nevertheless the word helps convey the idea of tenderness felt by the blossom. Sexual intimacy is a theme particularly well suited to Blake's purpose in establishing a gulf between Innocence and Experience. The event is either very wonderful or most distressing. The knowledge it brings is of sublimity or

164

disappointment, with no intermediate condition. The sublimity, moreover, results only from mutual enjoyment, and Innocence is always a condition of absorbed participation. Disappointment is a consequence of loneliness even when, as in unsuccessful sexual encounters, the loneliness is felt in the presence of another. 'The Blossom' does not bring out the sublime in sexual experience as successfully as other *Songs of Innocence* we shall examine. The blossom, herself, despite her tenderness, is rather disengaged, and tends to be aware of the male sexual organ almost as a sort of pet. The poem is delicate, but the attitude described is rather casual, (even though purity makes it so) when compared with that seen in such a poem as 'Cradle Song'.[1]

'The Sick Rose' is meant, perhaps, as a satirical depiction of an unhealthy attitude to sexual love, unhealthy by comparison with the attitude in 'The Blossom'. If this is the intention, the poem fails to achieve its end and succeeds, instead, in conveying a complexity and depth of appreciation superior to that found in the innocent poem. Elsewhere in the *Songs of Experience* sex is approached in a negative manner, and one suspects that the positive force of 'The Sick Rose' asserts itself in spite of Blake. We are told of the worm[2] that he

> . . . flies in the night,
> In the howling storm . . .

He is relentless and without pity, is secret and passionate, but not furtive or mean. He is said to destroy, but the destruction involves a 'dark secret love' which takes some of its character from the compassionate concern of the poet. This is felt in the opening line: 'O Rose, thou art sick!' which is an involuntary cry in which concern, intimacy and admiration are all felt. In the second stanza both the Rose (the bed 'Of crimson joy') and the 'dark secret love' are erotic and, in the context,

---

[1] Discussed on pp. 182 ff.

[2] For a discussion of the sources from which Blake probably derived his images in this poem and other experienced 'love poems' see Kathleen Raine, 'Blake's Debt to Antiquity', *Sewanee Review*, LXXI (1963), 380 ff.

even fierce, but they are also rich and wonderful. 'The Sick Rose' suggests the deep and intricate emotions that the sexual act involves despite the secrecy and the possessive taboos with which Experience surrounds the passion.

The illustration to 'The Blossom' is a very striking one. The leaves of a flame-like plant lie collapsed on the ground at the foot of the plate. A similar plant erects itself along one side of the plate and bends over the top. Among the upper leaves is a circle of finely drawn figures. In the centre a winged mother bends over a child in her lap. Other children (as cherubs or cupids) are variously engaged. One of them reads a book, two fly to embrace each other, two are embracing, and one (without wings) flies towards the mother. Wicksteed suggests that the leaves have a phallic significance, and that the winged figures trace the 'current of creation': birth, self-delight, attraction, embracing and generation.[1] The illustration to 'The Sick Rose' depicts the rose as having carried its stem down so that the bloom rests on the ground and the stem encircles the text. A small female figure bursts from the heart of the bloom as a worm enters it. Among the rose stems is a caterpillar, also two drooping human figures in attitudes of despair.

A poem did lie to hand that might have been included in the *Songs of Experience* in place of 'The Sick Rose'—one that, viewed superficially, might have fitted better with the general air of disillusion, sometimes disgust, found there. The symbolism of the poem is obvious, the emotions are crude, and the poem is thin, especially when one compares it with 'The Sick Rose'. Blake chose not to engrave it, and it is found only in manuscript:[2]

> I saw a chapel all of gold
> That none did dare to enter in,
> And many weeping stood without,
> Weeping, mourning, worshipping.

[1] *Blake's Innocence and Experience*, pp. 124 n., 125 ff.
[2] *Notebook*, p. 115. *Complete Writings* (1957), p. 163.

I saw a serpent rise between
The white pillars of the door,
And he forc'd & forc'd & forc'd,
Down the golden hinges tore.

And along the pavement sweet,
Set with pearls & rubies bright,
All his slimy length he drew,
Till upon the altar white

Vomiting his poison out
On the bread & on the wine.
So I turn'd into a sty
And laid me down among the swine.

This poem has a more obvious 'message' than 'The Sick Rose', as it refers to the religious and social prohibitions placed on sexual experience and then deals with the unfortunate consequence that when the prohibitions are broken (as they inevitably will be), the sanctuary is defiled. The implication is that it might have been better to have allowed unrestricted worship to those who 'stood without'. If the chapel had been standing open it could not have been entered in guilt.

The poem, which is composed of a wealth of references to Apuleius's 'Cupid and Psyche', deals with the complex emotions of sexual experience in too facile a way and Blake did not bother to use it. There is another poem, never printed, which deals more directly with sexual intercourse and which handles the theme most beautifully. Blake made a fair copy of this poem in the *Pickering Manuscript*[1] in about 1803, but its date of composition is not known:

THE CRYSTAL CABINET

The Maiden caught me in the Wild,
Where I was dancing merrily;
She put me into her Cabinet
And Lock'd me up with a golden Key.

[1] *Complete Writings* (1957), p. 429.

This Cabinet is form'd of Gold
And Pearl & Crystal shining bright,
And within it opens into a World
And a little lovely Moony Night.

Another England there I saw,
Another London with its Tower,
Another Thames & other Hills,
And another pleasant Surrey Bower,

Another Maiden like herself,
Translucent, lovely, shining clear,
Threefold each in the other clos'd—
O, what a pleasant trembling fear!

O, what a smile! a threefold Smile
Fill'd me, that like a flame I burn'd;
I bent to Kiss the lovely Maid,
And found a Threefold Kiss return'd.

I strove to sieze the inmost Form
With ardor fierce & hands of flame,
But burst the Crystal Cabinet,
And like a Weeping Babe became—

A weeping Babe upon the wild,
And Weeping Woman pale reclin'd,
And in the outward air again
I fill'd with woes the passing Wind.

The first five stanzas of the poem deal with the promise of sexual intercourse.[1] The cabinet contains a world within the world so that the experience is at once a departure from reality and a heightening of reality. Imprisonment by the maiden is a setting free in 'another England'. A new realm is gained, which is a renewal of the realm one already knows. The suggestion of an intensified reality is amplified in several ways. The cabinet is an artificial construction but it contains the whole natural world in miniature. It is made of materials that transmit the light and reflect it, dazzling the sense of place. The joy experienced is a sensual one and from the self,

[1] For a different interpretation of the poem see Kathleen Raine, 'Blake's Debt to Antiquity', *Sewanee Review*, LXXI (1963), 400.

but is known only because joy is given and so is that of another. Things become threefold, are intensified, yet less substantial. Like a flame, the lover consumes and is continuously renewed. The last two stanzas describe the culmination of the experience in orgasm. The identification of the self with another may go so far, but in striving to 'sieze the inmost Form' all is lost. The transport into the innermost world throws the lovers back on their own selves, emotionally spent.

'The Blossom' and 'The Sick Rose' do not quite fit into their respective series. The former poem tends to slight its subject, while the latter shows a depth and complexity of awareness unusual in the experienced songs. Blake is able to keep the intention seen in the *Songs* more clearly in mind in a series of *Songs of Experience* which deal, not with the sexual act, but with attitudes taken towards the social and religious aspects of sex. 'The Rose Tree', for instance, deals with marriage, and the apt choice of that tree as symbol of the state shows some humour. The tree is decidedly an inhabitant of the cultivated garden, is respectably instituted, and it can be relied on to produce flowers regularly, but it has sharp thorns as well:

MY PRETTY ROSE TREE

A flower was offer'd to me,
Such a flower as May never bore;
But I said 'I've a Pretty Rose-tree,'
And I passed the sweet flower o'er.

Then I went to my pretty Rose-tree,
To tend her by day and by night;
But my Rose turn'd away with jealousy,
And her thorns were my only delight.

The qualities of this little poem, and of several others we shall go on to examine, are not nearly often enough recognized in Blake. We have seen him in a vein of austere humour.

169

Here the humour is witty, ironical and combined with subtlety of insight. We are not always as aware of our motives as (being experienced and self-controlled creatures) we like to imagine we are. We do not disclose our more disreputable motives to ourselves and prefer to live (as the experienced nurse says) 'in disguise'. This does not always deceive other people though. Usually they are aware of the falsity, even though they may not exactly know what the disguise conceals. The rose tree knows that the speaker of the poem has been false to her, even though his conduct has been irreproachable. Blake allows his persona to be just frank enough for us to detect where his self-deception lies. In passing over the sweet flower for the reason that he 'has a Pretty Rose-tree' the speaker gives such a smug reason that his wife, one perceives, would have grounds for jealousy, even if she had no knowledge of the other woman. She would sense that the interest her husband showed in her was a proprietary one. He is not really capable of being attracted to anyone, and so the likelihood of his being impelled to love his wife is as remote as his being impelled into the arms of a mistress. In returning to his wife he is presented with her thorns—a well-merited snub.

'The Rose Tree' is a carefully controlled poem showing great delicacy of psychological insight. It may be compared with such poems as 'The Sick Rose', on the one hand, where there is less deliberate control, but which open up complex vistas in the soul, and, on the other hand, with poems which show too much control, tend to moralize (though the moralizing is on behalf of the devil's party) and which lack subtlety. The moralizing poems never leave the *Notebook*, and Blake did not print such poems as 'O Lapwing . . .', 'Soft Snow', 'To My Mirtle'[1] and other poems which work on an ideological level. Many show wit and many are sharply barbed, but they lack the human dimension.

There is a notable exception, a poem comparable to 'The

[1] In the *Notebook*. See *Complete Writings* (1957), pp. 168, 176.

Rose Tree' in depth of insight, which was not printed. It can be seen why Blake did not include the first version of the poem in the *Songs*, although he was interested enough to make a second try at writing it. It is the first attempt which is of greater interest. It reads:

> Never seek to tell thy love,
> Love that never told can be;
> For the gentle wind does move
> Silently, invisibly.
>
> I told my love, I told my love,
> I told her all my heart;
> Trembling, cold, in ghastly fears,
> Ah! she doth depart.
>
> Soon as she was gone from me,
> A traveller came by,
> Silently, invisibly:
> He took her with a sigh.[1]

It is possible that the speaker in this poem considers himself rather ill-used, the woman as ungrateful and, it turns out, a loose thing he is well rid of. There seems to be reproach in the 'I told my love, I told my love' of the second stanza. As in 'The Rose Tree', however, the speaker is allowed to be frank enough for us to see why any reproach to be made belongs to himself. He (unintentionally perhaps) gives himself away in saying:

> For the gentle wind does move
> Silently, invisibly.

The telling of love, unless it has already told itself so well that the utterance is unnecessary, is the forcing of an egocentric emotion on to the attention of another. Love is reciprocal, a shared emotion that seems to move from without, or else it

---

[1] The version given here is Sampson's reconstruction of what Blake first wrote down, and is taken from his *Poetical Works of William Blake* (1913), p. 109. It is worth noting, however, that Blake's version, like all the poems in the *Notebook*, is without punctuation (see Keynes's facsimile edition). We may, therefore, take line 7 ('Trembling, cold, in ghastly fears') as descriptive of the speaker, of the woman he addresses, or of both of them.

is not love at all. So the speaker has not declared a passion already 'in the air' but has exposed a greed. If he had sensed that the woman shared the emotion, was moved by the silent wind, he might be agitated in the telling, but not with 'ghastly fears', and there could be no fears on her part. A one-sided declaration such as has been made by the speaker might be acceptable to a woman who was silly and vain enough to be flattered by it, but the reaction is more likely to be alarm and disgust. The traveller who takes her so casually might not have 'serious intentions' but at least he is tactful enough to keep silent.

Blake did not use this poem, perhaps because the first stanza shows too much wistful insight to be an utterance of the aggrieved person of the second and third stanzas. He deleted stanza one. But without the first stanza the point of the poem is rather obscure. Blake took up the poem again in 'I asked a thief . . .',[1] which describes how the speaker is rebuffed when he makes 'immoral' suggestions, but has the chagrin of seeing the success of an angel whose suggestions are conveyed in winks and smiles. By now the original intention of the first version has been lost, and the poem has become a jibe at conventional morality instead of an exploration of experienced self-deception. It does not become one of the *Songs*.

The trend in the *Songs of Experience* that we have been examining (that of using the poems to expose motives and impulses normally concealed, even from the self) may be noticed in one or two of the *Poetical Sketches*, written more than ten years before the publication of the *Songs*. In 'How sweet I roam'd from field to field . . .'[2] the affection of the 'Prince of Love' is questioned:

> He loves to sit and hear me sing,
> Then, laughing, sports and plays with me;
> Then stretches out my golden wing,
> And mocks my loss of liberty.

[1] *Notebook*, p. 114. [2] *Complete Writings* (1957), p. 6.

This 'love' is unhealthily possessive, but though the victim complains, it is by no means certain that she dislikes her 'golden cage'.

In the poem that immediately follows, Blake's irony is very delicate:

SONG

My silks and fine array,
   My smiles and languish'd air,
By love are driv'n away;
   And mournful lean Despair
Brings me yew to deck my grave:
Such end true lovers have.

His face is fair as heav'n,
   When springing buds unfold;
O why to him was't giv'n,
   Whose heart is wintry cold?
His breast is love's all worship'd tomb,
Where all love's pilgrims come.

Bring me an axe and spade,
   Bring me a winding sheet;
When I my grave have made,
   Let winds and tempests beat:
Then down I'll lie, as cold as clay.
True love doth pass away!

One sympathizes with the girl, particularly as (so the middle stanza implies) lovers usually encounter an object that cannot return the love. Her own young man has a heart that is 'wintry cold', and he is the epitome of what all lovers come to worship. This coldness does not seem encountered by chance, though. Pilgrims are intent on finding a tomb, and they could not worship there if the saint were not dead and cold. Perhaps the girl (unknowingly) invites a lover who is unresponsive. This is not unlikely, seeing that she was rather affected about her love-affair in the first place:

My silks and fine array,
   My smiles and languish'd air,
By love are driv'n away . . .

After being rebuffed she must alter the role she plays, but perhaps that is no great matter as long as there is still an attitude to strike. The posture taken in the last two lines of the poem is not the same as that of the first two lines, but it is a similar one, and both are 'interesting'.

The irony in these two poems from the *Poetical Sketches* is very gentle and smiling. By the time he comes to write the *Songs of Experience* Blake is less tolerant of self-deception, as we have seen. Poems like 'The Human Abstract' are denunciatory, and 'The Rose Tree', although it is less vehement, is damning. 'The Lilly' is similar in tone to 'The Rose Tree'. Blake makes no denunciation, but forces a verdict on the evidence he presents.

THE LILLY

> The modest Rose puts forth a thorn,
> The humble Sheep a threat'ning horn;
> While the Lilly white shall in Love delight,
> Nor a thorn, nor a threat, stain her beauty bright.

The 'modest Rose' and 'humble Sheep' seem to expect an attack prematurely. As they cannot defend themselves, one wonders if the defensive motion might not be designed to invite harm or, at the least, to reassure themselves that harm is intended. Rose and sheep display their emblems of fear while the lily appears unafraid, though not because she is immune from attack. Where rose and sheep ask for the delights of 'Love' by showing their readiness to repel it, the lily invites it by appearing ignorant of what is intended. She is far from being innocent in 'Love' but she knows (or senses) that it is enticing to appear to be so, and assumes the appearance of a 'white', unknowing virginity. Plainly, 'Love' is regarded as something fascinating but indecent by all the creatures in the poem and they all show that they have nothing to do with indecencies. All three are insincere, but the lily shows a refinement of insincerity, for she pretends to know nothing of the passion, while the rose and sheep vulgarly insist on it. Small wonder, then, that the lily is more successful in attracting lovers.

Similar disguises to those in 'The Lilly' are seen at work in 'The Angel' where the maiden Queen hides, first behind a mask of 'witless woe', and later behind her 'fears':

THE ANGEL

I Dreamt a Dream! what can it mean?
And that I was a maiden Queen,
Guarded by an Angel mild:
Witless woe was ne'er beguil'd!

And I wept both night and day,
And he wip'd my tears away,
And I wept both day and night,
And hid from him my heart's delight.

So he took his wings and fled;
Then the morn blush'd rosy red;
I dried my tears, & arm'd my fears
With ten thousand shields and spears.

Soon my Angel came again:
I was arm'd, he came in vain;
For the time of youth was fled,
And grey hairs were on my head.

The illustration shows us the maiden queen and the angel represented as Psyche and Cupid. The maiden reclines in a position of woe, holding Cupid off with a strange gesture that at once keeps him at arm's length and caresses his cheek. Unlike the lily, the maiden uses her disguise of 'innocence', not to attract lovers, but to keep her young man in order, knowing that 'witless woe was ne'er beguil'd'. She is in love with him but hides her heart's delight, with the result that he leaves. She then changes her tactics. Wishing to encourage, not repel any advance, she puts on a false front of being alarmed by him when he returns. Alas! it is too late, for she is now past caring for anyone else, and so the fears she assumes in order to play the coquette are now translated into real fears.

'The Angel' does not show, as a poem, the self-sufficiency of 'My Pretty Rose Tree' or 'Never seek to tell thy love . . .'. The ironic humour lies in the way the situation changes, and in order to interpret the change the reader is obliged to do some reading between the lines, using his knowledge of other poems such as 'The Lilly'. Blake seems to have anticipated that the poem would be something of a conundrum when he wrote the first line, and the reader cannot be sure that he has answered the conundrum right. For instance, what significance does the title have in this especial context? It is ironical, of course, that such fears as the maiden experiences should be aroused by a male so honourable and gentle as 'angel' implies he is. But there remains some obscurity.

The maiden queen of 'The Angel' cannot give way to her heart's delight, she is confused about the state of her own feelings, and she hides her desire until it is no longer desire of a healthy kind. Her life is poisoned by the repression of an emotion just as in 'A Poison Tree' hidden feelings act to the detriment of the speaker.

A POISON TREE

I was angry with my friend:
I told my wrath, my wrath did end.
I was angry with my foe:
I told it not, my wrath did grow.

And I water'd it in fears,
Night & morning with my tears;
And I sunned it with smiles,
And with soft deceitful wiles.

And it grew both day and night,
Till it bore an apple bright;
And my foe beheld it shine,
And he knew that it was mine,

And into my garden stole
When the night had veil'd the pole:
In the morning glad I see
My foe outstretch'd beneath the tree.

It is not only the 'foe' who is poisoned here. The speaker's life is soured by the results of his caution, by the suspicions and anxieties of being at secret enmity and the strain of keeping up a friendly appearance which is known by both parties to be a sham. The 'foe' is aware of the dislike felt towards him, returns it in like manner and the mean contest begins in which the aim is to humble an enemy by getting him to show his spite first. He then has only himself to blame for the consequences, dramatically described (and depicted in the illustration) as death because that is the secret wish these 'friends' have for each other.

The enmity is established in the course of the poem, although the first stanza designates the foe. A foe is a person whom one cannot trust with one's feelings, and if one can trust oneself to utter one's feelings to no man, one can expect to make nothing but enemies. The distrust at the outset is a self-distrust, though the consequences are borne also by others. The original title of the poem given in the *Notebook*[1] was 'Christian Forbearance' because the cowardice described in the song is usually excused under that name. The poem does not describe the dissembling hypocrite, but a man who is self-deceived, who persuades himself that he is doing the right thing, though he soon finds that he is forced to play the hypocrite deliberately in order to hide his growing wrath.

In most of the poems we have been examining in this chapter there can be seen an intention to illuminate some dark corner of the mind, to show up some confusion or dishonesty in motives. 'The Garden of Love' appears, at first sight, to be more straightforward—an indictment of the 'system' and not an exposure of hypocrisy or deception in the individual.

THE GARDEN OF LOVE

I went to the Garden of Love,
And saw what I never had seen:
A Chapel was built in the midst,
Where I used to play on the green.

[1] P. 114. *Complete Writings* (1957), p. 165.

And the gates of this Chapel were shut,
And 'Thou shalt not' writ over the door;
So I turn'd to the Garden of Love
That so many sweet flowers bore;

And I saw it was filled with graves,
And tomb-stones where flowers should be;
And Priests in black gowns were walking their rounds,
And binding with briars my joys & desires.

The speaker describes the change brought about in the enjoyment of love by the effect of religious notions. What had been a region of pleasure and beauty has become a chapel and graveyard, a place of prohibitions, of mourning, of stifled desires. Love has been made sinful, and so a reminder of mortality instead of an expression of vigour. At a first reading, the intention of the poet seems to be to convey this rather superficial accusation.

If the poem speaks primarily of sexual love (as 'sweet flowers' seems to imply) then the speaker has, himself, exchanged a happy experience for an unhappy one. We must take him in one of two ways, then. Either he has allowed his experience of love to become tainted by a sense of guilt as the result of a religious conversion, or else he has become sexually disenchanted and, wishing to find the fault anywhere except in himself, blames the effect on religious prohibitions. In short, the speaker is a fool or a hypocrite, and whatever truth there may be in the social indictment he makes is spoiled by the distorted use made of it. The point is that we are not dealing with any corruption of Innocence, but a change within Experience. The 'Garden of Love' is, here, a realm of the mind, and if it is despoiled, the only person who can effect the damage is the individual concerned. If the speaker once enjoyed love which has now become degraded by religious and social pressures, it is he who has given way to the pressures, valuing the love too slightly to retain it. What is probable is that the 'Garden' which the speaker laments is not a garden of love at all, but a garden of self-indulgence.

There *is* something to be ashamed of in selfish gratification, and the half-obscured feelings of guilt involved are likely to attract second-rate religious notions. Perhaps this is just as well. The joys known to the speaker are bound with briars because it is necessary that, being distorted joys, they should be controlled. The priests who keep control base their morality on unhealthy repugnancies, but these are necessary checks to unhealthy impulses. Innocence needs no restrictions, but Experience can only control itself by writing 'Thou shalt not' over the door.

'The Garden of Love' is similar to 'London'. Both poems are written in the first person and both contain indictments of society in the Godwinian vein: it is his institutions that make man miserable. But there are important differences between the two poems in respect of their scope and complexity and of the degree of Blake's ironic detachment from the speaker. To take the latter point first: 'The Garden of Love' simply presents us with a Godwinian idea, and leaves us to make what we like of the argument. There is no indication in the poem that we are not listening to Blake talking in his own voice in an 'off' moment. In 'London', as we know, Blake's voice is to be heard counterpointing the theme of the wanderer, but in 'The Garden of Love' one listens for the ironical counterpoint in vain. 'London' is richer, also, in the complexity of its argument. The wanderer is in a miserable condition, but he knows that the situation is made more intolerable by the fact that he is forced to 'forge' it himself. He sees, also, that every aspect of his life is infected by the same malady. In 'The Garden of Love', the speaker petulantly assumes that the restriction is applied from without and makes no attempt to see the restriction as an aspect of a larger situation. His intelligence is limited, even within the bounds imposed by Experience—which cannot be said of the wanderer.

In 'The Blossom', which is an innocent song, sexual love is taken in a very matter-of-fact way, and it is only in the *Songs*

179   12-2

of Experience that furtive motives, shame, and fear make the experience of sex into a painful or disappointing one. Blake's treatment of sex has parallels in his treatment of birth, the underlying theme of two poems on infancy, one innocent and the other experienced:

INFANT JOY

'I have no name:
'I am but two days old.'
What shall I call thee?
'I happy am,
'Joy is my name.'
Sweet joy befall thee!

Pretty joy!
Sweet joy but two days old,
Sweet joy I call thee:
Thou dost smile,
I sing the while,
Sweet joy befall thee!

INFANT SORROW

My mother groan'd! my father wept.
Into the dangerous world I leapt:
Helpless, naked, piping loud:
Like a fiend hid in a cloud.

Struggling in my father's hands,
Striving against my swadling bands,
Bound and weary I thought best
To sulk upon my mother's breast.

Both these poems are spoken in the first person, but like the two 'Nurse's Songs', the one is a monologue, and broods over the speaker's inward vision of an event, while the other is a dialogue (the speaker provides both parts) in which delight is found in relationship with another person. In keeping with the habit of mind of the speaker, each poem seizes on one extreme emotion of the infant's limited range. The experienced poem prefers to dwell on sorrow, so the speaker, who describes his own birth, commences by talking of the groans he could not have been aware of, and goes on to talk of terror and resentment he cannot possibly remember. In the innocent poem the mother appears to have forgotten her pains of two days ago in the enjoyment of her child.

All events require interpretation, but in 'Infant Sorrow' interpretation threatens to thrust the event entirely aside. The speaker is not describing his own infancy, of course, but what can normally be observed: the convulsed movements of the baby, the expression on the face of a sucking child, but he is disposed to see these only as a protest against a hostile world. It must be added, however, that despite the speaker's pessimism the poem contains a recognition of the energy displayed by the child. The babe's advent is vigorously described as a leap into the world and even after being pent up in cloud and swaddling bands its subdued force is still apparent. There is an admiration here which is absent in, say, the experienced 'Nurse's Song', and it is possible that Blake allowed his theme to carry him beyond the grudging enthusiasms of Experience.

In the innocent poem, the mother is no less inclined to read the mind of her infant, and she goes so far as to put words into its mouth, making up the child's realization that it lacks a name, and then pretending that it gives itself a name which is a projection of the mother's pleasure:

> 'I happy am,
> 'Joy is my name.'

This is an interpretation of a different sort to the experienced one, for it is governed by an emotion springing from the occasion of being with the child. The interpretation is grounded on a real experience. The interpretation in 'Infant Sorrow', on the other hand, is grounded on a habit of mind, a dogmatic view of life, and so is all fantasy.

The illustration to 'Infant Joy' shows a mother sitting with a babe on her lap. She is attended by a fairy, and they are

181

placed in the half-open cup of a flower, similar to an anemone. Wicksteed is probably right in giving the flower sexual significance. Blake symbolically traces the baby to its origin, but whether we associate the flower with the uterus or with the gooseberry bush, whether we know how babies are made[1] or suppose that the fairies bring them, makes no difference to an appreciation of the poem. Its subject is the present enjoyment of the baby itself, and the symbols may be taken as the reader pleases. The illustration to 'Infant Sorrow' prosaically shows a mother about to pick up a struggling infant. In the background is the mother's curtain-hung bed.

Blake's finest achievement in presenting the difference between loves of the innocent and experienced sort is found in two poems both entitled 'A Cradle Song', although the experienced version is found only in the *Notebook*[2] and never became one of the *Songs*.

A CRADLE SONG

Sweet dreams, form a shade
O'er my lovely infant's head;
Sweet drèams of pleasant streams
By happy, silent, moony beams.

Sweet sleep, with soft down
Weave thy brows an infant crown.
Sweet sleep, Angel mild,
Hover o'er my happy child.

Sweet smiles, in the night
Hover over my delight;
Sweet smiles, Mother's smiles,
All the livelong night beguiles.

Sweet moans, dovelike sighs,
Chase not slumber from thy eyes.
Sweet moans, sweeter smiles,
All the dovelike moans beguiles.

[1] Compare 'A fairy leaped upon my knee . . .', *Complete Writings* (1957), p. 188.　　　　[2] P. 114. *Complete Writings* (1957), p. 164.

Sleep, sleep, happy child,
All creation slept and smil'd;
Sleep, sleep, happy sleep,
While o'er thee thy mother weep.

Sweet babe, in thy face
Holy image I can trace.
Sweet babe, once like thee,
Thy maker lay and wept for me,

Wept for me, for thee, for all,
When he was an infant small.
Thou his image ever see,
Heavenly face that smiles on thee,

Smiles on thee, on me, on all;
Who became an infant small.
Infant smiles are his own smiles;
Heaven & earth to peace beguiles.

A CRADLE SONG

Sleep, Sleep, beauty bright
Dreaming o'er the joys of night
Sleep, Sleep: in thy sleep
Little sorrows sit & weep.

Sweet Babe, in thy face
Soft desires I can trace
Secret joys & secret smiles
Little pretty infant wiles.

As thy softest limbs I feel
Smiles as of the morning steal
O'er thy cheek & o'er thy breast
Where thy little heart does rest.

O, the cunning wiles that creep
In thy little heart asleep.
When thy little heart does wake,
Then the dreadful lightnings break.

From thy cheek & from thy eye
O'er the youthful harvests nigh
Infant wiles & infant smiles
Heaven & Earth of peace beguiles.

In these two poems, as in other pairs, Blake uses identical words in order to mean very different things. 'Sweet', 'soft', 'peace', 'weep', 'beguile' have very different implications in the two contexts, and this is particularly noticeable in the case of the last line of the poems, identical except for a preposition. As the result of a trifling change 'beguile' alters its meaning from 'wins over' to 'defrauds'. This similarity in vocabulary but difference in signification reflects the larger picture: two mothers bend admiringly over their baby but they experience very different feelings and see different things, however similar their maternal activities may appear. The difference between the mothers is emphasized in the finest details of the poems. The experienced mother, who supposes that she knows all about the mind of her baby, though she merely projects herself on to it, calls it a 'beauty' (line 1), using an absolute term. The innocent mother, who makes no suppositions about her baby's soul, confining her statements to what she sees and feels, uses the word 'lovely', acknowledging the personal nature of the impression.

The opening words of the poems establish an immediate distinction between the mothers. The experienced one says:

> Sleep, Sleep, beauty bright
> Dreaming o'er the joys of night . . .

The words are almost a command, given as though the child can decide to remain asleep. The innocent mother also talks of dreams but, in doing so, makes no assertion about the mind of her child, for the dreams, like the expressions that haunt its face, hover over the infant, leaving it to rest undisturbed:

> Sweet dreams, form a shade
> O'er my lovely infant's head . . .

The lines are spoken as a blessing by a mother who is quite content to accept the baby in its strangeness without 'bending' it to her notions. Even when she refers to the infant as 'happy child' (line 17) she is not referring to its state of mind but to the appreciation she feels; to the good fortune of its being.

Blake's Criticism of 'Love'

The innocent mother talks of sleep as an 'Angel mild' (stanza 2). It is a benign influence hovering over the infant, like the shade-forming dreams, and, like them, is not the outcome of an exertion of will. The dreams wished for, in keeping with the nature of the sleep, are of places of calm influence. As she watches her babe the mother sees it smile (stanza 3) or hears it sigh and moan (stanza 4) in its sleep. These manifestations too, hover over the child rather than emanate from it. This is partly because, as the mother sympathetically responds to these utterances of the child they become movements in her own soul as she bends over the baby, also because the mother never wishes to go further than these outward manifestations. She participates so very sensitively in the movements she watches for, but the baby's soul is beyond her, and she shows no inclination to reach it. She knows nothing of the child's emotions and says nothing about them, being happy merely to watch the changes on the child's countenance.

There is something unpleasant in the experienced mother's feeling of the 'soft limbs' of the baby, for she does so in order to satisfy her sensuality. The child, 'softly' desirous, knows in its turn how to encourage the caresses it enjoys. Like a self-composed adult it is armed with 'wiles', and knows that it must please in order to be pleased. The mother comes very close to describing her babe as though its desires were sexual ones. The 'joys of night' are not specified, but like the 'secret joys', they sound indecently erotic, and in referring to the 'youthful harvests nigh', the mother seems to indicate later sexual experiences, to which the present self-gratifications of the babe are preliminary. Even sleep is spoken of as though it were a storing up of selfish energy which, like 'dreadful lightnings', breaks out destructively. The individual does not live in the warmth of contact with others, but coldly communes with himself, spending his animal heat in callous, impersonal bursts. The smiles of the infant in the experienced song do not hover between mother and child, but steal out of the baby.

They are the appearance of the 'cunning wiles' that 'creep' in the baby's 'little heart' and come furtively out, like lizards while the sun is shining. The mother centres the baby's world in itself, and assumes that it relates everything to its gratifications, just as she centres her world on herself. Joy is what can be got, is secret and sensuous, while sorrow is the frustration of such pleasures.

In the innocent poem emotions are not neatly definable. Some movement goes on in the baby which gives rise to 'sweet moans, sweeter smiles' (line 15), but both 'moans' and 'smiles' are sweet, for they manifest a whole and complex process. They are not indicative of a being who is built up of categories of emotion, but a living person. The mother smiles and sighs in sympathy, also she weeps over the child (line 20). The infant Christ of the last three stanzas both weeps and smiles. We cannot label the emotions that underly the weeping and smiling of mother and Christ, just as we cannot in the case of the baby. Such emotions involve a complete being and their texture is too complex and unique for easy generalities to be possible.[1]

The innocent poem cannot see man as the self-enclosed individual whose energies are released, like a flash of lightning into his world. On the contrary, men are quickened by their association with others, and the poem presents us with a complex of connexions. In the last four stanzas the mother associates her infant with the infant Christ:

> Sweet babe, in thy face
> Holy image I can trace.

She refers to the Old Testament creation of man in God's image, but there is a more direct reference to Christ, whose purpose in becoming man was to awaken man to the divine in himself. It is only if he can respond to God there, in the virtues of delight which make him reach out beyond himself,

---

[1] This is true of the type of self-expression seen as belonging to the piper (pp. 149 ff.). His words, like his music, carry the weight of his whole being. Compare also the weeping with joy in other *Songs of Innocence*.

that man can know God. An examination of the heavens returns only the blank stare of Nobodaddy.

As the child looks at its mother it, too, senses God, not because it carries any memory of a previous existence, like Wordsworth's child in *Intimations of Immortality*, but because it sees the face of its mother who loves it:

> Thou his image ever see,
> Heavenly face that smiles on thee . . .

In addition to 'seeing' God in the face of the child, the mother 'sees' its father at the time of procreation, and the child, when it sees its mother, also 'sees' its father's face on that occasion, because love is manifest now, as it was then:

> . . . Thy maker lay and wept for me,

> Wept for me, for thee, for all,
> When he was an infant small.
> Thou his image ever see,
> Heavenly face that smiles on thee,

> Smiles on thee, on me, on all;
> Who became an infant small.

The peace of the last line of the poem is that of 'The Divine Image', a mode of love. It is manifested in the relationship between the mother and child and is also the peace that accompanies and succeeds the sexual act. Unlike the categorical joys of the experienced song, this peace is complete, and always unique. It is referred to in the last three stanzas as a complex of weeping and of smiles, not because there is any rush of vague feeling, but because the emotion defies description or classification.

We noticed in 'The Divine Image' that men were unknown to one another and bound to respect each other's privacy. But also they were seen to yearn to each other. In the innocent 'Cradle Song' the mother accords the infant its privacy (unlike her experienced sister), yet Blake shows us poetically that they come together so that, though there can be no merging of individuals, their delights become one. In the first

two stanzas dreams and sleep are not seen as activities of the
baby, but as influences that hover over it. In the third stanza
the smiles that appear on the face of the infant are seen in this
way in the first two lines, but it becomes less clear as we pass
to the second two that the smiles referred to were not those of
the mother:

> Sweet smiles, in the night
> Hover over my delight;
> Sweet smiles, Mother's smiles,
> All the livelong night beguiles.

The child smiles in its sleep and the mother responds, but it is
not always possible to say who is responsible, for it is as if, in
the bond between mother and baby, smiling were a condition
that hovered between them. We are reminded of the sympathy envisaged in 'On Another's Sorrow', so close that a
common emotion was shared by separate persons:

> Can a father see his child
> Weep, nor be with sorrow fill'd?

Christ, in that poem, sits 'Wiping all our tears away', but it
is not at all certain whose face He wipes them from.

In the fourth stanza, the coming together of the manifestations of mother and child is even more marked:

> Sweet moans, dovelike sighs,
> Chase not slumber from thy eyes.
> Sweet moans, sweeter smiles,
> All the dovelike moans beguiles.

Does the mother hope that the child, in uttering its sighs will
not awaken itself, or does she hope that the sounds she makes
in response will not disturb it? Does she wish her sighs to
beguile away those of the child or does she state that the
child's sounds beguile her to peace? All these possibilities are
implied, for in her care and responsiveness the mother has
ceased to distinguish carefully between the sounds and
gestures expressed by the child and her own sympathetic
responses.

In the last four stanzas the child, Christ, the father and the mother are interchangeable in many places. The tears and smiles of one person become those of another, and the stanzas may be read in various ways. Although Blake is not stating the impossible: that these individuals *are* each other, he does mean to convey that there is a closer bond than similarity. All manifest the virtues of 'The Divine Image' and when they are together they transcend a mode of being in which we lurk within ourselves. The sympathetic bond does not destroy individuality (there is no merging), but in sympathy, in love, both individuals are moved by the same 'silent wind' from without. In the poem this shared influence is seen in the sleep, dreams, smiles, tears that hover between the mother and her child, between the mother and the father, between the divine images when they are divine. The manifestations belong to both persons, but are forced by neither, and without the other they would be impossible. There is no lightning flash of will here, but an energy that springs from intimacy.

The word 'love' may be used to refer to forms of self-gratification. The love of the experienced mother is of this sort, and the sexual loves that she predicts for her child are of the same variety. She emphasizes the secrecy and greed of our pleasures and the tensed and wilful nature of our energies. In passing to the innocent song we find human possibilities viewed in an altogether different way. As in the experienced poem, the love of a mother is described and this is related to sexual love but there is no hint of a selfish gratification here. There is something more, even, than shared pleasure. There is delight—an emotion that can only result from contribution to the delight of another, and the sexual dimension in the poem can refer us most successfully to this aspect. Blake introduces the sexual mode, not because he confuses it with other modes of love, but because, in referring to it, he can exemplify, in an understandable way, what, ideally, all modes of love have in common. In the sexual act the self is thrust into the background of the experience, and though the participants will eventually be thrown back into the 'outward air', self is subordinate to a being together, and, for a while, takes its significance from that conjunction. The experience is creative of the individuals that go to make it up, and not a forced creation of the will of each.

In the innocent 'Cradle Song' the mother is not isolated. She is an individual with her own secrets, and she realizes that her baby (which she does not suppose she can pry into) has its private and inexplicable inner self. But, in the moment of sympathy, these privacies have become secondary to a uniting experience, just as in coitus the union overcomes, for a while, the persons involved.

CHAPTER 7

THE POET AS MORAL CRITIC

IN writing the *Songs* Blake does not show that he has any interest in exploring religious questions in the abstract. In the same way, there is no interest taken in 'sex' as in itself a topic of interest. Instead, we see a study made of religious and sexual ideas as manifestations of man. This emphasis on the manifestation instead of on the topic has the result that, when the poetry is engaged with the sexual, the religious is never very far away, and vice versa, not because Blake confuses these subjects but because they are directions taken by the mind of a unified being. The *Songs of Innocence and of Experience* present us with a 'poetry of ideas', but, for Blake, ideas only become meaningful in the mind or mouth of a person. Without utterance or a human habitation any notion is a vague, shifting thing said by convention to have independent life, although the conventional nature of this 'existence' is usually forgotten. Blake does not forget—knows that it is absurd to present ideas as if they carried with them no colour and life from the mind that nourishes them.

Just as Blake is not in the least interested in making statements in the realm of pure theology, so, in moral and political matters, he is interested in ideas, not as something to be manipulated on their own account, but as the manifestation of a state of being, and as taking their quality from the mind that supports them. In the two 'Holy Thursdays' innocent and experienced moral reactions are seen being made to the same event, and we are invited to assess each reaction by forming some notion of the person who makes it.

HOLY THURSDAY

'Twas on a Holy Thursday, their innocent faces clean,
The children walking two & two, in red & blue & green,
Grey-headed beadles walk'd before, with wands as white as snow,
Till into the high dome of Paul's they like Thames' waters flow.

O what a multitude they seem'd, these flowers of London town!
Seated in companies they sit with radiance all their own.
The hum of multitudes was there, but multitudes of lambs,
Thousands of little boys & girls raising their innocent hands.

Now like a mighty wind they raise to heaven the voice of song,
Or like harmonious thunderings the seats of Heavens among.
Beneath them sit the aged men, wise guardians of the poor;
Then cherish pity, lest you drive an angel from your door.

HOLY THURSDAY

Is this a holy thing to see
In a rich and fruitful land,
Babes reduc'd to misery,
Fed with cold and usurous hand?

Is that trembling cry a song?
Can it be a song of joy?
And so many children poor?
It is a land of poverty!

And their sun does never shine,
And their fields are bleak & bare,
And their ways are fill'd with thorns:
It is eternal winter there.

For where-e'er the sun does shine,
And where-e'er the rain does fall,
Babe can never hunger there,
Nor poverty the mind appall.

On the occasions when the charity school children were taken to St Paul's, everything was done, no doubt, to make them show at their best. Sir Gilbert Elliot describes them at the National Thanksgiving for the recovery of George III in 1787 as follows:

Under the dome were piled up to a great height all round, 6000 children from the different charity schools in the city, in their different habits and colours . . . you may see this any year for they are brought to St Paul's and placed in the same order every year . . . when the King approached the centre, all the 6000 children set up their little voices and sang part of the Hundredth Psalm. This was the moment I found most affecting and without knowing exactly why I found my eyes running over and the bone in my throat, which was the case with many other people . . .[1]

The speaker in the innocent 'Holy Thursday' is moved by a scene that he finds at once magnificent and touching. In the first stanza the dignity of the occasion is emphasized by the gravity of the beadles and the decorum of the flow of children 'like Thames' waters'. In the second stanza the emphasis is on the delicate beauty of the children who are 'flowers', but the delicacy is combined with order and multitude. In the last line they raise their 'innocent hands' in gesture and prayer, but they do so in thousands and the effect is simultaneously one of simple, rather helpless gracefulness, and of grandeur. In the last stanza the grand aspect is emphasized as the children's voices rise to 'a mighty wind' and to 'harmonious thunderings'. In keeping with the greatness of the occasion the trustees of the schools are seen as 'wise guardians of the poor': humane, dignified and impartial men who may be relied upon to order things well.

The speaker in the experienced poem, on the other hand, is not 'taken in' by the spectacular nature of the occasion. He briefly dismisses what is meant to impress ('Is that trembling cry a song?') and explores the underlying significance of the event. His first words, picking up the title of the poem, are critical of the right of the gathering to be associated with anything holy. The great display of good works is seen, not as anything to feel proud of, but as flaunting in the face of God the fact that His commands are neglected. We are enjoined to love God and love our fellows. This great

[1] *Life and Letters*, I, 303. Quoted in M. G. Jones, *The Charity School Movement* (1938), p. ix.

gathering shows that we are prepared to carry out the easier
task of loving (or putting on a ceremony of loving) God, but
it is an insult to Him to lend splendour to the occasion by a
regimented display of failure to perform our duty to our
neighbour. The ceremony, with its impression of wise
guardianship and careful provision, is a lie to cover our real
situation:

> And so many children poor?
> It is a land of poverty!

It must be a land where there is a shortage of the necessities
of life, for if it were rich and men were capable of ordering
their affairs in a Christian manner there should be no need of
institutions for the relief of the poor. The existence of such
institutions is a symptom of a fundamental disorder, and the
last two stanzas of the poem are taken up by a rather vague,
rambling and rhetorical statement of the general moral
starvation indicated by the scene in St Paul's. The most
pointed accusation of the poem is made in the fourth line: the
babes are 'Fed with cold and usurous hand . . .'. The
charitable institution works in an impersonal and niggardly
manner and it expects a return. No doubt the speaker is
familiar with the apologies it was thought necessary to make
for charity schools from the time of their inception onwards.
Poor children, it was argued, were prevented from turning
criminal by being cared for, so the care was a good invest-
ment. They were taught to be useful without being given
ideas above their station and so made excellent servants. The
hand that feeds the children is usurous because the hope of a
return is the only effective incentive to charity that can be
seen at work in a wintry world.

The innocent poem, then, describes the scene in St Paul's
and is (rather naïvely, perhaps) impressed by what is seen.
The experienced poem tells us hardly anything about the
scene, and is chiefly concerned with interpreting it. The
interpretation is, however, very general, and the attack made
by the poem is not directed at any particular abuse or set of

persons. One receives the impression of the speaker that, if it were found that one single babe were hungry, he would have as much mental discomfort as now when there are thousands, and this would not be because he is taken up with the hunger or the babies but with the social pathology. He is concerned with the abstract circumstances of poverty. The poem ends by saying that:

> . . . where-e'er the rain does fall,
> Babe can never hunger there,
> Nor poverty the mind appall.

The word 'appall' seems to carry very much the same connotation that it did in 'London'. The mind, it is implied, blenches with horror when confronted with something that calls for relief, but which seems too large to be dealt with. The daunting scale on which poverty displayed itself in eighteenth-century London causes the speaker to retreat into a moral consideration of the subject and an appalled indictment of the climate in which misery can flourish. The speaker is so very concerned, so overcome by the awfulness of the problem, and yet he is paralysed, robbed of any duty he can perform in the face of an injustice built into the fabric of society. Whether the speaker's indictment is just or unjust is not as important as the fact that he has now taken the problem to a level where he need not do anything active about it because all personal action is futile. The problem is too large and it needs social, not personal manipulation. Acts of charity such as those of the 'wise guardians of the poor' are, willy-nilly, usurous, and merely countenance the evil which they keep within manageable bounds, but cannot eradicate. The speaker has turned to a contemplation, in isolated misery, of the horrors of poverty, of the right of poverty to exist. Into this realm poor people and acts or feelings of pity directed towards individuals need not enter.

The innocent poem is not concerned with the larger moral issues. It takes the general poverty indicated by the numbers of charity school children for granted, it regards the efforts to offset the poverty as necessary and, because something is achieved, regards them as well directed. Despite its simplicity, the poem ends with a statement which, though it might not acknowledge the complexity of the problem, shows that the speaker retains the sense of responsibility abandoned in the experienced poem:

Then cherish pity, lest you drive an angel from your door.

There is no attempt here to penetrate into social or religious significance, nor even to state a duty. The speaker merely concludes his description of the service in St Paul's and then makes the disarmingly simple statement of this last line. It is not a tag, because it gives the gist of no sermon. It contains no authority or rationale for pity, but relates any deed of pity only to the deed itself. There is no reward for pity and no punishment for not exercising it, but failure to show pity might turn away someone capable of receiving it. It is assumed quite without question that this is argument enough. Who could possibly wish to fail the offered occasion? Who would run a risk of doing an injury? The questions are not even asked.

The experienced poem is full of moral anxieties and accusations discussed on a religious and social level: 'Is this a holy thing to see . . .?' and can this be a 'rich and fruitful land . . .?' In spite of this preoccupation, the involvement of the speaker is with his own revulsions and criticisms and not with the charity children, with real poverty, or with responsible pity. His seizing the occasion, as he would seize any similar occasion to preach a sermon, shows that he substitutes skill in moral questions for a sense of what, morally, might be required of him. In the innocent poem, on the other hand, a fine moral sensibility is displayed without self-consciousness or fuss.[1]

[1] For a reading of these two poems which sees the innocent song as latent satire and the experienced one as a powerful and effective indictment see: D. V. Erdman, *Prophet Against Empire*, pp. 110–12; R. F. Gleckner, 'Irony in Blake's "Holy Thursday"', *Modern Language Notes*, LXXI (1956), 412–15; R. F. Gleckner, 'Blake and Wesley', *Notes and Queries*, CCI (1956), 522–4.

The Poet as Moral Critic

It would be wrong to draw from the two 'Holy Thursdays' the moral that abstruse political thinking should be, or can be, avoided. On the contrary, such thinking is a duty of experienced man. We may, perhaps, conclude that such thinking is very dangerous because not really responsible, however well informed or intricate, unless it is guided by pity. The speaker in the experienced song uses his generalizations to evade a knowledge of his duty, not to define it, and he breaks into a rambling condemnation. The innocent moral is drawn in one line, is drawn concisely, and makes itself perfectly clear. Pity must be cherished for its own sake. We have nothing else to guide us morally if it is let go, and our abstract moralizings, essential though they may be, must collapse or mislead us without it.

The speaker in the experienced 'Holy Thursday' is not wrong in the sense that his scepticism is necessarily misplaced. Perhaps all charity schools are unpleasant places and perhaps all the persons responsible for instituting them have unpleasant motives for doing so. A notion need not be erroneous in order to be detected as a prejudice, however, and the speaker is prejudiced because he slips automatically into a remote way of thinking after making the most cursory of observations. In the innocent poem the speaker hardly takes his fascinated eyes from the children. The experienced speaker barely sees them, and what he sees is subordinated to a social-political preoccupation.

We have seen Blake exposing a rather similar action of the experienced mind in 'The Garden of Love' where the speaker turns to social-religious recriminations in order to avoid an examination of his own shortcomings. In 'The Little Vaga-bond' similar recriminations are made, and, in a theoretical way, it is difficult to discount what the speaker says. But it is equally difficult to agree with him.

THE LITTLE VAGABOND

Dear Mother, dear Mother, the Church is cold,
But the Ale-house is healthy & pleasant & warm;
Besides I can tell where I am used well,
Such usage in heaven will never do well.

But if at the Church they would give us some Ale,
And a pleasant fire our souls to regale,
We'd sing and we'd pray all the live-long day,
Nor ever once wish from the Church to stray.

Then the Parson might preach, & drink, & sing,
And we'd be as happy as birds in the spring;
And modest dame Lurch, who is always at Church,
Would not have bandy children, nor fasting, nor birch.

And God, like a father rejoicing to see
His children as pleasant and happy as he,
Would have no more quarrel with the Devil or the Barrel,
But kiss him, & give him both drink and apparel.

The illustration to the poem, like that to the experienced 'Chimney Sweep', invites our pity and, as was the case in that poem, our pity becomes tinged with reservations when we read the text. A vagabond family is depicted, grouped in attitudes of despair about a fire blazing in the open. The only shelter known to such a family would be a temporary one supplied by the parish or by a tavern. If they could afford it, the entertainment of a tavern, where they might be allowed to huddle round the fire until morning, would be preferable to the harsh restrictions of a night in the workhouse. At the head of the poem Blake engraved a boy and an old man, both kneeling, apparently amongst trees. The boy has his head in the old man's lap and is being comforted. As there is an aureole of light round the old man's head, it is possible that these figures represent God and the Devil.

The child's attack on joyless religion has the force of being pointed and true. As he is a vagabond he has known charity administered as a duty by a cold hand, and has also observed, as anyone may, the austerities, repressions and disapprovals of religious bigots. Oddly enough there is an unpleasantly carnal aura about such people, who think too much of the flesh in giving it an inverted significance. They are mentally twisted and run the risk of becoming physically so:

> And modest dame Lurch, who is always at Church,
> Would not have bandy children, nor fasting, nor birch.

The little vagabond sees perversion of appetite as a feature of the teaching of any church, and suggests that if we allowed our bodies their comforts they might not turn against us. If we make our God-given faculties and inclinations into a Devil, they will plague and corrupt us, but if we would let them alone they might have an opportunity to assert their divine nature:

> And God, like a father rejoicing to see
> His children as pleasant and happy as he,
> Would have no more quarrel with the Devil or the Barrel,
> But kiss him, & give him both drink and apparel.

God could now accept and nourish the 'Devil' in his proper and pleasant form as healthy spontaneous desire. Blake initially wrote the last line of the poem as follows:

> But shake hands & kiss him & there'd be no more hell.[1]

This conveys the sense that the appetites should be brought into the fabric of religious thinking instead of being regarded as disreputable, but the later emendation adds the pathetic overtone that the Devil is poor. He is, like the vagabond, in want of drink and apparel, for the child has sensed that it is sinful to be hungry and dirty, or ill, or old, and that these will be punished by distaste and grudging assistance.

It is difficult not to respond to the pathos of the child who is so aware of being an outcast, so hungry for the petty gratifications that, in his deprived situation, have become an obsessive requirement. It is difficult, also, not to see that the little creature lacks any sort of beauty. Blake even seems to

---

[1] *Notebook*, p. 105. *Complete Writings* (1957), p. 180.

have gone to the length of making the poem the boy speaks as unattractive as possible. The other *Songs* are simple in vocabulary but show flexibility in their rhythm, placing the accent where strength is required. 'The Little Vagabond', on the other hand, shows an odd untutored crudity, too obvious not to be intended to jar upon the ear. When children make up verses extempore they will change the word order ineptly about in order to effect a scansion that, nevertheless, must often be forced. Disharmonies of this sort are very noticeable in such phrases as:

> . . . But if at the Church . . .
> . . . our souls to regale . . .
> . . . Nor ever once wish . . .
> . . . Would not have bandy children . . .

Blake's ear is a sensitive one and he would be aware of the juvenile rhythm and of the cliché in:

> And we'd be as happy as birds in the spring.

He would know that the extra rhyme in the middle of the third line of each stanza converts the terminal rhymes into a jingle, and lest this go unnoticed, he places a lame rhyme at the end of line four.

The clumsy and juvenile rhythm of the poem emphasizes its trite aspects, making us look more attentively at the sense of what the child says, and forcing us to examine his sincerity despite our awareness of his misery. No doubt Blake would agree with the gist of what his speaker says, would agree that the results of prurient self-denial are unhealthy. On the same page[1] of the *Notebook* as the draft of the 'Vagabond' appears, Blake wrote:

> Abstinence sows sand all over
> The ruddy limbs & flaming hair,
> But Desire Gratified
> Plants fruits of life & beauty there.

In spite of this apparent concurrence, however, we are not given, in 'The Little Vagabond', the impression of a speaker

---

[1] P. 105. *Complete Writings* (1957), p. 178.

who is honest or intelligent. His faculties are limited, perhaps, by his chronic condition of being in want. They are, nevertheless, limited. His dogmatic assertion of the proper role of the Church springs from the desire for comforts that he is desperately without, but one cannot help noticing that they are very private and limited satisfactions. One might agree with him that what should be offered at church should be more positively desirable and life-nourishing and yet find oneself in disagreement with the spirit in which the boy makes his proposals. He places too much emphasis on a mood of insistent pleasantness, and a church of drinking parsons and elated congregations does not seem more responsible or mature than one of 'fasting and birch'.

In 'The Little Vagabond', a desire for gratifications finds its expression through a reforming purpose. The 'drinking song' in *Songs of Innocence* is refreshingly ingenuous by comparison.

LAUGHING SONG

When the green woods laugh with the voice of joy,
And the dimpling stream runs laughing by;
When the air does laugh with our merry wit,
And the green hill laughs with the noise of it;

When the meadows laugh with lively green,
And the grasshopper laughs in the merry scene,
When Mary and Susan and Emily
With their sweet round mouths sing 'Ha, Ha, He!'

When the painted birds laugh in the shade,
Where our table with cherries and nuts is spread,
Come live & be merry, and join with me,
To sing the sweet chorus of 'Ha, Ha, He!'

The illustration to the poem shows a convivial group of men and women seated at a table beneath the trees. One of them, a man, stands facing the others, with both arms raised, singing, or leading a song. He waves his hat about in one hand, and raises a drinking cup in the other. Cups are held, also, by those seated at the table. The singer of 'Laughing

Song' is very pleased with himself and his company, perhaps even too easily pleased in a school-boy fashion:

> When the air does laugh with our merry wit . . .

The noisy chaff and tipsy jollity are possible, however, because he does what is impossible to the little vagabond: lets himself go, and, because he gives himself up, all nature seems to join in with his mirth. So universal is the laughter that the lines at the end of the poem, 'Come live & be merry, and join with me . . .' are less of an invitation than an expansive inclusion of his audience in a feeling of well-being. There is no desperate mood of longing here, such as the vagabond shows, but an easy, self-forgetful chiming in of youthful vigour with the heady intoxication of spring.

Although the song is lively, it runs with a more shallow flow than most of the *Songs of Innocence*, and it owes a good deal to earlier poetry in praise of the simple life, to *As You Like It* or to the sixteenth-century models which Shakespeare exploits in some of his comedies. The derivative nature of the poem is even more obvious in its earliest form written in a copy of *Poetical Sketches*.[1] Here it is a song by a young shepherd, contrasting with one by an old shepherd, whose theme is winter, not spring:

> When silver snow decks Sylvio's clothes
> And jewel hangs at shepherd's nose . . .

The old man sees warm-hearted Innocence persisting in age as a 'winter's gown' to protect against 'life's pelting storm'.

Blake is, as a rule, far more likely to pick up a theme or metrical form from Isaac Watts or the outline of an image from Mary Wollstonecraft, Mrs Barbauld or Apuleius than to echo an established poetic mode.[2] Yet in 'Laughing Song' he does very obviously write in a well-known and persistent convention. He probably wishes to bring into his study of

[1] *Complete Writings* (1957), p. 63.
[2] See the essays by Kathleen Raine and V. de S. Pinto (ed.) in *The Divine Vision* (1957).

Innocence whatever force and authority he can take from 'dead shepherds'. Blake's poetic predecessors had seen that rustic and simple lives had a grace and contentment not always possible to the more sophisticated. This is not the whole of Blake's Innocence, but it is a glimpse of it, and Blake, in writing 'Laughing Song', incorporates the glimpse in his *Songs*. Six years later the theme will be taken up once again by Wordsworth in the *Lyrical Ballads* where 'humble and rustic life' is described because: 'in that condition, the essential passions of the heart find a better soil in which they can attain their maturity'.

The experienced 'Holy Thursday' and 'The Little Vaga-bond' contain criticisms of the institutional aspects of man's life, yet we notice that the persons who make them have 'institutional' minds. The criticisms are made from a very definite standpoint and show a mechanical habit of thinking tending to isolate the speaker in his preoccupations and pre-conceptions. This isolation does not occur in the innocent poems even though the personae use conventional forms of thought. Their intellectual habit is not mechanical and they quicken those forms by making careful observations and taking an expansive interest. In the innocent 'Holy Thursday' the 'angel' of the last line is a lively conception pointing a fresh moral insight; is not a stereotype used to trick out a moral truism. Also, the speaker in that poem has become more human and less mechanical by being caught up in the ceremony at St Paul's. Whether the ceremony is worth his attention or not is less to the point than the fact that he has an attention to give, which is more than can be truly said of his experienced counterpart. In 'Laughing Song' the humour of the singer has allowed him to augment his feelings by expansively responding to the Spring. His mood is outgoing and sensitive, not self-centred and assertive. All of the *Songs of Innocence* emphasize this in some way (in the form of 'sympathy' in 'On Another's Sorrow', for instance) but two of the poems, 'Spring' and 'A Dream', seem designed to do so on the simplest level. Both depict an expansiveness similar to that of the singer in 'Laughing Song'.

SPRING

Sound the Flute!
Now it's mute.
Birds delight
Day and Night;
Nightingale
In the dale,
Lark in Sky,
Merrily,
Merrily, Merrily, to welcome in the Year.

Little Boy,
Full of joy;
Little Girl,
Sweet and small;
Cock does crow,
So do you;
Merry voice,
Infant noise,
Merrily, Merrily, to welcome in the Year.

Little Lamb,
Here I am;
Come and lick
My white neck;
Let me pull
Your soft Wool;
Let me kiss
Your soft face:
Merrily, Merrily, we welcome in the Year.

In 'The Little Vagabond' the rhythm of the poem was juvenile and the rhymes irritatingly lame. If it were necessary to demonstrate that the effect there was an intentional one by showing Blake's normal mastery of his medium, 'Spring' could be used for the purpose. The most childish form has been chosen for the poem, some lines are no more than one word in length, rhymes are in couplets, the allusions are to the most common things, and the speaker, or speakers, show the unaffected enthusiasm of simplicity. Blake has not departed very far from the cadences of:

> One, two;
> Buckle my shoe.
> Three, four;
> Knock at the door.

Despite this deliberately assumed elementary shape, the poem has an extraordinary vigour and movement, dependent largely on prosodic skill. The rhyme scheme is never obtrusive because most rhymes are imperfect. They help break the poem into short excited dashes of sound without ever making them seem artificial or forced. In the first two lines the rhyme is perfect:

> Sound the flute!
> Now it's mute.

Here, however, the staccato couplet wonderfully suggests the definite, sharply forced notes of an instrument that is abrupt by nature. After this first couplet, short lines and broken sentences indicate the bursts of energy of spring life: the pleased rush of a lamb which stands as suddenly still, the sudden start and equally sudden cessation of the lark's song. These bursts of energy form part of an organic flow, however. Each line is separate but the half-rhymes do not complete the separation—we are led from one line to the next, and on through the stanza to the steadiness of the long but vigorous refrain. The poem refers to the sporadic activities of different creatures, but the rhythmic pattern reminds us simultaneously of the underlying harmony of their mood and their movement as part of the season.

The poem is reminiscent of 'The Ecchoing Green' in that each thing mentioned is so much a centre of delight and a source of activity, and yet this activity is quickened by the ability to participate, to contribute to the general excitement. The illustration at the head of the poem shows a young woman seated beneath a tree. On her lap a child reaches excitedly towards a flock of sheep grazing nearby. There are bonds of delighted interest between creatures, each of which is so much itself. This is emphasized by the change in the refrain in the last stanza:

> Merrily, Merrily, we welcome in the Year.

In the previous stanzas each creature acted separately 'to welcome in the Year', but the last stanza depicts two creatures welcoming in the year by welcoming each other.

Mother and child decidedly welcome the year together. The first two stanzas seem to be spoken by the mother, but the third stanza belongs to the child who is illustrated as playing with a lamb at the foot of the poem. He is naked among the sheep and holds the wool of a lamb which licks his neck. The change in speaker in the course of the poem is barely noticeable. Perhaps the child's words are spoken for it by the mother, but, whether this is so or not, what is to be remarked is that, as in the 'Cradle Song', there is a bond of sympathy between mother and child bringing them into such harmony that we hardly observe when the speaker alters.

The responsiveness of all creatures to each other, and the quickening of their individuality by being part of a larger whole, is depicted also in 'A Dream'. In this poem Blake gives us an innocent world view, a 'metaphysical' statement that differs from such statements as are implicit in the experienced 'Holy Thursday' or 'The Human Abstract' in that it is not a preconception, mechanically applied, but an intuition realized in sympathetic response.

A DREAM

Once a dream did weave a shade
O'er my Angel-guarded bed,
That an Emmet lost its way
Where on grass methought I lay.

Troubled, 'wilder'd, and forlorn,
Dark, benighted, travel-worn,
Over many a tangled spray,
All heart-broke I heard her say:

'O, my children! do they cry?
'Do they hear their father sigh?
'Now they look abroad to see:
'Now return and weep for me.'

Pitying, I drop'd a tear;
But I saw a glow-worm near,
Who replied: 'What wailing wight
'Calls the watchman of the night?

'I am set to light the ground,
'While the beetle goes his round:
'Follow now the beetle's hum;
'Little wanderer, hie thee home.'

The poem is uttered by a young child, though it bears a close relationship to similar innocent poems representing the adult, such as 'On Another's Sorrow' or 'The Cradle Song'. Like them, this song is expressive of a knowledge, too deeply seated to be seriously questioned, that the world is ordered by the concern of creatures, one for another. Whatever other forces may operate, affection is certainly active. Not only is this true for every human being who sleeps in an 'Angel-guarded bed', but lowlier creatures, even down to an emmet, are cared for and watched. So powerful is the impulse of mutual solicitude that even the 'little mother lost' of this poem, in the middle of her bewildered struggles, thinks first of her children and husband, and knows that they have no thoughts but for her:

> 'Now they look abroad to see:
> 'Now return and weep for me.'

The speaker of the poem too, pities, and drops a tear, though unable to help. Someone can assist, though, for it would be strange if, in a world where pity was active, no relief could be found. All are provided for: the glow-worm and watchman beetle have their official duties, just as the angel-guardian has his; and the ant is sent safely on her way. Even these small creatures carry out their tasks in love and care and not as 'natural' functions, automatically performed.

The scene depicted in the poem is a quaint one, but it stops well short of being comical. The tremendous effort of an ant making its way frantically through the grass does succeed in being pathetic, and the poem has the sort of seriousness that a child can lend to any activity, even lying in the grass looking closely at one of the creatures there, and taking it at human level. We are, it would seem, meant to see the speaker as a child, and it is a peculiarly childish activity to make minute observations and to follow them with patient attention. The adult very seldom sees an emmet.

The first two lines of the poem take one's thoughts to the 'Cradle Song' where the mother wishes for sweet dreams to 'form a shade' over her infant, and sleep is seen as an 'Angel mild' hovering over the baby. In the present poem, the shade which hovered between mother and baby is seen from beneath instead of from above, but it is the same shade as in 'Cradle Song', made possible by maternal love and protection. It is not surprising that the little world described by a child in 'The Dream' is regulated by mutual care. As care is an active force in the speaker's own life it would be most surprising if he were to explain his cosmos in terms other than those of love and pity; if he were to use, instead, the terms of 'The Human Abstract'.

In 'Infant Joy' and 'Infant Sorrow' we found both speakers 'interpreting' the baby, but where the experienced poem did so in a categorical manner, the innocent explanation was in terms of the feeling the mother experienced in the presence of the baby. 'The Dream' is similar to 'Infant Joy' in that it is an interpretative poem—the speaker gives meaning to the movements of the insects—but it is not dogmatic, not a 'natural account'. There is nothing to be proved or tested in what is said because the love is intuitively known and its efficacy is implicitly asserted. The presence of the intuition, which proves itself, is all we need be sure of. If the speaker were making a dogmatic statement it would be necessary to find love in nature before assenting to it. Instead, the speaker makes a statement about nature that carries with it the colouring of his own state, a state that is aware of pity and love. This is sufficient demonstration that these forces exist.

The speaker in 'A Dream' must interpret his world, but manages to do so without imposing on it. He has no rigid notions which he has a vested interest in seeing realized, and if his intuition colours what he sees, it does so gently, not as an act of will blotting everything with overpowering tints. The poem is described as a dream because the knowledge of mutual care as a force active in the world has come as a dream would come, as something that is both of the speaker and from beyond him. Like the 'gentle wind' of love it is a force realized internally but comes only as a response. The explanation of the world contained in 'A Dream' is not a deliberate imposition but, instead, describes how the world would be obliged to whisper itself into the ear of such a person as the speaker.

The intuitions of Innocence leave it free to be quickened by the world in which it lives and to quicken its world. On the other hand, the preoccupations of Experience seek isolation in order to brood on themselves, away from disturbing influences. In the 'Holy Thursday' of Experience and 'The Little Vagabond', sociological and religious prejudices prevented the speakers from dealing candidly with the subjects they discuss. In 'Ah! Sun-Flower', a much more subtle temptation is described, the disposition to let the present moment slip, not on account of a prejudice, but in favour of thoughts about a future time.

AH! SUN-FLOWER

Ah, Sun-flower, weary of time,
Who countest the steps of the Sun,
Seeking after that sweet golden clime
Where the traveller's journey is done:

Where the Youth pined away with desire,
And the pale Virgin shrouded in snow
Arise from their graves, and aspire
Where my Sun-flower wishes to go.

This very direct and forceful little poem is given additional point if one keeps in mind 'Eternity', the fragment commencing 'He who bends to himself a joy . . .'.[1] The joy that is so longed for by the sunflower is not even one that is in sight, but one that is always to be. The sunflower wastes its life, not on a pleasure too greedily seized, but in considering the promise of pleasure. It turns its gaze all day at the sun, is always longing towards it, but the sun is never to be reached, and this 'traveller' is rooted in one spot. It waits for the future and finds the present a tedium that must be endured, counting the steps of the sun as the minutes and days drag through the season of its life. It is, like most of us, so much aspiring to some future ('Ah! when I am an adult'—'Ah! when this job is done') that the present can never be received with contentment. Our lives are 'pined away with desire', yet we remain virgins because we never reach any fulfilment. To emphasize this, Blake has built his poem of subordinate clauses only. There is no main verb in the long sentence which constitutes the song because nothing is ever to come to a resolution.

Primarily, the poem is about the mentality that allows life to be wasted in an endless and fruitless state of expectation, but it may be read as a particular attack on religious notions that suggest that life must be got through, unmeaning though it may be, for the sake of the fulfilment that will be offered in an after-life. There is mention of a celibate youth and maiden looking forward to a life beyond the grave and so, it is implied, inhabiting a cold and restricted grave in life. The sunflower longs for the sun she gazes at, but all that happens is that the sun sets. If the youth and maiden are rendered incapable of doing anything in their lives it is highly unlikely that they will be fit to travel to any other realm.

[1] See p. 151.

Blake is often misread because it is assumed that he speaks all the *Songs* in his own voice, when nearly always he causes his personae to do the speaking, interfering directly only when he draws the reader aside for a confidence. This misreading is less easy in 'Ah! Sun-flower' than elsewhere because Blake allows his own voice to break more closely to the surface of the poem. The irony is apparent and, although it is possible to read the poem in the voice of a persona whose pity for the sunflower is that of a commiserator, it is not long before amusement enters to tinge the feeling towards the dedicated flower whose concern about an hypothetical arrival prohibits any possibility of its travelling.

The temptation in Experience to allow hypothetical and dogmatic preoccupations to thrust aside the present occasion so that it is not really met, is so insidious that, in the case of two poems, Blake seems to have allowed them a place among the *Songs of Innocence* and later been obliged to transfer them. As they were not transferred at once, like 'The Little Girl Lost' and 'Found', it is not possible that he engraved them prematurely for *Songs of Experience* and gave them a temporary home in the earlier book. Perhaps he was taken in by the apparent sincerity of his own creations. The two poems are 'The School Boy' and 'The Voice of the Ancient Bard'.

THE SCHOOL BOY

I love to rise in a summer morn
When the birds sing on every tree;
The distant huntsman winds his horn,
And the sky-lark sings with me.
O! what sweet company.

But to go to school in a summer morn,
O! it drives all joy away;
Under a cruel eye outworn,
The little ones spend the day
In sighing and dismay.

Ah! then at times I drooping sit,
And spend many an anxious hour,
Nor in my book can I take delight,
Nor sit in learning's bower,
Worn thro' with the dreary shower.

How can the bird that is born for joy
Sit in a cage and sing?
How can a child, when fears annoy,
But droop his tender wing,
And forget his youthful spring?

O! father & mother, if buds are nip'd
And blossoms blown away,
And if the tender plants are strip'd
Of their joy in the springing day,
By sorrow and care's dismay,

How shall the summer arise in joy,
Or the summer fruits appear?
Or how shall we gather what griefs destroy,
Or bless the mellowing year,
When the blasts of winter appear?

This poem is illustrated at the foot by a picture of boys playing marbles. Other boys clamber amongst the intertwined branches that border the text on either side and all are enjoying themselves energetically. One thinks, when regarding children in their better moments, how pleasant it would be to be always like that. Education has its negative as well as positive results, and the inculcation of the knowledge and qualities of the adult, especially if the teaching is of the unimaginative variety, results in a premature driving out of enthusiasms and energies that one cannot help regretting, though there seems to be no help for the loss. There is no doubting the truth of the boy's statement that:

> . . . buds are nip'd
> And blossoms blown away . . .

Winter certainly is imposed upon children while they are still in their spring, and the poem might be quite an acceptable, if rather one-sided, statement of the results of education, pro-

vided it were made by anyone other than the schoolboy himself. It is a plea for the continuation of Innocence, and might
come well from an adult, but it is less convincing in the mouth
of a speaker who lays claim to the Innocence that is to be
preserved.

An innocent speaker would confine himself to a statement
of his own feelings such as is made here in the first and third
stanzas. This speaker also makes generalizations of a more
experienced sort, however, and he has an eye on the figure he
cuts. Stanza 2 commences in a convincingly innocent way, but
then the tone alters:

> Under a cruel eye outworn,
> The little ones spend the day
> In sighing and dismay.

There is no harm in the accusation of cruelty, if the boy has
felt himself cruelly used, but it is foreign to Innocence to
make the sort of interpretation contained in 'outworn' which
is representative of a theory of age and not a statement of
usage by a particular person. It is foreign to Innocence, also,
to see itself in the pathetic role of a 'little one'. The pathos is
further emphasized in the fourth stanza:

> How can the bird that is born for joy
> Sit in a cage and sing?
> How can a child, when fears annoy,
> But droop his tender wing . . .

Children do not think of themselves as tender unless they
have picked up an adult habit of thinking, and the comparison
with birds shut in a cage might be allowed only if it were not
designed to elicit sympathy, as it is here. There is a dogmatic
cast in the assertion that children are born for joy, for, though
the innocent welcomes what joy comes his way, he gives
himself no 'natural' claim to it.

The last two stanzas, eloquent though they are, fail to
convince one of the complete sincerity of the boy. He has far
too clear a view of unrealized possibilities ('how shall we

gather what griefs destroy . . .'), and far too appealingly sees himself as wronged:

> . . . the tender plants are strip'd
> Of their joy in the springing day.

Although one can sympathize with the plea made in the poem that Innocence should not be prematurely forced into Experience, it is difficult to give full sympathy to the particular speaker.

After 1815 Blake bound 'The School Boy' with the *Songs of Experience*,[1] and transferred with it 'The Voice of the Ancient Bard', another poem which is insidiously true until more closely examined.[2]

THE VOICE OF THE ANCIENT BARD

> Youth of delight, come hither,
> And see the opening morn,
> Image of truth new born.
> Doubt is fled, & clouds of reason,
> Dark disputes & artful teazing.
> Folly is an endless maze,
> Tangled roots perplex her ways.
> How many have fallen there!
> They stumble all night over bones of the dead,
> And feel they know not what but care,
> And wish to lead others, when they should be led.

In discussing many of the experienced poems we have noticed the adverse effects of the rigid mind, wilfully applied. A preoccupied mentality lay behind 'Ah! Sun-Flower', and in 'Infant Sorrow' and the experienced 'Cradle Song' fixed notions prevented immediacy of response. In Experience, sensitive intelligence is lost for the sake of an ordered subordination

---

[1] See the table given by Keynes and Wolf in their *Census of Blake's Illuminated Books* (1953), p. 55.

[2] Stanley Gardner expresses a similar view of the transferred poems, though he sees them as indicative of a 'transition from Innocence to Experience': 'In each poem there are intimations of true Innocence; but the Innocence is vitiated, and the flaw puts the poem among the *Songs of Experience*' (*Infinity on the Anvil*, p. 113).

of the world, but now, in 'The Voice of the Ancient Bard',
the 'opening morn' announced in the 'Introduction' to the
Songs of Experience is seen to be breaking, and the domination
of the abstracting mind is rolling away:

> Doubt is fled, & clouds of reason,
> Dark disputes & artful teazing.

A new truth is born, a spontaneous one particularly suited to
the 'Youth of delight', in place of truths which are gained by
a manipulation of other men's ideas. Burke, it might be
remembered, limited man's originality to making the best use
of what his tradition offered him, insisting that he could not
think creatively except by raising himself on established
modes of thought. This poem, like Paine, thrusts aside all
such 'truths' as a futile repetition.

There is not much point in attempting to find the basis of
the new truth or faith sung by the bard because he does not
say what it is. The message he brings is a negative one denying the validity of ratiocination and the poem merely says, in
effect, 'How fine it will be when we can get away from the
tyranny and delusions of the theorizing mind.' One might
agree—experienced persons certainly do allow their cerebral
life to dominate their senses and sympathies. But the ancient
bard offers no escape from this tyranny because his objection
to theory and abstraction is, itself, a theoretical one. Further,
if one's only influx of knowledge comes from an elaboration
of what is old, there is no point in ridding oneself of that
resource unless some other is available. The bard presents no
such alternative, and in all probability merely offers the same
rational round again, though he supposes it is something new.
He is, after all, the *ancient* bard. There always have been men
to decide that they have, at last, arrived at the absolute form
of truth and are sweeping aside centuries of wasted effort,
though it is not long before such 'truths' stimulate all the old
questions to assert their importance once again in a new
form. Godwin was such a man in Blake's time and, on a larger

scale, the 'truths' of the scientific eighteenth century, which had promised liberation from the knots of religious and metaphysical controversy of earlier centuries, were encountering problems in politics and epistemology instead.

It does not seem correct to find in this poem an announcement of some millennium seen by Blake himself. The promise made is too vague and is negative. Any 'new' programme would soon acquire perplexities if it were worth any attention at all. A life in which there were no problems, no moral decisions to be made, nothing to be learned or teased out might be possible for an animal or an angel, but seems neither possible nor tolerable for man. It is true that our problems become the province of the pedant or the fanatic with their:

> Dark disputes & artful teazing.

It is also true, however, that truth does not come 'new born' in the sense that the ancient bard seems to imply—does not come as a truth that may be had for listening to it. We must, each of us by our own efforts, arrive (and arrive again) at the realization of truths, even in the case of those that have been well formulated. Perhaps Blake first conceived the poem as an attack on pedantry, though it is difficult to see why he should do so for the benefit of Innocence. Later, he may have seen that it has relevance for Experience only, and seen also that the effect of the poem was to call all intellectual effort into doubt.

The *Songs* announce no millennium and explore the challenges of living without suggesting any way of escaping difficulty. It is true that they present us with Innocence, a state of perfection, but there is no possible way of winning to this state which is, essentially, unpremeditated. Our Innocence, and our innocent moments must be accepted as a gift on the occasions that they come to us. Experience can know Innocence only as an ideal that provides no programmes or definable truths, but acts as an awareness of a possible perfection which leads us to criticize our achievements. It cannot relieve us from the experienced responsibility of stumbling about over 'bones of the dead' in an attempt to find rational answers, and the responsibility of 'leading others' into adopting our mistakes instead of their own if we consider our reasons less dark.

It is true that Blake talks of a millennium in the *Songs*. In 'A Little Girl Lost' a future perfect age is addressed, but this is for the purpose of criticizing the present age. In 'The Little Girl Lost' and 'Found' a paradisial futurity is prophetically seen, but Lyca, who attains it, is made to fall asleep. Blake does not say anything positive about the girl's new state, and concentrates on the parents who have to help themselves to a proper adjustment. In the 'Introduction' to *Songs of Experience* the bard pleads with Earth to return, but this refers to a reorientation of her present self, and the Earth must help herself by understanding him if she is to benefit from his words. Blake is fully aware of the fact that, though Innocence is effortless, and though it provides us with an intuition of perfection, we are obliged to toil towards it, achieving it occasionally when we forget to toil. To lay down the toil, as the ancient bard suggests, could not render one innocent, but merely foolish, and that would be a step away from the sublime, not towards it.

'The Voice of the Ancient Bard' cannot be addressed to Innocence which, as it is not in the habit of doubt and disputation, cannot be reclaimed from these errors. If the poem is addressed to Experience its effect is to undervalue the disciplined and painstaking thought which is the mainstay of the experienced virtues. All that can be said for the message contained in the poem is that, although mistaken, it does have an apparent concern for 'truth'. One of the *Songs of Experience*, 'The Fly', also undervalues 'thought', but does so in a different spirit. Thinking is seen as the whole of life, but loses all value because the speaker flippantly finds life insignificant.

THE FLY

Little Fly,
Thy summer's play
My thoughtless hand
Has brush'd away.

Am not I
A fly like thee?
Or art not thou
A man like me?

For I dance,
And drink, & sing,
Till some blind hand
Shall brush my wing.

If thought is life
And strength & breath,
And the want
Of thought is death;

Then am I
A happy fly,
If I live
Or if I die.

Blake's intention in this poem is not very clear, but a paraphrase may be made as follows: the fly I have just idly killed and myself are very similar creatures. We go about our business, each according to our nature, as though there were nothing else in the world except ourselves, until some force we can know nothing about mechanically swats us. My nature is human and so my proper activity is thinking, a process which is like the buzzing of the fly. It goes on while I am alive because I can't help it, and it stops when I am squashed, also because I can't help it.

Thought is the 'life', 'strength', and 'breath' of the speaker. His flow of consciousness goes on continuously, that flow is what he recognizes as essentially himself, and it will stop only when he ceases to be. There is a shift here from the sort of awareness we saw in the piper whose clearly defined notions were no more than the visible part of a larger hidden complexity. His words expressed a larger self and he uttered more than he was aware of or consciously intended. By comparison, the thinking of the present speaker is a superficial business, happily playing over the surface of things, 'dancing', 'drinking' and 'singing'—a making merry, for tomorrow we die. He can answer for all his thoughts, he is the present sum of those thoughts, and that is all there is to him.

There are no inarticulate depths within the speaker and so he is like the giddy fly. The fly is like himself, as the second stanza insists, because both are subject to the operation of other forces, obviously with a mechanism of their own, but automatic, blindly operating under the law of nature. The thinker 'thoughtlessly' kills the fly, brushes it mechanically away without scruple just as his own thought will be brushed away by the larger 'thoughtlessness' of the universe. There is a different intuition of what is involved in 'thought' in 'The Ecchoing Green' where the liveliness of each being comes from its taking part in a larger movement. In 'A Dream' the innocent intuition manifests itself as an account of nature which shows all things, even the beetle and ant, caring for one another. Thought is not only a mode in which the complex and unknown depths within express themselves, but also a manifestation of the thinker's belonging to a complex, unknown and unified world beyond. Such thought is an expression of the depths of the universe as well as of the self. 'The Fly' on the other hand, depicts a universe of separate blind wills, necessarily destructive of each other, for all things die or disintegrate by the action of other things eventually.

The description of thought as reflex and self-contained given in 'The Fly' is well exemplified by the movement of the poem itself. It has a jerky, frivolous rhythm, the train of reflexion is started off by a chance action, and the game of thinking about the significance of the action is conducted according to conventional rules: there is a certain amount of verbal play, a syllogistic cast to the last two stanzas, and a pseudo-metaphysical direction in which conclusions are drawn. The illustration, however, has grace and liveliness despite the fact that it illustrates the 'summer's play' of the human being. Beneath a leafless tree a young woman is assisting a baby to take its first steps. Further away a girl plays with a racquet and shuttlecock all by herself.

'The Fly' presents us with a notion of the nature of 'thought' consequent on the confined sympathies and superficiality of the experienced state. Blake takes his examination of experienced 'thinking' a stage further in 'The Clod & the Pebble', a poem which exposes a fundamental contradiction in the experienced account of the way the mind works.

THE CLOD & THE PEBBLE

'Love seeketh not Itself to please,
'Nor for itself hath any care,
'But for another gives its ease,
'And builds a Heaven in Hell's despair.'

So sang a little Clod of Clay
Trodden with the cattle's feet,
But a Pebble of the brook
Warbled out these metres meet:

'Love seeketh only Self to please,
'To bind another to Its delight,
'Joys in another's loss of ease,
'And builds a Hell in Heaven's despite.'

The liveliness of the speakers in the innocent songs we have examined is increased by their ability to participate wholeheartedly in the situation of the moment and to sympathize. This sort of self-forgetfulness leads to a heightening of individuality and not, as in the case of the clod, to a squashy plasticity. Both loves depicted in the poem are of a limited kind. The pebble is hard, crystalline, and has an organization of its own. However, it receives no impressions, nothing is communicated to it, and so it has nothing to love.

The clod, on the other hand, receives all impressions, but has no mind to retain them and so insufficient individuality to be capable of loving. Both clod and pebble make assertions about the nature of love in accordance with their personalities—that love is selfless, that love is selfish—but love is beyond both of them.

Neither clod nor pebble know what it is to love, in any full sense of the word, and neither of them know what it is to think, except in a very limited way. The pebble cannot perceive and so cannot think to any purpose, despite its organization, while the clod does nothing but perceive and has no character of its own to think with. Thinking that has any point at all is indicative of a significant relationship between the thinker and his world (just as love is a relation), but there can be no question of any organic interaction here, only an inert reception of meaningless impressions on the part of the clod and an elaboration of empty systems on the part of the pebble. Although we think of our sense organs as designed merely to record, they can do so only because we are intelligent (in the organizing sense of the word), and although we think of our mind as designed merely to think, it does so only because we are intelligent (in the receptive sense of the word).

Innocence can make the assertions of neither clod nor pebble because it is intelligent in the best sense, it neither tyrannizes over its world nor is enslaved by it. The mother in 'Cradle Song', for instance, observes her child intently and is sensitive to the silent wind that blows between them; she is most perceptive and without dogmatism, but only because she is capable of active enjoyment. There is nothing supine and nothing domineering in her thought or affections, and she shows neither the flabbiness of the clod nor the rigidity of the pebble.

Blake's illustrations to the poem show us the world of the brook. At the head of the poem cattle and sheep are depicted drinking from the stream, while beneath the text are some creatures of the river-bank: a duck, frogs, a worm and plants. All these creatures are, at least, alive, which the clod and pebble are not. Yet Experience likes to explain itself as both clod and pebble, as mechanically servile in respect of its senses and as mechanically tyrannical in regard to its will and mind, though these mechanical attributes, added together, cannot make up a living whole.

CHAPTER 8

BLAKE'S CRITICISM OF RELIGION

In this chapter we will discuss some of the *Songs* that might be called religious, though, as we have seen, Blake pays no heed to the topic as an abstract study. He presents us with diverse ideas on the subject as manifestations of different states of mind and, when he makes (or implies) a judgement of the idea, the evaluation is made, not according to any abstract criterion, but according to the qualities of the mind in association with the idea. Strictly speaking, Blake's interest is in 'love', not theology, and he evaluates religious notions by asking if they demonstrate a soul capable of love or not.

Students of Blake, reading such poems as 'The Divine Image', sometimes conclude that the poet is asserting that God is in man, not in the heavens—that, somehow, man is God. Blake would not suppose that, apart from showing the presumption of the speaker, such a statement could have any meaning at all. He makes no categorical statements about God in the *Songs*, contenting himself with the implication that if a man knows anything about God, what he knows will be determined by his state, by his capacities for knowledge.

Hobbes describes our notion of God as the outcome of superstition and credulity. The propagandist finds it easy to instil in fearful man ideas of God to suit his purpose, which is a political one. The most enlightened notion of God, Hobbes suggests, is one that confesses Him altogether beyond man's powers of comprehension. Blake presents such a God in the *Songs of Experience*, in the mystery of 'A Little Boy Lost' for instance, because the mind that is confined in its self-consciousness (like the speaker of 'The Fly'), the mind that is isolated in the prison of its thoughts (like the wanderer), cannot possibly conceive God as anything but a dark unknown beyond its intelligence. It cannot, however, resist making assertions about the supernatural any more than it can about the 'natural'.

Innocence also makes categorical assertions about God, as in 'The Divine Image' but, in doing so, confines itself to what it knows from listening to its own emotions. Experience can talk of God only as an hypothetical being whose existence is suggested logically and He may, with equal logic, be denied. Innocence makes assertions about God in the same manner that the mother in 'Infant Joy' makes statements about her baby.[1] In telling of God it makes no statements that are not, in fact, descriptions of the feelings of the speaker. Logically such feelings cannot be denied. They exist, and they are given without theoretical elaboration. The most striking example of this is, perhaps, 'On Another's Sorrow' which is cast in the form of a logical inquiry into the nature of love, and yet keeps falling back to the faith of the speaker:

> O! no never can it be!
> Never, never can it be!

Even when, in this poem, the speaker seems to be making a dogmatic statement, he is using it as a vehicle for his sure knowledge of the efficacy of sympathy. He knows God because he knows of sympathy:

> Think not thou canst sigh a sigh
> And thy maker is not by . . .

The innocent mind knows God because it knows the virtues of delight. The experienced mind, which has lost these virtues, reconstructs them as a function of the understanding, as the 'mercy', 'pity', 'peace' and 'love' of 'The Human Abstract', or the 'natural' justice of Hobbes and Hume. God, also, is constructed as a function of the understanding, as the contradictory and autocratic creature placed in nature by man as its law-giver and controller, who is super-human yet shows all the frailties of experienced man.

[1] See p. 181.

Experience, of course, regards Innocence as an ignorant
and unfilled version of itself, and subjects it to the teaching
necessary to elevate it to a better understanding. The mind of
Innocence understands the experienced lessons according to
its own capacities, however. The Father can only be communicated as one who protects, and 'love', 'mercy', 'pity'
and 'peace' are taken to mean care for another and not for the
self. Christ, who shows the innocent virtues, was the founder
of a great church for just these reasons, perhaps. His message
is carried by the sword, by reasonable argument and by
propaganda; by 'control' of the militant type. Such power
would be short-lived, however, if the message it carried were
not continually responded to by that part in man which is
innocent, which is responsive, not to physical and rational
compulsion, but to 'control' of a sympathetic kind. The
especial significance of Christianity is that, fundamentally, it
shows a faith in the presence in man of virtues which are
products, not of the understanding, but of sympathy.

In 'A Dream' the faith of Innocence in the effectiveness of
loving care was illustrated in the way the activity of the
insects was interpreted. The reference to the angel was the
only hint at a religious mythology. We move closer to a
specifically religious statement of this faith in 'The Shepherd',
though there, too, we are given the merest hint of the
Christian form of the idea. Blake, as we have said before, is
not really interested in religions as such, but in the qualities
of men, which support religious notions.

THE SHEPHERD

How sweet is the Shepherd's sweet lot!
From the morn to the evening he strays;
He shall follow his sheep all the day,
And his tongue shall be filled with praise.

For he hears the lamb's innocent call,
And he hears the ewe's tender reply;
He is watchful while they are in peace,
For they know when their Shepherd is nigh.

Blake achieves his effects by means of very confident strokes. The bold repetition of 'sweet' in the first line, for instance, establishes the ingenuous tone of the poem in a completely convincing way. The 'lot' of the shepherd is 'sweet' because he confers 'peace', but the peace that is given does not arise from any determinative exertion on the shepherd's part. Just as his life is his 'lot', is something given which he accepts as it comes, so his peace is conferred by his presence and by his being *led* as he follows 'his sheep all the day'.

His role is not to direct, but, in 'straying', to give way, yet this is not a passive activity. The illustration shows a sturdy, alert man looking over his flock. His stance, as he leans on his crook, is a relaxed one, his glance is easy, and his presence is itself a guarantee that his strength will never be needed. His sheep realize this, and their sense of his presence keeps them at peace. He 'controls' his flock, but in the sense of the word we saw used by the bard of the 'Introduction'. He is not required to make them do anything, but to give them his care which allows them freedom. This care is the theme of the poem. The shepherd is aware of the bond of affection between the lamb and the ewe whose 'call' and 'tender reply' he hears. The sheep are aware of the care of their shepherd. In their dumb way the flock know of the existence of a force which, in the case of the shepherd, fills 'his tongue . . . with praise'.

The reference to 'praise' is the only indication in the poem that it has a dimension of religious significance. It has the effect of giving the whole poem an added meaning, yet not a meaning which can be forced to suit any dogma. The praise is not reduced to any religious pattern and it is not necessarily addressed to a Deity. Even when the shepherd has no deliberate intention of praying formally, he cannot help, in all his speech, uttering his intuition of peace and care. His tongue is filled with praise by virtue of his being alive and aware in the way that he is. Blake's poem preaches nothing, and though we might call it a Christian one it is informed, not so much by Christian thinking as by the underlying reality of love on which much of that thinking is established. Blake is not attempting to set aside Christian thought, we are free to see a relationship between the shepherd and Christ the Shepherd if we wish, but we are expected, first, to see the operation of watchfulness and affection on which the relationship is based, and there is no important reason why this perception should not belong to 'heathen, turk or jew' as well as to Christian. Blake is, in short, attempting to get down to the roots of religion in the human soul, rather than follow the branches and twigs of ramifying doctrines. This idea is one that Experience finds blasphemous, its religions are rooted in a Divinity who controls man from without, and to suggest that religion is rooted in the soul is to suggest that God is an arbitrary notion. Experience is quite right in finding the idea repellent, for if the soul is isolated, knows no contact or love, any God it creates must be a manufactured article, abstract and lifeless. Such a soul requires a tyrant. The innocent soul, however, 'creates' God by being in touch, by manifesting the virtues of delight, which are virtues of participation. As it does not impose itself, it does not produce a subjective notion, an outcome of the 'imagination' (in Hume's sense of the word). Religious ideas take new root in the innocent soul because it can afford them nourishment.

'The Shepherd' very gently hints that the impulse in man the poem describes may take the direction indicated by some specific religion, but it does not attempt to define the shepherd's 'praise' in any detail. This is true of most of the *Songs of Innocence*. Many of them are religious, but only three of them mention God and none mentions Christ by name. Blake is unwilling to show the force that enlivens religion as being committed to any particular form, presumably because this might distract attention from the force itself, from the responsiveness which confirms the truth of our best religious ideas. In practice, of course, Innocence has no option but to fructify the religious notions that come its way, and we have seen the innocent chimney sweeper doing this with the Christian myth. The poem in which Blake shows Innocence most closely associated with specifically Christian ideas is 'The Little Black Boy', although even here the association is rather a loose one.

THE LITTLE BLACK BOY

My mother bore me in the southern wild,
And I am black, but O! my soul is white;
White as an angel is the English child,
But I am black, as if bereav'd of light.

My mother taught me underneath a tree,
And sitting down before the heat of day,
She took me on her lap and kissed me,
And pointing to the east, began to say:

'Look on the rising sun: there God does live,
'And gives his light, and gives his heat away;
'And flowers and trees and beasts and men recieve
'Comfort in morning, joy in the noonday.

'And we are put on earth a little space,
'That we may learn to bear the beams of love;
'And these black bodies and this sunburnt face
'Is but a cloud, and like a shady grove.

'For when our souls have learn'd the heat to bear,
'The cloud will vanish; we shall hear his voice,
'Saying: "Come out from the grove, my love & care,
'"And round my golden tent like lambs rejoice."'

Thus did my mother say, and kissed me;
And thus I say to little English boy.
When I from black and he from white cloud free,
And round the tent of God like lambs we joy,

I'll shade him from the heat, till he can bear
To lean in joy upon our father's knee;
And then I'll stand and stroke his silver hair,
And be like him, and he will then love me.

The doctrine presented by the little boy's mother is a strange mixture. To start with, it is heathen: 'Look on the rising sun: there God does live.' It contains, also, echoes of the 'Song of Solomon', pagan in its tone: 'Come out from the grove, my love & care . . . .' In addition, her words are reminiscent of the quasi-metaphorical descriptions by Swedenborg of God in terms of a sun, of love in terms of its heat, and of wisdom as its light.[1] Finally, the teaching is traditionally Christian, suggesting that the true life is with a loving Father in Heaven and that earthly life is a necessary preparation for a time when the cloud of the body will be dispersed. The poem makes a wide cast for its religious notions, although we may, if we wish, associate the mother's teaching with Christian ideas, and Blake's illustrations encourage one to do so. The first shows the boy being instructed by his mother. They are seated in a grove and the sun can be seen on the horizon. The other illustration shows the two little boys leaning on God's knee. God is represented as Christ the Shepherd.

The teaching in the poem deals with the roles of body and soul and the meaning of earthly and heavenly existence. On earth we receive God's benefits, not directly, but through the agency of His sun and His creation and, as His love comes indirectly to us through light and heat, we receive it by means of the physical body. The physical world mediates between God and the soul, and the body has a most necessary function. Although it eventually dies, that function is a part of the Divine purpose:

> . . . we are put on earth a little space,
> That we may learn to bear the beams of love . . .

Blake significantly puts these sentiments affirming the positive role of the body into the mouth of a black boy, a member of a race who, as slaves, were obliged to undergo the most

---

[1] These are in degrees above the natural or 'dead' sun perceived corporeally. Man, as he is a spirit, knows this sun too, but not in the highest degree. See *Divine Love and Wisdom*, Part II.

appalling physical hardships.[1] The boy is aware of his ill-usage, he knows that the 'English boy' regards him as one 'bereav'd of light' and so not susceptible of love, and yet he uses even his sufferings as an excuse to affirm his duty of loving. If God's sun burns him a little it is so that he will be better fitted to meet God at the latter day. The eternal joy offered then is that of love, and the hardships he undergoes give him a present opportunity of loving denied the more comfortably situated white boy. If eternal bliss is to be enjoyed in the 'beams of love', how wise to anticipate that joy by exercising love now. Loving is certainly no passport to heaven, the charitable black boy and the untried white boy are both the 'love & care' of God and both are summoned alike to rejoice about the 'golden tent'. But the black boy has been more fortunate, has been obliged to suffer more on earth and, by showing charity despite his treatment, had an opportunity to acclimatize beforehand.

Although the poem deals with the destination of the soul, its whole impact is to affirm a present duty, and to emphasize the significance of the body which allows us to perform it. Heaven is the common destination of all and we can leave it to God to summon us from the 'grove' in His own time. Until then, the body will protect us in its shade, and our earthly existence offers us opportunities of showing charity, which anticipate the later joys of love.[2] There is no bemoaning an earthly lot, no looking forward to the joys of heaven where we will exist with our undesirable and inconvenient elements shed away. Indeed, the English boy needs protection from the

[1] The undesirability of the slave-trade and the treatment of slaves were anguished questions of the time. D. V. Erdman gives an interesting account of the effect on Blake's work of the slave question in his *Prophet against Empire*, ch. 10.

[2] Blake's innocent religious impulses are recognized in our own day by such thinkers as Dietrich Bonhoeffer: 'Our relation to God not a religious relationship to a supreme Being, absolute in power and goodness, which is a spurious conception of transcendence, but a new life for others, through participation in the Being of God. The transcendence consists not in tasks beyond our scope and power, but in the nearest thing to hand' ('Outline for a Book', *Letters and Papers from Prison*, 1959 edn.).

joys of heaven when he gets there because he has not used his earthly existence to anticipate them.

The song presses the metaphor of the sun very hard indeed, and it is not at all clear why an excess of love should burn, but the point of the poem is that the love comes first by being established in the mother and the little black boy, and the particular explanation they give to account for and sustain their knowledge of love is indicative of their humanity. They regard even God with the utmost of tolerant understanding, and it is implied that we are not to know Him only by His more fortunate manifestations but also by the shade where He is partly obscured, where His care seems diminished.[1]

In some of the *Songs of Innocence*, in 'The Lamb' for instance, it might appear as if the intuition of love as a principle actively at work were being sustained by an ignorance of pain and injustice. This is not Blake's idea—the little black boy and his mother are very much aware of suffering and neglect, they live, physically, in the shadow, but take even the half darkness as a proof of light. They look forward to a time of resurrection, while accepting their present state gladly, and even their thoughts about resurrection are the occasion for a real and present feeling of charity, an increase in their sense of responsibility towards those who do not love them. In Experience, on the other hand, even the idea of resurrection may be used to avoid responsibility, reject the affections and, in an odd way, both disclaim and clutch at the life of the body. This tendency is depicted in 'To Tirzah', one of the *Songs of Experience*.[2]

---

[1] The duty of the boy and his mother is, perhaps, described in the lines:
> The Angel that presided o'er my birth
> Said, 'Little creature, form'd of Joy & Mirth,
> 'Go love without the help of any Thing on Earth.'
>   (*Notebook*, p. 31; *Complete Writings*, 1957, p. 541.)

[2] Keynes suggests that this poem was added in about 1801. He says: 'This plate does not appear in three of the earliest copies of the book . . . Sampson, in the Oxford edition, 1913, has pointed out that the symbolism of *To Tirzah* suggests that it was written and etched some years later than the rest of the *Songs of Experience* . . .' (*Complete Writings*, 1957, p. 894).

TO TIRZAH

Whate'er is Born of Mortal Birth
Must be consumed with the Earth
To rise from Generation free:
Then what have I do to with thee?

The Sexes sprung from Shame & Pride,
Blow'd in the morn; in evening died;
But Mercy chang'd Death into Sleep;
The Sexes rose to work & weep.

Thou, Mother of my Mortal part,
With cruelty didst mould my Heart,
And with false self-decieving tears
Didst bind my Nostrils, Eyes, & Ears:

Didst close my Tongue in senseless clay,
And me to Mortal Life betray.
The Death of Jesus set me free:
Then what have I to do with thee?

It is Raised a Spiritual Body

The text of the poem is completed by some words that appear in the illustration. This depicts the body of a naked man with the torso raised and supported by two young women. An old man bends forward and is about to empty the contents of an ewer over the body. The figure of the young man, the position in which he is placed and the grouping are reminiscent of representations of the body of Christ after being taken down from the cross. On the robes of the old man, where there is a clear space, are written the words: 'It is Raised a Spiritual Body'.

The little black boy says that he will eventually be free of the shadow of the body, but though he makes a distinction between body and soul, they do not function separately, and he does not think of one part of himself as being debased or without ultimate significance. In 'To Tirzah', on the other hand, the speaker draws a distinction between a 'me' and a 'generated' part. The word 'soul' is not mentioned though the 'me' is an immortal, confined for a while in the meaning-less flesh:

> Thou, Mother of my Mortal part,
>
> ... ...
>
> Didst close my Tongue in senseless clay,
> And me to Mortal Life betray.

He has been trapped in this world which contributes nothing to his essential self, a self with its proper existence in the land to which the sunflower aspires.

The poem confronts us with a knot in Christian thought, firmly tightened by Paul in 1 Cor. xv, and never loosened since. Fortunately, Blake is interested less in theological matters than in psychological, and we are asked to look at the tangle made by the speaker in his attempts to unravel the problem, rather than to attempt an unravelling of our own.[1] The song derives much of its imagery as well as its theme from Paul's Epistle, but with this difference in emphasis, that where Paul is attempting to show that there is a significant 'spiritual' life to follow the 'natural' one, the speaker in 'To Tirzah' takes the future spiritual life as his reality and derives from this the conclusion that the natural has no significance. Also, there is a decided difference in tone between Paul and the song, for though Paul describes the 'natural' as sown in 'corruption' and 'dishonour' and the 'spiritual' as raised in 'incorruption' and 'glory', he is characterizing and placing the two 'bodies', and has not undergone the revulsion against the natural that we may detect in 'To Tirzah'. Far from diminishing the significance of earthly life Paul regards it as the basis of his knowing:

If in this life only we have hope in Christ we are of all men most miserable.[2]

---

[1] The poem is usually read as Blake's own affirmation of Christian truth. See: S. Foster Damon, *William Blake: His Philosophy and Symbols* (Boston, 1924), p. 281; Wicksteed, *Blake's Innocence and Experience*, pp. 183–6; Kathleen Raine, 'Blake's Debt to Antiquity', *Sewanee Review*, LXXI (1963), 399.   [2] 1 Cor. xv. 19.

St Paul's premiss is that Christ sets free in this world, and from this it is concluded that He sets us free in the next as well, but 'To Tirzah' interprets this as a release from this world into the next:

> The Death of Jesus set me free:
> Then what have I to do with thee?

Paul attempts to add something to earthly life, while the speaker, seizing on the addition, rejects the present reality. In doing so he attempts to give authority to his pronouncements by quoting from the Gospels, but travesties Christ's words to his mother at Cana: 'Woman, what have I to do with thee?'

Paul talks of the first man, Adam, who was 'made a living soul', who is 'of the earth, earthy', and the last Adam, Christ, who 'was made a quickening spirit' and 'is the Lord from Heaven'. Again, Paul is making a distinction in order to prove that the dead (those who have 'fallen asleep') may be raised up:

As is the earthy, such are they also that are earthy, and as is the heavenly, such are they also that are heavenly.[1]

Paul claims, merely, that in the two states there are two natures and that we may bear the image of each in turn. 'To Tirzah' also refers to Adam, but as the man who fell from a more blessed condition to the degraded one we know. The Fall is associated here, as it often is, with the discovery of the sexual pleasures which are regarded as too soon ripe and very quickly gone. They are 'Blow'd in the morn; in evening died'. The discovery of this knowledge is punishable by death ('For in the day thou eatest thereof thou shalt surely die') but this is commuted to a life imprisonment of drudgery and sorrow in the 'senseless clay' of a fallen body.

The denunciation of the Mother (as human mother or as Mother Earth—both of whom introduce man to his fallen state) contained in the last two stanzas is made to ring false by

---

[1] Verse 48.

the querulous tone of the accusations made, the pompous way in which Christ is quoted (the quotation is repeated), and the smug affirmation of the penultimate line: 'The Death of Jesus set me free . . . .' This sentiment, in its context, is a horrible one. To point the horror Blake has completed the poem by depicting the broken corpse of the man whose agony is the occasion for the present self-congratulation.

The words written on the robes of the old man ('It is Raised a Spiritual Body') are most unpleasant as they occur in the poem. They do not hint at Paul's image of the seed which must die in order that a new thing may grow, but instead illustrate the negative doctrine of the speaker. The preoccupation with the natural body in the poem is unhealthy, the speaker cannot find satisfaction of an 'earthy' sort but hangs on to the idea that he will obtain it. He is at once repelled and fascinated by the flesh and his notion of eternity is of endless time spent in a body that is, somehow, not a body. The dead youth, Christ, lies at the feet of the old man who pronounces this 'truth' and is still alive. He carries a jug in his hand, as though he bore the water of life.

St Paul's Epistles are not always free of a dislike of the 'earthy', but the passage on which 'To Tirzah' is based leads in the direction taken by 'The Little Black Boy' rather than into the negative state of mind that is shown here. The idea of resurrection and an after life may encourage any one of a great variety of attitudes taken towards life itself. Life is often looked upon as a period of probation for heaven. The speaker in 'To Tirzah' seems to look upon it as a nuisance to be got out of the way, and rests on the assurance that Christ has ensured his passage to heaven. This is obviously not a trust placed in Christ but a rather stupid form of conceit which does not even suppose probation necessary. The black boy looks on life, not as a probationary period, but as one that has its own importance, is suffused with God's love. We may the better prepare ourselves for heaven by a present enjoyment of love, but neither preparation nor probation are the present object, which is to seize the opportunity of knowing charity.

The title of 'To Tirzah' is rather obscure, but it may refer us to the Song of Solomon:

Thou art beautiful, O my love, as Tirzah, comely as Jerusalem . . .[1]

If this is so, the reference might be made by the speaker in derision of the loving forms of address found in the Canticles (and used so effectively in 'The Little Black Boy'). He would certainly find the analogy between married love and divine love a grotesque one.

The speaker of 'To Tirzah' asserts that the divine presence is concentrated in the land of the sunflower's aspiration, although the power of God extends into the natural world, which He created as a place where man could serve his alternative to the death sentence. Jesus has reclaimed us from that prison of clay. The earthy sphere, then, comes under the dominion of God, but He is removed from it, and we cannot know Him or His blessings in our present state. The little black boy, on the other hand, knows the blessing of the divine presence while on earth, even though it might be darkened for him. Other *Songs of Innocence* also recognize the influence of loving care on earth, extending it beyond man to all created things. In 'A Dream', the insects look after one another, and in 'Night' there is not only divine care for all creatures, but an eternal life awaits every one of them.

NIGHT

The sun descending in the west,
The evening star does shine;
The birds are silent in their nest,
And I must seek for mine.
The moon like a flower
In heaven's high bower,
With silent delight
Sits and smiles on the night.

[1] vi. 4.

Farewell, green fields and happy groves,
Where flocks have took delight.
Where lambs have nibbled, silent moves
The feet of angels bright;
Unseen they pour blessing
And joy without ceasing,
On each bud and blossom,
And each sleeping bosom.

They look in every thoughtless nest,
Where birds are cover'd warm;
They visit caves of every beast,
To keep them all from harm.
If they see any weeping
That should have been sleeping,
They pour sleep on their head,
And sit down by their bed.

When wolves and tygers howl for prey,
They pitying stand and weep;
Seeking to drive their thirst away,
And keeping them from the sheep;
But if they rush dreadful,
The angels, most heedful,
Recieve each mild spirit,
New worlds to inherit.

And there the lion's ruddy eyes
Shall flow with tears of gold,
And pitying the tender cries,
And walking round the fold,
Saying 'Wrath, by his meekness,
'And by his health, sickness
'Is driven away
'From our immortal day.

'And now beside thee, bleating lamb,
'I can lie down and sleep;
'Or think on him who bore thy name,
'Graze after thee and weep.
'For, wash'd in life's river,
'My bright mane for ever
'Shall shine like the gold
'As I guard o'er the fold.'

The religious mythology of the poem is consistent with, and amplifies the intuitions of such poems as 'The Ecchoing Green' and 'The Shepherd'. It is an outcome of the same sense of belonging, of participating and of caring. This is a sense that at once steadies and enlivens, as we saw particularly in 'The Ecchoing Green', and the prosodic elements of 'Night' suggest this rhythmically. Each stanza changes subtly in the second half from the equable stability of longer iambic lines with alternate rhymes to the quickened tempo of shorter anapaestic couplets. The more weighty impetus of the first half of each stanza gathers liveliness in the second part.

The first three stanzas of the poem describe the work of supernatural agencies in conferring pity and peace on the creatures of the world. It is surprising—when we pause to reflect on it—that, though most of the *Songs of Innocence* are spoken by persons with a strong sense of the efficacy of the virtues of delight, there are only two or three which mention the supernatural. The poems are shot through with a sense of benign influences at work, without there being any need to identify the influence exactly. 'Night' is more specific. Not only are the agents named as angels, but their role is defined. The angels who 'pour blessing' and who 'look in every thoughtless nest' appear in the other innocent songs but only in the illuminations to the text where they are seen amongst the letters as small figures, flying about their business or at rest in various postures, sometimes of elation or despair.

The second half of the poem turns from a description of the work of pity to a consideration of the frustration of this work. Innocence is not, as has been stated, maintained by remaining in ignorance of harm. It does know that the lamb is eaten by the tiger and the knowledge does not act as a threat to its faith. There can be no threat because the faith is not vested in force but in love. The angels do not control by asserting their will and any effect they have is only through the exercise of love. They 'seek to drive' the thirst of wolves and tigers away, but they do not restrain them if they 'rush dreadful'.

The poem is carefully worded, it is an innocent song, and it avoids 'natural' arguments. It is to distort the perspective of the poem to say, as one commentator does: 'The angels are doing their duty and they *are* heedful of the wolves' and tigers' *right* to follow their divine instinct and the lambs' *right* to die and inherit new worlds.'[1] No reason whatever is given for the limitation of the power of the angels, and it does not occur to the speaker to find one. The question of whether the angels have the power to check harm, but for some reason do not use it or, alternatively, have no power at all, is not at issue in the poem. The speaker does not think in terms of power or imposition of will, does not associate his angels in any way with this sort of action, and, while it is relevant to ask why he does not, it is not relevant to go into the natural history of angels. We must remind ourselves that we are looking at the poem, not in order to discover abstract metaphysical verities, but to observe the qualities of mind that will support the belief stated.

In the 'Introduction' of the *Songs of Experience* we were presented with the 'Word' and the 'Soul' that 'might controll' each other by love. Earth, in her 'Answer' could not understand this and saw love as an imposition of the will of the lover, saw control as enforcing obedience. The speaker in 'Night' does not understand 'love' in the second sense. Love has nothing to do with making another do what is wanted, but only with allowing affection to be felt and any further interference is unthinkable. 'Love', plainly, has more than one meaning; may, on the one hand, involve sympathy, benevolence and self-forgetfulness, but may, alternatively, involve an assertive interference with less regard of the person than of the principles involved. The former love may, if looked at in a certain light, appear helpless, just as the angels in 'Night' appear helpless, but it is, at least, the real thing, and it is a knowledge of the real thing that informs the mind of the person who speaks this poem. That is at the centre of the

---

[1] Gleckner, *The Piper and the Bard*, p. 123.

poem, and the accuracy of the speaker's statements about the agents of love depends entirely on the accuracy of his intuition of love. We may accept these angels as being divine.

The same real (if undefined) knowledge of what love is also lends support to the notion of heaven contained in the last two stanzas. The 'new world' is different chiefly in this respect, that values not in the ascendancy in the present one come into their own. It is the kingdom of God because 'pity' and 'meekness' are the impulses that direct it:

> . . . 'Wrath, by his meekness,
> 'And by his health, sickness
> 'Is driven away
> 'From our immortal day.'

Pity and meekness are not absent from the present world, but they are not always effective, and may even be looked on as a weakness. They may also, being concealed in Innocence, be disregarded altogether, and the world be quite satisfactorily explained and organized on principles of fear, strife and the understanding, in the manner of Hobbes. The 'new world' to be inherited is a genuine and proper world in this respect, that the values of the speaker are realized there. He knows the virtues of delight and so a place where they could be universally effective, governing both lamb and lion, is normal and healthy. 'Wrath' is a departure from the normal, is a 'sickness', so a Hobbesian explanation of the world in terms of strife is a description only of its pathology. Wild beasts do rush upon the creatures 'controlled' by the angels, but after the onslaught, whatever its outcome, the proper state of peace is returned to in some world, this or the next. The 'new world' is not, in this poem, a place to be aspired to. It is not the residence of God, and the lion thinks about Christ, just as he could think about Him in this world. The animals feed themselves and the lion even has the task of guarding 'o'er the fold' against an unspecified disaster. The only difference put forward is that the lion knows pity and meekness as well as the sheep, and knowledge of pity, as the black boy makes clear, is a delight that can be enjoyed in all worlds. The nature of the 'new world' is to confirm and extend the virtues of delight which are enjoyed in this. Such a heaven may be realized in the present unlike the heaven of 'To Tirzah' which is a release from the dark and sunless prison of the earth.

Blake etched 'Night' on two plates. The first shows a slender tree starting at the bottom of the page, enclosing the text on one side and arching over it. A creeper spirals up the trunk to the top. Amongst the branches are small figures of angels and of birds, and at the foot of the tree a lion lies asleep in its cave. This design is graceful, but the illustration for the second half of the poem is even more so. At the foot of the text five tall human figures walk on the sward. Their carriage suggests that they are the angels of the poem. Part of the bole of a tree is seen on the left, and there are suggestions of the bole running up past the text. The tree is given body and its size is indicated by the leaves and smaller branches which sweep down from the right-hand edge of the text almost to the ground. The whole effect is of soaring greatness and dignity achieved with the lightest and easiest touch.

Hobbes suggests that the least offensively superstitious notions of God admit that He is incomprehensible and, no doubt, such a notion is best suited to Experience which knows nothing of the divine virtues, and requires the idea of something frightening and powerful to keep its self and its world in order. Heaven, also, is unknown but is consistent with such a God because it is associated with the idea of punishment and reward. The innocent God and His heaven are not unknown and, instead of being associated chiefly with the end of life and the end of time, are most decidedly present in both. Even when heaven is thought of as a place where the dead go, they are translated in order to continue the enjoyment of their energies. They do not go there to receive a reward but in order to continue to fulfil obligations that are felt in this life.

Thoughts of God and heaven are such that they turn innocent attention to the present moment. In 'The Tyger' of the *Songs of Experience* the theme of the poem is the 'distant deeps' beyond space and before time where a mysterious Being undertook the creation, whereas ideas of God in 'The Lamb' are about someone whom the speaker knows intimately as if He were a constant companion.

THE LAMB

Little Lamb, who made thee?
Dost thou know who made thee?
Gave thee life, & bid thee feed
By the stream & o'er the mead;
Gave thee clothing of delight,
Softest clothing, wooly, bright;
Gave thee such a tender voice,
Making all the vales rejoice?
   Little Lamb, who made thee?
   Dost thou know who made thee?

   Little Lamb, I'll tell thee,
   Little Lamb, I'll tell thee:
He is called by thy name,
For he calls himself a Lamb.
He is meek, & he is mild;
He became a little child.
I a child, & thou a lamb,
We are called by his name.
   Little Lamb, God bless thee!
   Little Lamb, God bless thee!

THE TYGER

Tyger! Tyger! burning bright
In the forests of the night,
What immortal hand or eye
Could frame thy fearful symmetry?

In what distant deeps or skies
Burnt the fire of thine eyes?
On what wings dare he aspire?
What the hand dare sieze the fire?

And what shoulder, & what art,
Could twist the sinews of thy heart?
And when thy heart began to beat,
What dread hand? & what dread feet?

What the hammer? what the chain?
In what furnace was thy brain?
What the anvil? what dread grasp
Dare its deadly terrors clasp?

When the stars threw down their spears,
And water'd heaven with their tears,
Did he smile his work to see?
Did he who made the Lamb make thee?

Tyger! Tyger! burning bright
In the forests of the night,
What immortal hand or eye
Dare frame thy fearful symmetry?

In 'The Lamb' the child is very proud of his knowledge and is delighted to instruct, in play, the lamb which knows less than himself, which does not know, even, how to speak or understand what it is told. But the child can understand the account he has been given, and sees what is, for him, the sensible and obvious truth that a gentle creature created the world. When he tells the lamb about the 'meek' and 'mild' Lamb of God the child is very sure that he knows the truth, and repeats his assurance: 'Little Lamb, I'll tell thee.'

The child knows that his Creator is like himself but 'The Tyger' opens with a question and closes with the question unanswered. 'What immortal hand or eye' could frame or dare frame the symmetry of this beautiful but terrifying beast? Every sentence and utterance of the poem is a question, to which no answer seems humanly possible, and the most obvious point of contrast between 'The Lamb' and 'The Tyger' is that the speaker in the former poem is quite sure of his understanding, while in the latter the speaker can do no more than wonder.

The wonder about the Being who could create the tiger

comes to a climax in the penultimate stanza where the speaker refers to the possible reaction of the immortal Maker on viewing His handiwork. In asking if a human reaction was evoked, the speaker is speculating on the nature of the Creator:

> Did he smile his work to see?
> Did he who made the Lamb make thee?

Even the inhuman stars who are already created have thrown down their spears and wept in pity and regret that such a thing as the tiger should come into being and if the Creator can smile it is either because He can afford to do so or because He is above pity; either because He knows more than the stars and can see a place for this new creature in the light of His superior understanding, or because the sight of the voracious tiger appeals to His inscrutable nature. In either case the mind of the Creator is beyond the speaker's comprehension. Anyway, the speaker just does not know what happened. Perhaps there is more than one Creator: the lamb made by a gentle Being and the tiger by a fierce one.

The questions asked in 'The Tyger' are posed in such a way as, finally, to be unanswerable for they search a realm altogether beyond human experience.[1] The creation takes place outside time and it is effected by a Being who is, by definition, incomprehensible. We do, however, learn something about the speaker of the poem: first, that he likes speculation of a highly abstract sort for its own sake and, secondly, that as such speculation must have some point of departure in reality, his mind finds that reality in the existence of the terrifying. A universe that contains beasts of prey must be a ruthless one, and his questions are so framed that any possible answer must first explain that. Religious notions erected on such an awareness as the speaker displays can only be mysterious (to satisfy his love of the abstract) and awe-inspiring (to satisfy his preoccupation with the dreadful).

---

[1] Kathleen Raine explores the cosmological significance of the poem in: 'Who Made the Tyger?', *Encounter* (June 1954), pp. 43–50.

'The Lamb' hardly departs from the realm of what may be experienced and God is seen as a child, as gentle and loving. We may look on the poem as a description of the world by a person who is protected, and so cannot take into account the harm from which he is shielded. The mild experience and kindly usage known to the child lead him to believe what he is told about the benign nature of the Creator, we may say, and when the child knows more he will think differently. No doubt this is true—the child will think differently, but his new thought will not necessarily be more constructive or realistic. An increase in the habit of the remoter forms of abstraction, which is usually accompanied by a loss of the powers of appreciative observation, does not necessarily improve the quality of the intelligence, and a demand that the explanation of its terrifying manifestations be made the first condition of any account of the universe does not necessarily lead to a greater insight. The speaker in 'The Lamb' may know less, in a worldly sense, than the speaker in 'The Tyger', but the preoccupation in the latter poem, to the degree that it is a theological one, is more unreal, deals with a topic too remote, and so is more superficial. 'The Lamb', furthermore, does not say the last word for Innocence which, as we have seen in such poems as 'Night' and 'The Little Black Boy', *is* aware of the depradations of wolf and tiger, but does not find it necessary to fix this knowledge at the centre of attention.

We have been looking superficially at 'The Tyger', at its place in the framework of the *Songs of Experience*, and at its nominal theme, but on going more deeply into the poem it becomes apparent that Blake has allowed his song to take its own growth and that it has burst the bounds of Experience. The speaker is not exclusively aware of the harmful even though, in contrast to the lamb, the tiger seems, symbolically, to represent the presence of evil in the universe. On reading the poem we are aware, primarily, of the power and the beauty of the animal. We are also aware of the fact that though the nominal theme of the poem is the mystery of the act of creation, its real theme relates that creation to the grandeur and wonder of the created world. If Blake intended to write a song showing the blindness, isolation and self-deception of the experienced state, his own creation exceeded the purpose he had in mind, and shows an appreciativeness that exemplifies, not Experience, but an occasion of innocent delight. Perhaps Blake realized this but allowed the poem to remain in Experience to show that the state has its better moments. Perhaps he decided that the nominal preoccupations of the poem did not allow it a place amongst the *Songs of Innocence*, but that it was too fine not to be included somewhere in the *Songs* even if, like 'The Sick Rose', it is not, properly, experienced in its scope,[1] and has eluded a determinative 'control'.

The first stanza presents the tiger as a wonderful creature, even though it is one to shrink from, like the fire it is compared with. The speaker cannot even guess at the powers of the Being who could conceive the tiger and bring it into existence though the animal has symmetry, has proportions that may be recognized as fitting. The first stanza is collected, is a single question, but the questions become more breathlessly urgent in the three stanzas that follow as the speaker pursues the trend of his speculation about the Creator. These questions all reflect the wonder felt at the tiger which could only be formed in fire and fierceness, the substance of its being fetched in difficulty and daring from undefinable 'deeps or skies'. Once the material is available, only a Being of great power could manipulate it:

> And what shoulder, & what art,
> Could twist the sinews of thy heart?
> And when thy heart began to beat,
> What dread hand? & what dread feet?

[1] In his interesting analysis: 'Blake's Revisions of "The Tyger"', M. K. Nurmi says that the first draft shows Blake primarily aware of the dreadfulness and horror of the tiger and asking pointed questions concerning its origin. The second draft, he says, emphasizes the divine origin of the beast, while the third restores some of the dreadfulness to establish a synthesis of the two drafts. See *Publications of the Modern Language Association*, LXXI (1956), 669–85.

The twisting of the sinews conveys not only the strength of the Creator, but also the necessarily savage and implacable nature of a beast formed in something akin to agony. The tense power of the tiger is taken up into the concentrated activity of the Maker, so intent on the task that He is seen only in His active members: as the feet that move about the anvil and the hand that executes the task of the smith.[1] Now the sentences that form the questions are broken off in gasps of breathless wonder as the intensity of the process of creation and the degree of force involved increase, and as the purpose of the workman becomes manifest in a creature that defies full understanding.

'The Tyger' is a *Song of Innocence* rather than of Experience, for though the speaker does not, on a first reading, seem to know God through the virtues of delight, his knowledge does come through his breathless wonder at the tiger. He shows amazed reverence, which is love of a sort. Experience is woken to wonder only by something very startling, perhaps, as by the tiger, but it *can* be woken, and if its waking here takes the form of a preoccupation with an unknown and hypothetical Creator this does not gainsay the real excitement felt in the poem. The theology is an accident that must not only be forgiven but accepted, for we have seen, in the *Songs of Innocence*, that the spontaneous being must accept the materials that come to hand, must take the jaded religious, political and moral notions that are given it and by contributing its enthusiasm renew the notions so that they are once more fit for use. In 'The Tyger' an experienced speaker has

---

[1] Blake originally wrote:

> What dread hand & what dread feet
> Could fetch it from the furnace deep
> And in thy horrid ribs dare steep
> In the well of sanguine woe . . .

The shortened version indicates the attention of an observer held in fascination by the movements of the smith. Blake's extensive revisions of the poem are discussed by: Wicksteed, *Blake's Innocence and Experience*, p. 246; Stanley Gardner, *Infinity on the Anvil*, pp. 123–31; M. K. Nurmi, 'Blake's Revisions of "The Tyger"', *loc. cit.*

been startled into Innocence. The wonderful beast of the
created world has surprised the speaker into finding new
resources of meaning in his myth of the Creator.

'The Tyger' presents us with the movement of a mind,
experienced in its regular habits, slipping into the mode of
Innocence in a moment of breathless contemplation. In the
poem, the formulae of Experience become the vehicle for a
more vital energy. It would be well, in concluding this study,
to emphasize the fact that the Innocence shown is not sought
in any special way, but has come while pursuing the forms and
thoughts proper to Experience. This reminds us that there is
no programme for releasing the innocent energies, that there
is no formula for attaining Innocence. The 'gentle wind'
inspires us when it can, but there is nothing to be gained from
longing for it or attempting to force it. We can respect it
when we recognize it in others, but there is nothing we can do
to induce it in ourselves, and our duties and programmes
must be executed in the realm of Experience. It is only when
we are meeting the duties of that realm that the spirit is able
to find us.

Blake is most careful to make a separation between
Innocence and Experience. Innocence, it is true, provides
Experience with its ideals of justice, love, charity, and so on,
but Innocence itself knows no ideals, needs no constraints of
that sort. Experience, with some sense of the loves and
sympathies it once knew and may know again, sets up its
substitute: an orderly structure of aims, and it does well to
make these consistent, and soundly based on 'nature' and the
understanding, as Hobbes does. In our better moments,
however, we transcend such structures.

The greatest danger to the student who sees Blake's distinction between Innocence and Experience is, perhaps, to
attempt to ignore Blake's separation; to suppose that as
experienced beings we can take Innocence into our scheme of
things instead of respecting it as a joy that flies on its own
wing. As experienced beings (outsiders and spectators in our

own lives) we can force nothing, must take our responsibilities in our own laboured way and hope for the occasional invitation to enter. But even hoping should not be engaged in too anxiously, and it is better to be content with the powers we do have, while realizing their limitations. It is only by taking our experienced ideas seriously, in the knowledge that they must always be imperfect, that we are likely to transcend the state.

THE DATE OF COMPOSITION OF THE SONGS

BLAKE'S NOTEBOOK

THE *Songs of Innocence* and the *Songs of Experience* appear to have been engraved at different periods. The title-page of *Songs of Innocence* bears the date 1789, though Sampson suggests that this was the year in which etching was begun, not completed. Some sets of *Songs of Innocence* were issued separately, but once the *Songs of Experience* were completed the two sets were always bound together under the inclusive title, each with its own title-page. In some copies the title-page of *Songs of Experience* carries the date 1794, although the *Prospectus* dated 10 October 1793 advertises the work as 'published and on Sale'.[1] Once the *Songs* were assembled, Blake moved the plates about within the sets but kept each series distinct. The only transferences made were 'The Little Girl Lost' and 'Found', which were moved from *Innocence* to *Experience* when the latter series was completed, and 'The School Boy' and 'The Voice of the Ancient Bard' which came to be placed, as a rule, among the *Songs of Experience*, after starting life as innocent poems. A detailed description of the arrangement of the plates in extant copies of the *Songs* is given in *A Census of William Blake's Illuminated Books*, compiled by Geoffrey Keynes and Edwin Wolf (New York, 1953). Sampson gives a census in tabular form in his 1905 edition of the *Works*.

It seems likely that the two series were written as well as engraved at different times, and it is usually assumed that Blake wrote the *Songs of Innocence* in 1789, or not long before

[1] *Complete Writings* (1957), p. 207.

then, and the *Songs of Experience* in 1793. These dates cannot be firmly fixed, though it seems reasonable to suppose that Blake finished the composition of the *Songs of Innocence* before commencing work on the plates.

The assumption that 1793 is the date of composition of the *Songs of Experience* is based on the existence of nearly all of them in manuscript form with other similar poems, complete and incomplete, in a section of Blake's *Notebook*. By reference to the preceding section of this *Notebook* a date is ascribed to the section from which *Songs of Experience* were drawn. Most editions of Blake's writings include extracts from this manuscript book (sometimes called the *Rossetti Manuscript*). Geoffrey Keynes divides it into sections (according to the date of the entries) in his *Complete Writings* of 1957. Wicksteed gives a facsimile of seventeen of the pages from which *Songs of Experience* were taken in his *Blake's Innocence and Experience*. A facsimile and transcript of the whole book is given in *The Notebook of William Blake*, ed. Keynes (London 1935).

The *Songs of Innocence* and of *Experience* are conceived as a whole, yet a period of three or four years must have intervened between their times of composition if the date 1793 is accurately ascribed to the relevant part of the *Notebook* and if the poems were written there for the first time and not, as Sampson suggests, transcribed 'apparently from earlier rough drafts'.[1] Sampson ascribes the date 1793 to the part of the *Notebook* from which the *Songs of Experience* are taken on the assumption that the sketches in the *Notebook* precede these verse entries. The sketches include designs for works composed subsequently to the *Songs of Innocence* and the *Book of Thel*, but none for these two works.[2] Geoffrey Keynes agrees with this date: 'Having used the volume as a sketch-book consecutively from his brother's beginnings until about the

---

[1] 'Bibliographical Preface to the Rossetti Manuscript', in *The Poetical Works of William Blake*, ed. John Sampson (Oxford, 1905), p. 139.
[2] *Ibid.*

year 1793, Blake then turned it round and began to write poems in it from the other end. This group of poems, including the first drafts of several of the *Songs of Experience*, occupies pages 115–98 of the reversed book.'[1]

An examination of the facsimile edition of the *Notebook* shows that the poems under discussion are so written as sometimes to obliterate, sometimes to avoid obliterating, sketches made in the book. None of these sketches, however, is of such a nature that they may be firmly ascribed to any particular date. What is noticeable is that they are all done across the page and are sprawling, unlike the small, centrally placed and more carefully done sketches of the preceding pages. With one exception which might have been added at a later date, none of them is upside down in relation to the reversed text. Might these large sketches not have been done in the intervals of poetic composition? As the book was reversed and turned upside down for this section, which is a distinct one and obviously meant for a distinct use, it does not seem impossible that the pages were filled in prior to those that precede them. The manuscript poems of Experience might have been written before 1793. The last of the poems written in this section of the *Notebook* contains allusions to events in France of 1791–2.[2] Because of its terminal position, however, this poem can give us only a terminal date.

[1] *The Notebook of William Blake*, 'Introduction' by Geoffrey Keynes, p. vii.
[2] Discussed by D. V. Erdman in *Prophet Against Empire*, ch. 8.

INDEX TO CITED POEMS

GENERAL INDEX

General Index

General Index

Fall, the, 128–32, 142, 148, 234
Foss, Martin, 6 n.
Frye, Northrop, 3 n.

Gardner, Stanley, 2, 155 n., 214 n., 247 n.
George, M. Dorothy, 99 n.
Gilchrist, Alexander, 113 n.
Gleckner, R. F., 2, 155 n., 196 n., 239
God
  and the divine virtues, 71–7, 79, 86, 156
  experienced view of, 156–62, 198–9, 223–4, 241–8
  Hobbes on, 53–4, 223
  innocent view of, 104–10, 156–62, 186, 224–31, 242
Godwin, William, 4, 15, 17, 20, 179, 215

Harding, D. W., 2 n., 152
Hermetic tradition, the, 3
Hirsch, E. D., 2
Hobbes, Thomas, 37, 50–61, 63, 64, 67–9, 77–9, 81–3, 85, 111, 133–6, 223–4, 240, 241, 248
Housman, A. E., 155 n.
Hume, David, 49, 79, 111–12, 114, 116, 127–8, 134, 224, 227

Innocence, the state of,
  affectionate nature shown in, 100–2, 132, 189
  whole-hearted attention shown, 91, 120, 138, 184–5, 193–6, 203, 209
  in child and adult, 118–22, 124–6, 136
  clear mindedness shown, 70–3, 104–10, 224
  precarious existence of, 19, 121–2
  fellow-feeling in, 41–4, 107–11, 197, 207–9, 230–1, 239
  knowledge of harm, 109, 133, 231, 238, 245
  as a state of perfection, 6–7, 125–9, 138, 156, 217, 248–9
  seen in the poet, 124–5, 136, 137
  organic relationship with institutions, 21–7, 38, 110, 203
  grasp of realities, 92–4, 97
  self-forgetfulness of, 4, 26–7, 40, 48, 73, 112, 137, 180–1, 189–90

sensitive awareness shown, 26–7, 110, 185–6, 221
spontaneity shown, 150–3, 202–3
sufficiency of, 24–7, 205–6
toleration shown, 34–6, 138, 150

Jones, M. G., 193 n.

Keynes, Geoffrey, vii, 171 n., 251–2
  and Wolf, Edwin, 214 n., 231 n., 250
Knights, L. C., vii, 153 n.

Leavis, F. R., 123, 155 n.
Locke, John, 50, 79, 85–6, 116
love, 10, 189, 220–1
  and prostitution, 13–14, 19
  doctrine of, 84, 88–9
  see divine virtues, social virtues, sexual love

mercy, *see* divine virtues, social virtues
Milton, John, 23 n.
mystery, 61, 65–6, 69, 71, 77, 83, 85, 89, 92–4, 135

natural law, 51–9
natural man, 53, 95, 112, 127
nature, 67–9, 79, 80, 86–7, 99, 239, 248
Newton, Sir Isaac, 50
Nurmi, M. K., 246 n., 247 n.

original character of man, theory of the, 6, 16–17, 20–2, 28, 37, 56–9, 74–5, 127, 133–4, 137, 138
Ossian, 96

Paine, Thomas, 16–17, 20–2, 28, 37, 49, 57, 58, 215
peace, *see* divine virtues, social virtues
Pinto, V. de S., 202 n.
pity, *see* divine virtues, social virtues
poetry, function of
  in Experience, 149, 153, 155
  in Innocence, 149–53
Pope, Alexander, 57, 64, 68, 79, 84–6, 127–8, 134–6
priestcraft, 82–8, 92, 179

General Index